THE *Cliff Richard* FILE

To Carol
love
Cliff Richard

Also by Mike Read
Mike Read's Rock and Pop Quiz Book
The Story of the Shadows
The Aldermoor Poems

With Tim and Jo Rice and Paul Gambaccini
The Guinness Book of Hit Singles, Vols. 1 – 5
The Guinness Book of Hit Albums, Vols. 1 & 2
The Guinness Book of Hits Challenge, Vols. 1 & 2
The Guinness Book of Hits of the '60s
The Guinness Book of Hits of the '70s
The Guinness Book of 500 No. 1s

MIKE READ

THE *Cliff Richard* FILE

Roger Houghton
London

First published 1986

© Mike Read 1986

Front cover photograph by
Simon Fowler;
back cover photograph by
LPA International Photo Services Ltd

All rights reserved. No part of this
publication may be reproduced, stored
in a retrieval system, or transmitted, in
any form or by any means, electronic,
mechanical, photocopying, recording or
otherwise without the prior permission
of Roger Houghton Ltd

Set in Linotron Gill by Gee Graphics Ltd
Printed and bound in Great Britain by
Butler & Tanner Ltd, Frome
for Roger Houghton Ltd, in association
with J. M. Dent and Sons Ltd, Aldine
House, 33 Welbeck Street, London W1M 8LX

Picture Acknowledgements

The author and publishers are grateful to
the following for permission to reproduce
illustrative material in this book: John
Timbers; David Willis; Richard Young; the
BBC Picture Library; Syndication
International; Rick Richards; the *New
Musical Express*; *Film Review*; Hinkson
Photographics; Comic Relief; Simon
Fowles and Michael Page. Every effort has
been made to trace picture copyright
holders; the author and publishers
apologise for any inadvertent omissions.

Author's Acknowledgements

My grateful thanks to Julie Farrant and Gail Norman for invaluable help with typing; to Gill Snow and all at Cliff's office, to Margaret Wells, and to Aruna Mathur who designed the book.

The author and publishers would also like to acknowledge the help given by two of the largest of Cliff's many fan clubs: Janet Johnson of The Cliff Richard Fan Club UK, 234 Winchmore Hill Road, London N21 1QR and The International Cliff Richard Movement, PO Box 2BQ, London W1A 2BQ.

British Library Cataloguing in Publication Data

Read, Mike
 The Cliff Richard file.
 1. Richard, Cliff
 2. Singers – Great Britain
 Biography
 I. Title
 784.5'0092'4 ML420.R5

ISBN 1 85203 002 X

FOREWORD

by Cliff Richard

'Gosh! My own diary! At last I can find out what I got up to over the years! I'm usually so busy looking forward that there's hardly any time to look back. But this book will bring back all the memories of the dozens of different countries around the world I've played in, all the people I'd forgotten and some who have probably forgotten me . . . the tv and radio shows, films, records, stage productions, successful times and not so successful times, kind words from the fans and harsh words from the critics.

'Who knows, I could become the Samuel Pepys of the twentieth century . . .!'

1940-1958

OCTOBER 14   Harry Rodger Webb is born in Lucknow, India to Rodger and Dorothy Webb.

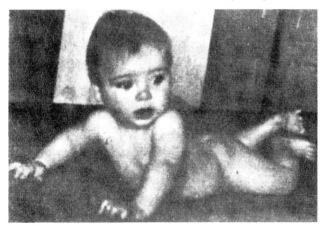

■ Naked Cliff aged five months

■ Cliff the leader, aged 18 months

1943
Harry's sister Donella is born.

1945
Harry attends his first school which is attached to St Thomas's church in Lucknow, where he sings in the choir.

1948
Harry's second sister Jacqueline is born.
7-year-old Harry and his family undertake the three-week voyage to Tilbury, England on the *SS Ranghi*.

SEPTEMBER ☐   With just £5 to their name the Webb family move in to a single room in Carshalton, Surrey.

SEPTEMBER ☐   Harry is enrolled at Stanley Park Road primary school in Carshalton.

1949
For much of the year Harry's father is unemployed and finds it hard to make ends meet.
Harry's first girlfriend is pony-tailed school friend Elizabeth Sayers.

1950
The Webb family move to Waltham Cross in Hertfordshire where Harry's father starts work for Ferguson's Radio at Enfield and his mother works at a factory in Broxbourne.
Harry enrols at his new school, King's Road Primary in Waltham Cross.
Harry's third sister, Joan, is born.

1952
Harry fails his eleven-plus and goes to Cheshunt Secondary Modern School. The Webb family move into a red-brick three-bedroomed council house in Hargreaves Close, Cheshunt, where Rodger Webb makes furniture for their new home out of packing cases.

1953
Harry plays 'right-back' for the school and Hertfordshire under-14 football teams.

1954/55/56
Harry becomes a leading light in the school dramatic society, taking on the role of Ratty in *Toad of Toad Hall* and Bob Cratchit in Dickens' *A Christmas Carol*. Harry becomes friends with two of the teachers at his school, Mrs Norris and Bill Latham.

1957
Harry is stripped of his prefect's badge for playing truant from school to go to a cinema in Edmonton to watch visiting American Rock 'n' Roll stars Bill Haley and the Comets.

Harry leaves Cheshunt Secondary Modern School with a GCE 'O' level in English.

Harry and some of his school friends, Beryl Molyneux, John Vince, Freda Johnson and Betty Clark perform as The Quintones at the local Holy Trinity Church Youth Club.

Harry works as a credit control clerk at Atlas Lamps Enfield for £4 15s 0d a week.

1958
Drummer Terry Smart co-opts Harry into the local Dick Teague skiffle group as a vocalist and rhythm guitarist.

Terry Smart and Harry break away from the skiffle group to form the Drifters in order to play more rock 'n' roll-based music. They enlist an old school friend of Harry's, guitarist Norman Mitham and rehearse at the Webbs' house.

18-year-old teddy boy John Foster, an employee at the local sewage works, is so impressed by Harry after watching him perform at The Five Horseshoes in Hoddesdon that he offers to become his manager. Harry agrees.

A ballroom manager at a hall in Derby where Harry and the boys were appearing said he couldn't bill them as Harry Webb and the Drifters as it wasn't a particularly good name for a rock 'n' roll singer. After initial suggestions of Cliff Russard and Russ Clifford, John Foster suggests Cliff Richard.

Following an appearance by Cliff at the 21's Club in London's Old Compton Street, guitarist/bass player Ian Samwell joins the group.

EARLY SUMMER ☐ John Foster's parents put up £10 for Cliff to make a demonstration record of 'Lawdy Miss Clawdy' and 'Breathless' at a recording studio in London's Oxford Street.

MID-SUMMER ☐ Cliff closes the bill at a Carroll Levis talent contest at the Gaumont Theatre in London's Shepherd's Bush, and a month later, at another appearance there, agent George Ganjou attends and is impressed.

LATE SUMMER ☐ Record producer Norrie Paramor agrees to take Cliff and the Drifters on after hearing their demonstration record.

LATE SUMMER ☐ Cliff and the Drifters record 'Schoolboy Crush' and 'Move it' (written by Ian Samwell) at Studio Two at Abbey Road studio with Norrie Paramor.

■ Cliff and the Drifters play Clacton-on-Sea, Butlins

■ Drifters Ian Samwell and Terry Smart with Cliff (second from right)

AUGUST ☐	George Ganjou signs them to his agency. With Ken Pavey replacing Norman Mitham, Cliff and the Drifters play a 9-week residency at Butlin's holiday camp, Clacton-on-Sea.
AUGUST 9	Cliff signs a long-term contract with Columbia records.
AUGUST ☐	Cliff's first single 'Move it'/'Schoolboy Crush' is released.
SEPTEMBER 12	'Move it' enters the chart.
SEPTEMBER 13	Cliff makes his TV debut on ABC TV's 'Oh Boy!' singing 'Move it' and 'Don't bug me baby!'.
SEPTEMBER ☐	Through contacts at the 2 I's coffee bar, Cliff recruits two more Drifters Hank B. Marvin and Bruce Welch. Formerly with the Railroaders skiffle group, and the Chesternuts, they join Terry Smart, Ian Samwell and Cliff to become the new line up of the Drifters. Ken Pavey is no longer a member of the group.
OCTOBER 5	Cliff begins a tour with the Kalin Twins. The Most Brothers, who are also on the bill, loan Cliff their bass player Jet Harris for some appearances during the tour.
OCTOBER ☐	Immediately after the tour, Ian Samwell leaves the Drifters to concentrate on songwriting and is replaced by Jet Harris.
OCTOBER 19	The *Oh Boy* album is recorded and features Cliff, Neville Taylor and the Cutters, the Dallas Boys, the Vernons Girls, John Barry, Peter Elliot, Vince Eager and Cuddly Dudley. Cliff performs shortened versions of 'TV Hop', 'Rockin' Robin', 'Early in the Morning', 'High School Confidential', 'I'll try', 'King Creole' and 'Somebody Touched Me!'.
OCTOBER ☐	Franklin Boyd becomes Cliff's manager but John Foster still continues to work with Cliff in a similar capacity.

THE CLIFF RICHARD FILE 1940-58

OCTOBER **25**   Cliff makes his radio debut on the BBC Light Programme's 'Saturday Club'.
NOVEMBER ☐   Columbia release Cliff's second single 'High Class Baby'/'My Feet hit the ground'.
NOVEMBER **17**   Cliff makes his variety debut at the Metropolitan, Edgware Road in London.
NOVEMBER **21**   'High Class Baby' enters the chart, eventually peaking at No.7.
DECEMBER ☐   Cliff rehearses for the part of Curly Thompson in the forthcoming movie 'Serious Charge'.

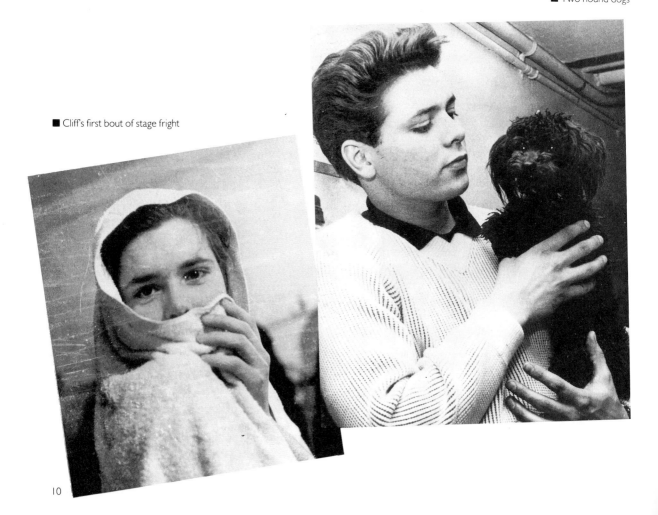

■ Two hound dogs

■ Cliff's first bout of stage fright

FOR THE RECORD — AN EMI BIOGRAPHY

COLUMBIA   CLIFF RICHARD   COLUMBIA   COLUMBIA
COLUMBIA   COLUMBIA

Cliff Richard, born in Lucknow, India, on October 14, 1940, has been interested in music since the age of three, when he was given an old-fashioned phonograph.

He came to this country at the age of eight to live with his grandparents, and it was at this time that his musical interests began to fade - firstly because there was no gramophone and, secondly, because most of his time was taken up with sport. He was in the Hertfordshire Junior Football League and held the school championship for javelin throwing.

As a member of the school dramatic society he appeared in many plays, and after one of these in which he sang, he was persuaded by enthusiastic friends to take up singing. This, plus the fact that he had now moved with his parents to Cheshunt - where he had a radiogram - sparked off his interests in music again.

Joining a vocal group, Cliff appeared at local dances and clubs and built himself quite a reputation, which prompted him to form his own accompanying group, which he called "The Drifters." This group consisted of Terry Smart (drums), Ian Samwell (electric guitar) and Cliff (vocals & guitar).

"The Drifters" were heard by John Foster, now their manager, who took them to Soho's 2 I's coffee bar. This was followed by a number of bookings, the first being at the Regal, Ripley. Whilst appearing at the Gaumont, Shepherd's Bush, Cliff was introduced to Columbia recording manager Norrie Paramor.

A most successful recording test followed and within a few days Cliff and The Drifters cut two sides for Columbia - namely "Schoolboy Crush" and "Move It" (DB.4178).

With the compliments of
Syd Gillingham,
Press Relations Officer,
Popular Repertoire,
E.M.I. Records Limited.

LANgham 5544

8.8.58.

1959

JANUARY ☐   Cliff makes his first appearance with the new Drifters at Manchester's Free Trade Hall. On the bill with them at the various appearances which follow are the outrageous singer with the flaming orange hair, Wee Willie Harris, Tony Crombie and His Rockets, and 'the sensational new comedian from Liverpool', compère Jimmy Tarbuck.

JANUARY ☐   Franklin Boyd and John Foster receive dismissal letters from Cliff's father.

JANUARY ☐   Cliff's third single 'Living Loving Doll'/'Steady With You' is released. Despite Hank Marvin, Bruce Welch and Jet Harris making their debut on a Cliff single it only reaches No.20 in the chart.

JANUARY 30   'Living Loving Doll' enters the chart, which is also a historical moment as it's the first time the current group have played on a Cliff Richard single. The Drifters also release their debut single 'Feelin' Fine'/'Don't Be A Fool With Love'.

FEBRUARY ☐   Despite the *NME*'s comments about Cliff's allegedly disgusting gyrations on ABC TV's 'Oh Boy' he wins the 'Best New Single' award in the paper's annual poll.

FEBURARY ☐   Tito Burns is appointed Cliff's manager.

FEBRUARY ☐   Terry Smart leaves the Drifters, eventually joining the Merchant Navy and is replaced by a drummer suggested by Jet Harris – Tony Meehan. Tony had previously played with the Worried Men skiffle group behind Adam Faith, Vince Eager, Vince Taylor and the Vipers.

APRIL ☐   The first album is released, simply entitled *Cliff*.

MAY 8   Cliff's fourth single 'Mean Streak' enters the charts, only to be followed into the hit parade the following week by the other side 'Never Mind'.

MAY ☐   Cliff appears in the film *Serious Charge* starring Anthony Quayle, Andrew Ray and Sarah Churchill. Cliff says, 'The people who made the film must have been daft. I was cast as Curly, but instead of simply changing the name of the character, they went through the painful and complicated procedure of curling my hair with hot tongs every morning before the day's shooting.'

JUNE ☐   *Cliff No. 1* EP released.

JULY 10   Cliff's fifth single 'Living Doll', written by Lionel Bart, enters the chart and goes on to win him his first Gold Disc.

JULY ☐   *Cliff No. 2* EP is released. Due to confusion with the American Drifters, Cliff's backing group change their name to the Shadows. This is suggested by bass guitarist Jet Harris.

AUGUST 21   Cliff appears on the front cover of the *NME* 'as you will see him in the film *Expresso Bongo*'. Classified small ads in the paper offer '12 different pictures of Cliff in action for only 2/9d'.

AUGUST 29   Cliff is best man at the wedding of Drifter Bruce Welch to Anne Findlay at St Stephen's Church, Westminster.

SEPTEMBER 4   Cliff meets Michael Delamar, producer of *Serious Charge*, to discuss his next film.

THE CLIFF RICHARD FILE 1959

SEPTEMBER 18 — *NME* describes Cliff as, 'The most electrifying and dynamic vocal talent to emerge in recent years'.

SEPTEMBER 25 — Only a year after his first hit and the article in which they had referred to him as 'a crude exhibitionist', the *NME* include a four-page tribute to Cliff in their September 25 issue. In the supplement Cliff pays tribute to his producer Norrie Paramor, the guy who is by now his manager Tito Burns, his agent George Ganjou and TV producer Jack Good. Cliff says, 'One short year and yet I seem to have accomplished so much – I've been very lucky. Without the public there would be no Cliff Richard success story – I shall *never* forget what they've done for me.'

SEPTEMBER 25 — Cliff says: 'Marriage is my ultimate aim – but not until I'm 27.' 'In spite of all the insults hurled at today's teenagers, I think they're a great crowd. I should know after all, I'm one of them.'

SEPTEMBER ☐ — **Cliff gives his own top 10:**

Elvis Presley – 'Heartbreak Hotel'	'This was Elvis's first record to break really big.'
Connie Francis – 'Sailor Boy'	'Connie is one of my favourite female artists.'
Frank Sinatra – 'It Happened in Monterey'	'This was the first Sinatra disc that I ever bothered to listen to.'
Ricky Nelson – 'I Believe What You Say'	'Ricky is a big favourite of mine . . . this is one of the best beat numbers ever recorded.'
Lena Horne – 'At The Waldorf Astoria' (LP)	'There is really only one thing you can say about her. Perfection.'
Drifters – 'Jet Black'	'Jet Black is one of my favourite instrumentals.'
Carmen Jones (LP)	'I like opera, but I listen to it in a way that's understandable to me.'
Elvis Presley – 'Don't Be Cruel'	'I just like it.'
Ferlin Husky – 'Boulevard Of Broken Dreams' (LP)	'This man is one of the sincerest singers I know.'
Marty Wilde – 'Fire Of Love'	'Marty is a close friend of mine. This is one of his best records.'

Quotes about Cliff:

Marty Wilde — 'We aren't rivals.' 'One of the few things we have in common is a liking for Chinese food.'

Craig Douglas — 'Cliff is so good-looking, I'd hate to have to follow him on a show.'

Lionel Bart — 'I think Cliff & the Shadows' unique rendition of my "Living Doll" is merely a rung on the ladder towards far bigger things.'

THE CLIFF RICHARD FILE **1959**

Jack Good	'One of the greatest performers in the country.' 'He always knows the keys in which he sings!'
Jayne Mansfield	'I think Cliff Richard is the "Most".'

SEPTEMBER ☐ 'My ultimate ambition is to make a Western with Elvis.' 'If I had the choice to pick any girl actress to play opposite me in a film, I'd pick Sandra Dee without hesitation. I think she's just fabulous.'

SEPTEMBER/OCTOBER ☐ Cliff films *Expresso Bongo* in which he plays the part of up-and-coming rock 'n' roller 'Bongo Herbert'. Laurence Harvey portrays his manager, who is decidedly more keen on his percentage than his protégé's well-being. A more sympathetic ear comes from Harvey's girl-friend in the film, Sylvia Sims. Yolande Donlan is cast as a fading singer who becomes the rising star's would-be seductress. The film, which runs for 1 hour 48 minutes, is produced and directed by Val Guest with screenplay by Wolf Mankowitz.

SEPTEMBER 28 National headlines proclaim: 'Military help Glasgow police control Cliff Richard crowds.'

OCTOBER 2 Keith Fordyce reviews Cliff's new single 'Travellin' Light': 'Cliff Richard's latest is very good, but not tipped for the top spot.'

'Living Doll' enters the US *Billboard* Top 100 at No. 80.

OCTOBER 9 Cliff is voted 'Top British Male Singer' in the *NME* annual poll, while 'Living Doll' is voted 'Disc of the Year'.

OCTOBER 9	Both sides of Cliff's sixth single 'Travellin' Light/Dynamite' enter the charts.
OCTOBER 14	Cliff is given a surprise birthday party in Leeds. Among the guests are his parents, manager Tito Burns, impresario Arthur Howes, fan club secretary Jan Vane and the Shadows. Cliff receives over 2,000 cards and presents. 'I can honestly say it is the happiest day of my life.'
OCTOBER 26	Cliff broadcasts live from Radio Luxembourg with DJs Barry Alldis, Don Moss and Ted King.
OCTOBER 30	*Cliff Richard Picture Parade Album* is published containing more than 120 photographs of his friends, car, girl-friends, family and other candid shots – and all for just 3/6d!
OCTOBER 30	The natural consequences of a 'B' side getting as high as No. 16 in the charts would be that the sales and Top 30 positions of the 'A' side would be seriously affected. Regardless of logistics, 'Travellin' Light' zooms to No. 1, deposes 'Mack The Knife' and stays on top for five weeks. For the second time in a row, Cliff knocks Bobby Darin off the pole position. 'Travellin' Light' eventually earns Cliff a Silver Disc.
OCTOBER ☐	Cliff and the Shadows tour Scandinavia. Drummer Tony Meehan is hospitalised with appendicitis and his place is taken by Laurie Joseph.
NOVEMBER 1	Millions of television viewers see compère Bruce Forsyth present Cliff with a Silver Disc for 'Living Doll' during the singer's debut on 'Sunday Night at the London Palladium'. Shadow Tony Meehan is allowed out of hospital for a few hours to appear on the show.
NOVEMBER 6	Cliff necklets and heart lockets become available at the knockdown price of 4/11d.
NOVEMBER 13	Cliff writes an article for the world's top film magazine *Photoplay*, in which he insists that he's *not* another Elvis and gives his reasons.
NOVEMBER ☐	*Cliff Sings* LP is released.
NOVEMBER 20	*Expresso Bongo* is premièred at the Carlton in London. The critics comment: 'Not enough numbers.' 'Not enough professionalism.' 'No colour.'
DECEMBER 6	Cliff voted 'King of Rock 'n' Roll' on Radio Luxembourg's Swoon Club.
DECEMBER ☐	Cliff and the Shadows appear in the pantomime *Babes in the Wood* at the Stockton Globe. Cliff takes the part of the Sheriff's troubadour.
DECEMBER ☐	*Expresso Bongo* EP is released, three of the tracks having been written by Cliff's producer Norrie Paramor, and by Christmas passes the 30,000 sales mark.
DECEMBER 25	Cliff appears on Hughie Green's AR-TV's Christmas Day Special singing 'Living Doll' to thank the viewers who had voted him the artist they wanted most in the world to appear on the show.
DECEMBER 28	Cliff is voted 'Best British Male Vocalist of the Year' on the TV pop programme 'Cool For Cats'. Because of pantomime commitments his mother collects the 'Cat's Whisker' award on his behalf.

1960

JANUARY 1 — Cliff, Lonnie Donegan, Marty Wilde and Russ Conway outstrip all their American counterparts (including Elvis) by taking the top four places in the *NME* end-of-year points table.

JANUARY 15 — 'A Voice In The Wilderness' is released. Keith Fordyce reviews the record and says, 'It's a great pity that an artist of Cliff's calibre should be burdened with a song that many people will find a bit distasteful.'

JANUARY 17 — Cliff tops the bill on 'Sunday Night at the London Palladium', which also stars the Platters, and shatters previous viewing records when 19½ million viewers in 6,853,000 homes become the biggest audience for a light entertainment show in the history of British TV.

JANUARY 18 — Despite a car crash on January 7, involving two of the Shadows, Hank Marvin and Jet Harris, Cliff and the group fly to America for their first tour of the United States, scheduled to run for 38 days and including shows in Pittsburgh, Milwaukee, Oklahoma City, Kansas City, San Antonio and Houston.

JANUARY ☐ — The American tour is advertised as having 'the biggest stars of 1960', and features not only Cliff and the Shadows but Frankie Avalon, Freddie Cannon, Clyde McPhatter, Sammy Turner and the Clovers.

JANUARY 21 — Cliff appears on the Pat Boone Show on American TV singing 'Forty Days', 'Living Doll', 'Dynamite', 'Voice In The Wilderness' and 'Whole Lotta Shakin', Pat Boone introduces Cliff as 'Britain's most important singing and record star — a young British lad — terribly young, terribly rich, who tonight makes his television debut. Welcome, Cliff Richard!' Cliff's opening number 'Living Doll' draws comments of 'Wizard', 'Smashing' and 'Top-hole' from Pat Boone. A conversation ensues:

Cliff: 'What? What'd he say?'
Pat: 'I simply said, "Wizard, smashing".'
Cliff: 'Excuse me a moment, please (consults American-English dictionary). Oh, you mean crazy!'
Pat: 'Well, yes, if you prefer technical terminology. You know, Cliff, I've been reading up on you and I see that you were born in India, but left for England at the age of one. How come?'
Cliff: 'Frankly, Pat, when you've shot one elephant you've shot them all. Besides, I was getting to be quite a burden on the family. A year old and I hadn't had a single hit record yet!'
Pat: 'That's the most tragic story I've heard since *Death of a Salesman*. By the way, we're all looking forward to your new picture *Expresso Bongo*.'
Cliff: 'Oh, thank you Pat, it was a fun thing to make.'
Pat: 'Fun thing? Oh, dangerous, eh? But what does the title *Expresso Bongo* mean?'
Cliff: 'Don't know exactly. I believe it has to do with Italian coffee served in a drum.'
Pat: 'Oh, that's a fun joke. I love British humour, it's so quaint.'

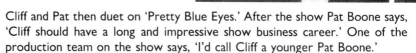

Cliff: 'Thank you! You know, one of England's favourite humorists happens to be an *American* star?'
Pat: 'Oh, really?'
Cliff: 'Oh, *indeed*! Matter of fact, I'd like to sing a little tribute to him – if you'd care to join me.'
Pat: 'Charmed – what'll it be?'
Cliff: 'It's called "Pretty Blue Eyes". I hope you like it, Mr Jack Benny ... '

Cliff and Pat then duet on 'Pretty Blue Eyes.' After the show Pat Boone says, 'Cliff should have a long and impressive show business career.' One of the production team on the show says, 'I'd call Cliff a younger Pat Boone.'

JANUARY 23   A member of the official Elvis Presley Fan Club of Great Britain meets Elvis in Paris and says of Cliff Richard: 'He's at the top in Britain at present, but no doubt you will put him back in his rightful place when you get back to the civilian life.' Elvis is not pleased with the statement and retorts, 'There is room at the top for everyone.'

FEBRUARY □   *Cliff Sings No.1* EP released.

FEBRUARY 5   Cliff's manager Tito Burns comments on his return from the American tour: 'The entire company (including Frankie Avalon, Freddie Cannon, Johnny and the Hurricanes and Sammy Turner) stood and cheered Cliff.'

■ Cliff and Frankie Avalon

THE CLIFF RICHARD FILE 1960

FEBRUARY 12 Pop TV producer Jack Good, speaking out in an interview, says, 'I don't think Cliff would have existed at all as a singer without Elvis. He certainly wouldn't be the singer he is today. The initial impetus of Cliff's singing was entirely due to Elvis's influence.'

Cliff forms his own publishing company Eugene Music. His parents Mr and Mrs Rodger Webb are among the directors.

FEBRUARY 19 Marty Wilde supports Jack Good's theory when he comments in an interview: 'Without Elvis Presley the main influence of rock 'n' roll would never have appeared, so neither would Cliff Richard.'

Tito Burns disagrees: 'Tommy rot! I can't believe Jack really meant it in his heart.'

Michael Holliday: 'Cliff undoubtedly had the quality to enable him to develop on his own.'

Norrie Paramor: 'Absolute nonsense! In fact, but for fate decreeing that Elvis should come on the scene first, the Presley-Richard situation could easily have happened in reverse.'

Lionel Bart: 'I must concede that Jack Good is perfectly reasonable when he states that Cliff was considerably influenced by Elvis.'

FEBRUARY 19 Cliff leaves Wichita, Kansas by plane.

■ Cliff and his parents flying to America

FEBRUARY 20	At 10pm Cliff arrives at London Airport four hours late after running into bad weather, and goes home to Cheshunt. The Shadows remain in the States, committed to fulfil tour dates.
FEBRUARY 21	Cliff appears at the *NME* Poll Winners' Concert before 10,000 people, with a group called the Parker Royal Four backing him. He shares the No. 1 dressing-room with Marty Wilde.

In the evening Cliff appears on 'Sunday Night at the London Palladium', again with the Parker Royal Four, who comprise 20-year-old car mechanic Norman Sheffield on drums, two 18-year-old clerks Norman Tracey and John Rogers on guitar and bass respectively and leader Brian Parker, a 20-year-old accountant who was once a member of the same skiffle group as Cliff. Cliff says, 'They come closer to the Shadows than any other group I've heard.' The group is Cliff's choice, as opposed to that of manager Tito Burns who had hoped to arrange an accompaniment which included Cherry Wainer and Don Storer, as well as three guitarists and a percussionist!

Cliff has the last word on the Elvis/Cliff controversy; 'I feel that without Elvis I certainly wouldn't be the singer I am today. I'd like to go on record as saying that in my opinion Elvis is the greatest.'

MARCH □	*Cliff Sings No.2* EP released.
MARCH 4	In an interview in Germany just prior to leaving the army, Elvis singles out Cliff, Marty Wilde and Tommy Steele as three British singers with whom he is specially familiar and whose records he has.
MARCH 14	Cliff receives the Carl-Allan Award for the artist who made the most popular record during 1959 ('Living Doll').
MARCH 15	*Expresso Bongo* opens at the Sutton Theatre, New York.
MARCH 18	Cliff's 8th single 'Fall In Love With You/Willie and the Hand Jive' is released. It eventually sells enough copies to earn Cliff a Silver Disc. Reviewing it, Keith Fordyce says, 'It's a pretty ditty that will appeal to a wide audience.'
MARCH 19	Cliff stars in ATV's 'Saturday Spectacular' with Peter Elliott, Janette Scott and Al Saxon as his guests.
MARCH 22	Cliff stars in the BBC's Royal Albert Hall concert with Ted Heath, Edmundo Ros and Chris Barber.
MARCH 28	Cliff is presented to Prince Philip, the Duchess of Kent and Princess Alexandra at the Royal Film Performance at Leicester Square Odeon.

Prince Philip: 'How long have you been back from America and was it hard work?'

Cliff: 'Yes, it has been.'

Prince Philip: 'Yes, I know work doesn't seem to stop.'

Cliff: 'It's a good job it doesn't, sir!'

MARCH 30	Along with sixteen other artists, Cliff helps to raise £3,750 at a Wembley concert in aid of spastics.
MARCH 31	Cliff is the guest of Eamonn Andrews on BBC TV's 'Crackerjack'.

APRIL ☐	*Cliff Sings No.3* EP released.
APRIL ☐	Cliff moves into a semi-detached corner house in Winchmore Hill with his parents and three sisters. The dining-room has a 1960 Design Award mahogany suite with red upholstery. The kitchen floor is covered in grey lino with harlequin colours on the chairs and pink wallpaper. Cliff's bedroom wallpaper is green at one end of the room, with natives and yaks all over it, the other three walls being sunshine yellow. By the side of his bed is a reading lamp presented by the 59 Teenage Club of the Eton Mission in Hackney Wick. Cliff's youngest sisters Jacqueline and Joan share a bedroom, while Donna has her own room with a little balcony. Cliff's grey Sunbeam Alpine sports car is invariably parked outside.
APRIL 4	Cliff starts a week of variety at the Glasgow Empire. The crowds create traffic chaos, and national press coverage follows.
APRIL 11	Week of variety at Coventry Theatre.
APRIL 13	'Me and My Shadows' ten-minute ATV show.
APRIL 17	Six and a half thousand people pack Blackpool's Opera House to see Cliff and the Shadows. Several hundred fans smashed down a side floor in an attempt to get to their idol.
APRIL 18	Week of variety at Sheffield Lyceum.
APRIL 30	The coach driver taking Cliff and the other artists from Norwich to Bradford turns up three hours late, and three thousand fans chant 'We Want Cliff' at Bradford's Gaumont Theatre when the show starts two hours late.
MAY 2	Cliff's Sunbeam Alpine, worth £1,000, disappears in Derby.
MAY 3	The Sunbeam Alpine turns up 300 miles away in Dundee.
MAY 13	On being told that he has again been chosen for the Royal Variety Show, Cliff says, 'When I was chosen for the last Royal Variety in Manchester, I felt that I had then reached a peak, so I'm completely knocked out at being selected again! In fact, everything is going so well at the moment I'm scared to breathe in case something goes wrong. Nervous? Of course I am. My stomach is turning seventy-five cartwheels every minute at the thought of next Monday'.
MAY 14	Series of one-night-stands comes to an end at Clacton Essoldo.
MAY 16	Cliff appears on a Royal Variety Show which includes Russ Conway, Diana Dors, Lonnie Donegan, Liberace, Max Bygraves, Adam Faith, Nat King Cole and Billy Cotton.
MAY 19	Cliff's discovery Dave Simpson enters the charts with a song called 'Sweet Dreams'. He is backed by his group the Hunters – previously the Parker Royal Four who had deputised for the Shadows backing Cliff in February.
MAY 21	Cliff has Bobby Rydell as his guest on ATV's 'Saturday Spectacular'.
MAY 23	Columbia throw a party for eighty teenagers to help them decide which of the twenty-four sides recorded by Cliff the previous month will be his new single. The teenagers are drawn from youth organisations, Cliff's Fan Club and EMI staff and after listening to the tracks vote for their favourites.

After allotting their respective marks, the four most popular are evaluated.

1	'Please Don't Tease'	758 points
2	'Gee Whiz It's You'	714 points
3	'Nine Times Out Of Ten'	708 points
4	'I'm Willing To Learn'	672 points

■ Cliff announces the result of the ballot to his fans

THE CLIFF RICHARD FILE **1960**

JUNE ☐ Cliff and the Shadows – along with Joan Regan, Russ Conway, Edmund Hockridge and Des O'Connor – open in the long-running London Palladium season *Stars In Your Eyes*. Cliff performs five numbers a night with the Shadows, as well as appearing in a novelty song 'Open Up the Doghouse' with David Kossoff.

JULY 1 *NME* publish the British chart entry score for January-June 1960 with 30 points for No.1., 29 for No.2., 28 for No. 3. etc. down to 1 point for No. 30.

1 Adam Faith	779
2 Cliff Richard	713
3 Anthony Newley	609
4 Johnny Preston	531
5 Emile Ford	471

JULY 7 'Me & My Shadows' 13-week Sunday night series on Radio Luxembourg commences. Each show runs fifteen minutes.

THE CLIFF RICHARD FILE **1960**

JULY 11   The London *Evening News* starts a series 'What Are They Really Like – the pop stars Adored by Millions?', inviting the readers to 'look behind the glossy façade'. They feature the personal story of Cliff.

JULY 15   Columbia A & R manager and Cliff's producer Norrie Paramor says he's confident that the sales of 'Travellin' Light' will pass the million mark within a few weeks, making him only the second British artist to win *two* Gold Discs. (The other was pianist Winifred Atwell.)

JULY 22   'Please Don't Tease' knocks Jimmy Jones' 'Good Timin'' off the No. 1 spot.

Fans notice that the Cliff crucifix normally around Cliff's neck has recently been replaced by a St Christopher. Cliff answers: 'The crucifix was given to me when I first began in show business, but when I heard a false rumour that I condemned Protestants and that I was Catholic, I left it off. I'm a Protestant myself, but I have many good friends in other denominations and wouldn't dream of condemning any religious body.'

When asked who he thinks his biggest rivals will be by the summer of 1961, Cliff replies 'Kenny Lynch and Dave Sampson'.

JULY 23   Cliff admits that he would like to have recorded two songs that are current hits – 'Angela Jones' and 'When Johnny Comes Marching Home' – and that if he had to select any personality to entertain him for one evening, it would be Ray Charles.

JULY ☐   The Shadows have the first of many hits which are to span more than two decades.

JULY 29   Cliff approves the story for his third film, which it is announced is to be adapted from Margery Allingham's novel *Hide My Eyes*. Negotiations are under way to secure American actress Carol Lynley as co-star. Cliff says, 'I've been an admirer of Carol since I saw her in *Blue Jeans*. She is my automatic idea of a co-star.'

JULY 31   Cliff Richard stars in 'Saturday Spectacular' for ATV, where producer Norrie Paramor presents him with a golden car mascot.

AUGUST 5   'Please Don't Tease' is No. 1 for the third week running.

AUGUST 12   Cliff buys a new Ford Thunderbird from Lex Garages in London's Lexington Street.

AUGUST 19   'Please Don't Tease' deposed by the Shadows' 'Apache'.

AUGUST 26   The music press pays tribute to Cliff's second anniversary in show business.

SEPTEMBER 1   Cliff meets American actress Annette Funicello after learning that she couldn't get tickets for his Palladium review *Stars In Your Eyes*. He invites Annette and her mother to be his guests at the show and takes them out for dinner afterwards. Annette says, 'Cliff is very like Paul Anka, who is a great friend of mine; his manner is almost identical.'

SEPTEMBER 16   Cliff's 10th single 'Nine Times Out Of Ten/Thinking of our Love' is released and sets up a new record for advance sales for a single in Britain (nearly 180,000).

SEPTEMBER 22   'Nine Times Out Of Ten' goes straight into the Top 10, while 'Please Don't Tease' is still well-placed in the Top 20.

THE CLIFF RICHARD FILE 1960

SEPTEMBER ☐	*Cliff Sings No. 4* EP released.
OCTOBER 1	Cliff and the Shadows appear on TV's 'Oh Boy' and among other tracks perform 'Evergreen Tree' from their new album.
OCTOBER 3	Cherry Wainer, making her first tracks for EMI, records a song written by Cliff, 'Happy Like A Bell (Ding Dong)'.
OCTOBER 7	The album *Me & My Shadows* is released, and the music paper headlines boldly proclaim, 'No home should be without this album by Cliff.' The sixteen tracks comprise what is thought by many fans of Cliff and the Shadows to be their greatest LP together.
OCTOBER 9	Cliff receives an early birthday present of a silver St Christopher for his car from the Mayor of Bexhill.
OCTOBER 14	It is announced that Cliff will star in his own TV series on ATV, commencing in the early part of 1961. Six half-hour shows are envisaged, on which he'll be supported by the Shadows and the Vernons Girls, with Jack Parnell as musical director.
OCTOBER 16	Cliff co-stars in ATV's Sunday afternoon show 'Birthday Honours' with unknown science student Fred Chiftenden. Hosted by Godfrey Winn, the programme traces the careers of the two young men, both born on October 14 1940 – Cliff, the £1,000 per week singing star, and Putney-based Fred, a student at the Imperial College of Science living on £6 per week.
OCTOBER ☐	Cliff signs a new contract with manager Tito Burns.
OCTOBER 19	EMI managing director, Len Wood, reveals that in the two years since his career started, Cliff has sold a remarkable 5½ million single records.
OCTOBER 21	Cliff receives a solid silver St Christopher key-ring from his South African fan club, and a box of Polynesian cakes from fans in Honolulu.
OCTOBER 28	Cliff's first published composition 'Happy Like A Bell (Ding-Dong)' is released on Columbia. Performed by Cherry Wainer, it features Shadow Bruce Welch on guitar and Cliff singing the 'ding-dongs'!
OCTOBER 28	*NME* poll results are published, and Cliff receives the following positions: World Male Singer – 2nd to Elvis Presley British Male Singer – 1st British Vocal Personality – 2nd to Lonnie Donegan World Musical Personality – 5th behind Duane Eddy, Elvis, Sammy Davis, and Russ Conway Best British Disc of the Year – 'Please Don't Tease' is 2nd to the Shadows' 'Apache'. His 'second to Elvis' in the World Male Singer section is the highest position ever attained by any British artist in a world category.
OCTOBER 28 OCTOBER ☐	Cliff's autobiography *It's Great to be Young*, Souvenir Press, at 12/6d. Secret transatlantic negotiations under way for Cliff to make a film in Hollywood. Names linked with the venture are Elvis's manager Colonel Tom Parker and Hal Wallis (who has Elvis under an exclusive film contract).
OCTOBER 30	Cliff and the Shadows appear at the annual concert at Cliff's old school in Cheshunt, in aid of the town's youth club building. Also featured are Cliff's cousin Johnny Carson and singer Neil Christian.

THE CLIFF RICHARD FILE **1960**

■ 'Do I really have to sign the back of a Drifters picture?'

NOVEMBER 1	Casting scheduled to commence for Cliff's third film based on the novel *Hide My Eyes*, a murder thriller in which he'll sing at least three songs. Shooting is due to start at the end of January.
NOVEMBER 20	Cliff is featured in a 40-minute broadcast on the BBC's Home Service, in conversation with Steve Race and poet Royston Ellis. He discusses his career, private life, Elvis, girl-friends and money.
NOVEMBER 25	Cliff's 11th single 'I Love You/'D' In Love' is released. The 'A' side is written by Shadow Bruce Welch.
DECEMBER 1	'I Love You' moves straight into the Top 10, and goes on to earn a Silver Disc.
DECEMBER 1	*Cliff's Silver Discs* EP released.
DECEMBER 1	Cliff performs in front of the Queen Mother in a Royal version of 'Stars In Your Eyes' with Judy Garland, Bruce Forsyth, the Shadows and the Norrie Paramor Orchestra.
DECEMBER 2	Cliff buys himself out of his film contract with producer Mickey Delemar, allegedly for a sum running well into five figures.
DECEMBER 9	Cliff vows, 'After being at the London Palladium for six months, I shall never, never stay at the same theatre for more than two weeks in future.'
DECEMBER 11	Cliff records two songs in German at the Abbey Road Studios.
DECEMBER 12	Cliff takes his first holiday for eighteen months when he flies to Spain with his mother, two of his sisters and road manager Mike Conlin.
DECEMBER 27	Cliff's father Rodger Webb, ill with heart trouble, enters a North London hospital.
DECEMBER 28	EMI chairman Sir Joseph Lockwood claims that the company had no less than a quarter of the world's total sales during 1960, and Cliff is their best-selling artist having topped the charts not only in Britain but Australia, Holland, New Zealand, Sweden, Singapore and South Africa.

1961

JANUARY 6	*NME*'s analysis of the best-selling charts for 1960 is published. With 30 points for each week at No.1, down to 1 point for the No.30 position, final placings are:

1 Cliff Richard	1,416
2 Adam Faith	1,386
3 Elvis Presley	1,104
4 Everly Brothers	965
5 Anthony Newley	965
6 Connie Francis	915
7 Jimmy Jones	758
8 Duane Eddy	732
9 Johnny & the Hurricanes	684
10 Shadows	655

JANUARY 6	Cliff places an ad in the music press:

'My sincere and grateful thanks to all of my friends who sent such wonderful cheery letters and gifts to my father Rodger Webb in hospital. These gestures have been most appreciated, and I am certain will help him on the road to recovery. Once again, my sincere thanks.'

JANUARY 7	ATV announce that Cliff's half-hour series will start on 16 February. Among the guests on the show will be Alma Cogan, Marty Wilde, Cliff's cousin Johnny Carson and Dave Sampson.
JANUARY 15	Cliff headlines a show at the Royal Albert Hall for the dependants of Jack Conway (recently killed in a car crash), an associate of Cliff's manager Tito Burns.

Cliff opens his act with 'Whole Lotta Shakin', followed by 'Willie And The Hand Jive', 'Please Don't Tease', 'I Love You' and finishes with his version of Ray Charles' 'What'd I Say'. Also on the bill are the Shadows, Cliff's protégé Dave Sampson, Bert Weedon, the Kaye Sisters, Cherry Wainer, the Vernons Girls, Jackie Rae and Janette Scott, Chas McDevitt and Shirley Douglas.

JANUARY 16	Cliff's producer Norrie Paramor goes into Abbey Road Studios to produce 'Please Don't Treat Me Like A Child' for 14-year-old schoolgirl Helen Shapiro. She joins the Columbia label and becomes Cliff's stablemate.
JANUARY 18	Cliff records two programmes for the BBC's transcription service, backed by Ted Heath and his Orchestra. Cliff is also featured in sketches with Dickie Valentine.
JANUARY 19	Cliff appears on the BBC TV children's programme 'Crackerjack', hosted by Eamonn Andrews.
JANUARY 20	Cliff and the Shadows' manager Peter Gormley meet for talks in Peter's office.

■ Cliff meets the fans

JANUARY 23	'Cliff and Elvis choose their favourite love songs for you,' reads the newspaper advertisement for the *Mirabelle* girls' magazine. A special song supplement pull-out includes the lyrics of 'Nine Times Out Of Ten' and 'Living Doll'.
JANUARY 28	Cliff's father leaves hospital.
JANUARY 29	Cliff reveals that he's a great fan of Dakota Staton.
FEBRUARY 5	Cliff begins a tour starting at the Birmingham Hippodrome, headlining a bill that includes Cherry Wainer, Chas McDevitt and Shirley Douglas, Dave Sampson and the Hunters and Norman Vaughan.
FEBRUARY 10	A banner headline in the music press asks, 'Should the Shadows part from Cliff?'
FEBRUARY 16	Cliff begins a TV series which is to include Marty Wilde, the Kaye Sisters and Jill Browne – star of TV's 'Emergency Ward 10' in which she plays nurse Carole Young – with whom Cliff sings a duet.
FEBRUARY 17	T. Birckby of Huddersfield sparks off a mini-storm with his letter of the previous week to the music papers, which ended '. . . Cliff Richard, Adam Faith and Fabian are poor singers and the songs they record are trash.' Hundreds of letters pour in to the music press – some agreeing, but most up in arms. Ruth Esau of Virginia Water in Surrey has the most sensible remark to make, stating in her letter that 'One man's meat is another man's poison.'
FEBRUARY 18	Cliff has five songs in India's Top 10!
FEBRUARY 18	Impresario Leslie Grade reveals that Cliff could earn around £30,000 from a forthcoming film which is planned. The picture will co-star actor Robert

Morley and feature the Shadows, but is as yet unnamed.

FEBRUARY 19 — Cliff dines with American singer Bobby Rydell.

FEBRUARY 23 — Cliff duets with Marty Wilde on 'Rubber Ball' on ATV.

FEBRUARY 24 — Cliff's 12th single 'Theme For A Dream/Mumblin' Mosie' is released. One reviewer calls it, 'A light and pretty number, easy on the ear, with a good tune which will set you humming or whistling.'

FEBRUARY 24 — Cliff appears on a BBC Home Service radio documentary 'Teen Beat' hosted by Steve Race. The programme is subtitled, 'A survey of a teenage idol and his music!'

FEBRUARY 27 — Cliff and the Shadows receive Carl-Allan Awards at London's Lyceum Ballroom. Cliff's trophy is in recognition of the best vocal record of the year for dancing.

FEBRUARY 27 — EMI reveal that advance orders for 'Theme For A Dream' exceed 200,000.
FEBRUARY □ — Columbia release *Me And My Shadows No.1* EP.

■ Me and my Shadows

MARCH 1 — Cliff on BBC's 'Parade of the Pops'.

MARCH 1 — It is announced that Australian Peter Gormley, who came to Britain at the end of 1959 with Frank Ifield, is to be Cliff's new personal manager. Peter has already been looking after the Shadows since July 1960.

MARCH 5 — In the afternoon Cliff appears at the *NME* Poll Winners' Concert at Wembley's Empire Pool. In the evening he tele-records a London Palladium Special for NBC to be networked across the United States. Comedian Charlie Drake and the Tiller Girls are also on the show, which is compèred by Laurence Harvey.

MARCH 6	Cliff and the Shadows experience a 4½-hour delay at London Airport as they attempt to fly to South Africa, and end up going to see a horror film in Hounslow. They eventually take off 6 hours late. The tour takes in South Africa, Australia, New Zealand, Singapore and Malaya.
MARCH 7	Cliff and the Shadows arrive in Salisbury, Rhodesia, to be greeted by a 3,000-strong crowd.
MARCH 10	Cliff reveals that the co-star in his new but as yet unnamed film will be a German girl, Heidi Bruhl. He says, 'She sings extremely well and looks a million dollars. My own thought is that I would like to see young Helen Shapiro in the film. She's only 14 years old, but she has immense potential and could well become one of the biggest names in show business.'
MARCH 13	Cliff is nominated 'Star of Stars' by *Weekend* magazine. As he's in South Africa, his sister Donella collects the award on his behalf at London's Lyceum Ballroom.
MARCH ☐	*Me And My Shadows No.2* EP released.
MARCH 13/14	Ten thousand teenage fans disrupt traffic in Johannesburg as they surround Cliff's hotel, causing scenes never before witnessed in South Africa. Police, the Flying Squad and the traffic department combine to maintain a constant guard on the Carlton Hotel, to prevent girls getting in. At one stage Cliff addresses the massive crowd from the balcony, but can hardly be heard except for the words '... this is the most fantastic sight I've ever seen.'
MARCH 15	EMI South Africa record Cliff's entire act before a capacity audience at the Johannesburg Colosseum. This is the first time that Cliff and the Shadows have been recorded at a public concert.
MARCH 17	The March issue of *Hit Parade* magazine (2/-) features an article personally written by Cliff.
MARCH ☐	Top South African DJ Bob Holness interviews Cliff for his Durban 'Calling to Youth' show, prior to leaving the Union to seek a broadcasting career in Britain.
APRIL 7	On his return from South Africa Cliff talks to journalist Derek Johnson: 'The only minor upset of the tour was the controversy over the colour bar, which prevented some of the non-Europeans from seeing our show. When we were first offered the contract to go to South Africa, we didn't realise there would be those problems, and when they arose we found ourselves in rather an awkward position. We overcame this situation to the best of our ability by offering to do a couple of shows especially for the non-Europeans, with the proceeds going to charity. Those shows took place in Cape Town and Salisbury. Despite this colour-bar policy I found that the whites were very tolerant towards the coloureds.'
APRIL 7	'Gee Whizz It's You/I Cannot Find A True Love' enters the Top 20. So many copies were unofficially imported into this country that EMI recognise its potential and belatedly release it as Cliff's 13th single.
APRIL ☐	*Me And My Shadows No.3* EP released.
APRIL ☐	It is announced that Cliff and the Shadows will undertake a season at Blackpool Opera House, commencing on Monday 28 August.
APRIL ☐	A mail order firm starts selling the 'Cliff' two-way shirt in black and white for 32/6d.

THE CLIFF RICHARD FILE 1961

APRIL 8	Cliff makes his debut on BBC TV's 'Juke Box Jury', discussing the week's new releases along with Dora Bryan, Janet Munro and DJ Ray Orchard. There are a couple of hiccups for normally unruffled chairman David Jacobs, as he wrongly announces that Dave King's 'Young In Love' is a remake of Tab Hunter's 'Young Love', and then plays 'Intermezzo', the 'B' side of Mañuel's 'Mountain Carnival'.
APRIL 9	Cliff begins a short series of one-night stands, headlining with the Shadows on a bill which includes the Brook Brothers, Ricky & Geoff, and Patti Brooks. After the opening show at Liverpool Empire all the artists celebrate Geoff Brook's birthday at a back-stage party.
APRIL 21	Cliff has two discs in the Top 10: 'Theme For A Dream' and 'Gee Whiz It's You'.
APRIL 21	*Listen to Cliff* LP is released. Cliff is accompanied by the Shadows on eight of the tracks, by the Norrie Paramor Orchestra on four numbers, and on the remaining four by the Bernard Ebbinghouse Band.
APRIL 22	Cliff appears on BBC Light Programme's 'Saturday Club'.
APRIL 26	Cliff is on BBC's 'Parade of the Pops'.
APRIL 28	In an interview with journalist Mike Hellicar, Cliff speaks out about the fact that for the first time in his career he has two records in the Top 10: 'I wasn't at all pleased when I found that "Gee Whizz It's You" was available as a single in Britain. I thought quite honestly that the decision to release the disc in Britain was a bad one.'
APRIL 28	It is announced that the shooting of Cliff's as yet unnamed new film will be delayed until the end of May. Also revealed is that Robert Morley – cast as Cliff's father in the film – probably won't be available and the role may be taken by veteran actor Stanley Holloway of *My Fair Lady* fame.
APRIL 30	Listeners to BBC's Network Three magazine programme 'Sound' hear part of an actual Cliff recording session in progress, with the voices of producer Norrie Paramor conducting the orchestra, recording engineer Malcolm Addy and his assistant David Lloyd. The songs being recorded are 'Lover' and 'It's Almost Like Being In Love' for the album *Listen to Cliff*.
MAY 8	Network Three programme 'Sound' is repeated.
MAY 11	Cliff, along with the Shadows, is featured in a 20-minute cabaret spot at the NSPCC Pied Piper Ball. Cliff's appearance is at the specific request of Princess Margaret who attends with her husband Anthony Armstrong-Jones.
MAY 12	It is revealed that Cliff's new film is to be called *The Young Ones*, and there is likely to be a major role for Diana Dors. Robert Morley is reinstated in the part of Cliff's father in the film.
MAY 12	Christine Porter of Reading and Gloria Vingue of Wembley, both BBC TV employees leaving for jobs in the United States, have a 'last request' granted when they are taken to meet Cliff at BBC's Television Theatre.
MAY 15	Cliff's father Rodger Webb dies, aged 57.
MAY 19	A virtually unknown actress from London's East End is named as Cliff's co-star in *The Young Ones*. She is 21-year-old Annette Robertson, who was in the

original production of *Fings Ain't Wot They Used T' Be!* On the same day Cliff talks about Radio Luxembourg on their 30th Anniversary: 'I feel sure that thanks to Radio Luxembourg, I have made a whole army of new friends. I have the greatest possible admiration for this organisation, which is an absolute boon to the youngsters – and, of course, a blessing to recording artists like me!'

MAY 26   South African Carole Gray, a dancer in *West Side Story*, is signed up to play Cliff's girl-friend in *The Young Ones*, while Annette Robertson (originally reported as starring in the role) will have another part in the film. The same day Cliff presents awards at the Methodist Association of Youth Clubs annual get-together at London's Royal Albert Hall.

JUNE 2   Cliff takes part in a charity show in aid of the African Bureau at London's Victoria Palace. Also in the show are Georgia Brown, Cleo Laine and the casts of *Fings Ain't Wot They Used T' Be!* and *Beyond The Fringe*.

JUNE ☐   In the June issue of *Hit Parade*, Cliff describes his dream year.

JUNE 9   Cliff talks about *The Young Ones*: 'It's not often that I get nervous, but boy, those butterflies really got at me for the whole of the first day's shooting – and stayed for almost the rest of the week.'

JUNE 12   Cliff buys a powder-blue Hillman Automatic for his mother Dorothy Webb.

JUNE 16   Cliff's 14th single (the 13th being the imported 'Gee Whizz It's You') is released – 'A Girl Like You/Now's The Time To Fall In Love'. A favourite song of Cliff's late father, it is described by one reviewer as 'the prettiest song that Cliff has got hold of since "Living Doll" – it stands every chance of getting to Number One.'

JUNE 17   Cliff sings his new single on BBC's 'Saturday Club'. His projected tour of Scandinavia is confirmed for August.

JUNE 25   In top hat and tails, Cliff duets with Russ Conway on BBC TV's 'Billy Cotton Band Show'.

JUNE 26   Along with Helen Shapiro, Cliff stars in Radio Luxembourg's hour-long 'Monday Spectacular', hosted by Muriel Young and Shaw Taylor. The show is recorded in front of a hundred teenagers.

JUNE 30   'Theme For A Dream' tops the charts in New Zealand.

JULY 3   Cliff's producer Norrie Paramor and his wife Joan celebrate their 18th wedding anniversary.

JULY 7   Cliff is booked for the 'Jo Stafford Show' being recorded at ATV's Elstree Studios for transmission in the United States.

JULY 7   The *NME*'s chart points table for January-June 1961 is published, with 30 points for each week at No.1, down to 1 point for each week at No.30.

1 Elvis Presley	916
2 Cliff Richard	581
3 The Shadows	519
4 Everly Brothers	488
5 Matt Monro	374
6 Adam Faith	365
7 Bobby Vee	356
8 Temperance Seven	355
9 Duane Eddy	341
10 Allisons	314

JULY ☐   Robert Hofschroer and Kevin Sparrow, winners of the National Deaf Children's Society film script competition, win a visit to Elstree to watch *The Young Ones* being shot and to meet Cliff.

AUGUST 4   As pictures from the set of *The Young Ones* are released, Cliff admits, 'I have benefited enormously as a result of working with such a fine actor as Robert Morley. I've been getting along wonderfully with Carole [Gray] – she's a great girl and everyone likes her. In fact, the other evening she invited the company to a barbecue at her home.'

AUGUST 6   Cliff attends the marriage of his 18-year-old sister Donella to Paul Stevens at Waltham Abbey in Essex. Norrie Paramor and the Shadows are guests at the wedding.

AUGUST 9/10   Cliff records tracks for *The Young Ones*.

AUGUST 11   Discussing their forthcoming debut LP *The Shadows*, on which Hank Marvin performs a solo vocal 'Baby My Heart', Hank jokes, 'Cliff's scared to death as a result of this unexpected competition.' And on the subject of Bruce Welch's vocal solo, Hank adds, 'Cliff's not so worried about this one!'

AUGUST 13   Cliff hosts a birthday dinner for his mother Dorothy Webb.

AUGUST 18   *The Young Ones* producer Kenneth Harper reveals that, 'Interest in the advance prints of the film has been so great that we had no hesitation in beginning an immediate search for a new script for Cliff and the Shadows – we have decided to start production in May or June 1962.'

AUGUST ☐   Cliff buys a record shop for his newly married sister Donella and her husband Paul.

AUGUST ☐   In Norway, Cliff is presented with a Silver Disc for 'Living Doll' at a concert in Oslo. He becomes the first British artist to win the award, which is made by the Norwegian newspaper *Arbeiderbladet* and handed to him by DJ Erik Heyerdahl.

AUGUST 28   Cliff and the Shadows start a six-week season at Blackpool's Opera House.

SEPTEMBER 1   Cliff's 'A Girl Like You' is at No.7 in the British charts and No.3 in New Zealand. His version of 'Beat Out Dat Rhythm' is at No.5 in Holland, and in South Africa 'Gee Whiz It's You' is also at No.5.

SEPTEMBER 5   Cliff's protégé Dave Sampson leaves the Columbia label to join Fontana.

SEPTEMBER 9   An enteritis epidemic – which has been causing havoc among many artists appearing in Blackpool summer shows – lays low Bruce Welch. Lonnie Donegan's guitarist Les Bennett joins the Shadows to back Cliff for one night only.

SEPTEMBER 10   Bruce Welch recovers sufficiently to rejoin Cliff and the Shadows at *NME*'s all-star concert at Wembley's Empire Pool. Many girls vault the protective rail separating the stage from the auditorium to throw roses at Cliff.

SEPTEMBER □   During the Blackpool season, Cliff shares a house with the Shadows a couple of miles down the coast at Lytham St Annes, which had been prepared by his mother during their Scandinavian tour.

SEPTEMBER 14   A fan sends Cliff a 303-page letter!

SEPTEMBER 15   'A Girl Like You' tops the charts in Hong Kong. A newspaper claims that Delia Wicks, who sings in John Leyton's backing group the Angels, is a 'close' friend of Cliff's.

SEPTEMBER 17   Cliff appears at the Royal Albert Hall with the Shadows, Adam Faith, Helen Shapiro and the John Barry Seven at a concert promoted by the *Daily Mirror* for the printers' pension fund.

SEPTEMBER 22   The wives of Shadows Hank Marvin and Bruce Welch arrive in Blackpool. Shadow Jet Harris moves into a bungalow with Cliff.

SEPTEMBER 29   Connie Francis reveals that she would like Cliff or Adam Faith to make a guest appearance in her forthcoming film tentatively titled *Cook's Tour*, which would feature pop talent from Britain and the Continent.

SEPTEMBER 29   Southport fans present Cliff with a ten-week-old Pyrennean Mountain puppy.

SEPTEMBER 30   Cliff watches Preston North End play Leyton Orient at Preston's Deepdale ground as a guest of impresario Leslie Grade.

SEPTEMBER □   In a New Zealand disc popularity survey, Connie Francis comes top, followed by Elvis Presley with Cliff third.

OCTOBER □   *Listen To Cliff No.1* EP released.

OCTOBER 6   Cliff's 15th single is released: 'When The Girl In Your Arms Is The Girl In Your Heart/Got A Funny Feeling'. Both tracks are from the Associated British film *The Young Ones*. On the same day, Drummer Tony Meehan leaves the Shadows and is replaced by Krew Kats drummer Brian Bennett.

OCTOBER 7   Cliff appears on 'Thank Your Lucky Stars', his first television programme since 'The Billy Cotton Band Show' on 24 June.

OCTOBER 13   Cliff and his *Young Ones* co-star Carole Gray appear on the front cover of the *NME*. The paper includes a four-page tribute to Cliff as he comes of age the following day.

Mr Ludovic Stewart, Music Advisor for Cambridgeshire schools, says in his annual report: 'Mr Cliff Richard and his associates have done more to continue some children's musical education than the whole world of music teachers and administrators. There is no doubt that some outlay on guitars would benefit an enormous proportion of the secondary school community.'

OCTOBER 14   Many stars pay tribute to Cliff on his 21st Birthday.

Cliff's producer Norrie Paramor recalls the early days of his career in

 Johnny Weissmuller eat your heart out

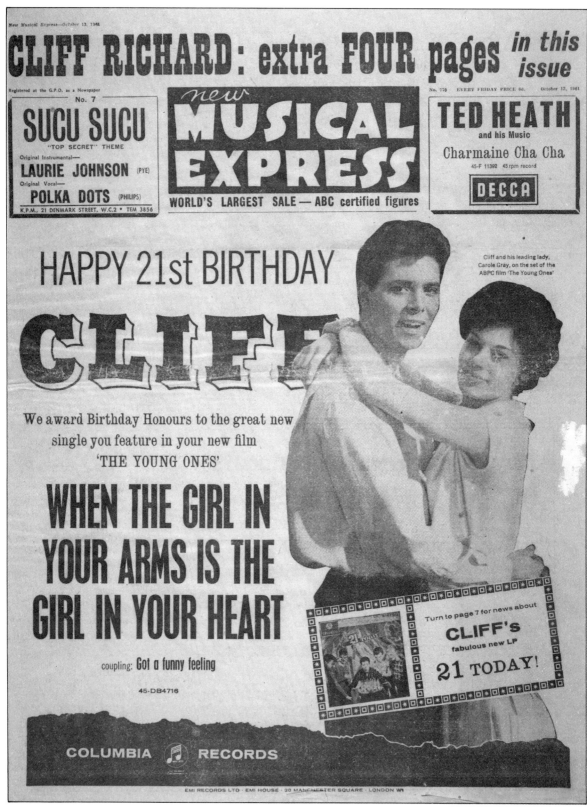

Elvis to return to the Army?

1958: 'He was broke, scared and wondering whether "Move It" would ever really move! I find Cliff exceptionally easy to get along with and I would give him full marks for his ability to take direction, his genuine humility and his directness of opinion.'

Jet Harris, leader of the Shadows, says, 'Cliff's whole character was summed up for us when our recording of "Apache" became a hit ... Cliff's attitude was one of sheer delight ... we were really touched by the real pleasure he derived from our record hit.'

Hank Marvin of the Shadows: 'Cliff has been the perfect ambassador of British show business wherever he has travelled.'

Bruce Welch of the Shadows: 'Despite all the success that has come his way, he hasn't become the slightest bit big-headed.'

Tony Meehan, former Shadows drummer: 'He is undoubtedly one of the finest people character-wise with whom I have ever come into contact. He has great quality and patience, and is a wonderful example to all the young people who admire him.'

Cliff himself looks back over the previous three years: 'It seems incredible that so much has been crammed into such a short spell. If I was asked to nominate the supreme highlight of my career to date, I expect I would settle for the day when I received my Gold Disc for "Living Doll" at the London Palladium.'

A London palmist and clairvoyant scrutinises a photograph of Cliff's hands without knowing who they belong to: She says: 'I feel the subject is very famous, but although he is a very big personality, he is very humble and never forgets people who have helped him, nor does he consider himself too big to mix with ordinary people. He gets very nervous and tensed-up at times. He is religiously minded, and I foresee that anything he prays for will be answered in time. He will marry at one stage in his career and continue to be successful while he enjoys personal happiness. Although this subject is slightly psychic and would enjoy doing this sort of work, he doesn't know that a protective spirit is watching over him. It tells me he will rise to take on even more power. When he marries he will choose someone of refinement and taste. He will have three big romances and lots of little ones, and on his security finger there is a blonde woman, slim and of medium build. There are lots of "sevens" jumping around him, but I am confused to say why. Some of the sevens are forming into groups of five ... the number fourteen keeps recurring. I feel it is very important to him. It is as though he lives two lives, but this could be because he probably has two names. I can see various letters, but I can't identify them as they are such a jumble. I see H–R–Y though!' (Cliff's real name is Harry.)

OCTOBER 14　At Cliff's 21st Birthday Party at EMI's headquarters in London, Sir Joseph Lockwood – the head of EMI – presents him with a Silver Disc for sales of more than 250,000 albums, and a camera.

OCTOBER 14　Jane Maughan of Sanderstead in Surrey presents Cliff with a letter containing 700 sides of writing and 56,000 words on his departure from London Airport.

OCTOBER 15　Cliff and the Shadows are involved in a drama at Singapore Airport when their airliner makes two unsuccessful attempts to land in heavy mist.

OCTOBER 16/19	In Singapore and Kuala Lumpur.
OCTOBER 19/20/21	Cliff appears at Sydney, Australia in front of 12,000 people each night, before going on to Melbourne, Perth, Adelaide and Brisbane. New Zealand appearances in Auckland, Wellington, Dunedin and Christchurch follow.
OCTOBER 20/21	The *Sydney Daily Mail* says: 'Cliff Richard proved a good entertainer and an engaging personality in his Sydney Stadium show. His voice too, was pleasing – when you could hear it above the din of screaming, screeching fans.'
	Noted violinist Florian Zabach, on the bill with Cliff and the Shadows at Sydney, is booed by the audience while he is playing. Florian says, 'I would have been much happier appearing with the Sydney Symphony.'
OCTOBER □	Cliff and Mark Wynter are guests of honour at a Melbourne Teenage Ball.
NOVEMBER 10	Connie Francis releases a cover version of 'When The Girl In Your Arms Is The Girl In Your Heart' in the United States, with a change of gender.
NOVEMBER 17	It is announced that Cliff's next film will probably be called *Summer Holiday*.
NOVEMBER 20	On their return to Britain, Cliff reveals that during the 35 days they were away, he and the Shadows undertook 28 different aircraft flights.
DECEMBER 1	In the annual *NME* poll, Cliff appears in the following categories:

British Male Singer – 1st
World Male Singer – 2nd to Elvis Presley
British Vocal Personality – 2nd to Adam Faith
World Musical Personality – 4th behind Elvis Presley, Duane Eddy and Sammy Davis
Best British Disc of the Year – 4th with 'When The Girl In Your Arms Is The Girl In Your Heart'.

Cliff says, 'I simply can't explain to you how an artist feels when he reads that he has won an honour of this magnitude.' The same day, Norrie Paramor says that he plans five recording sessions for Cliff and the Shadows before Christmas.

DECEMBER 2	Cliff is impresario Leslie Grade's guest at Leyton Orient v Norwich football match.
DECEMBER 8	*The Young Ones* is heralded by the critics as 'The best musical Britain has ever made – and the finest teenage screen entertainment produced for a long time – anywhere!' The plot of *The Young Ones* revolves around a youth club which is due to be torn down in a redevelopment scheme by a company owned by Nicky's (Cliff Richard) father Hamilton Black (Robert Morley). Inevitably Nicky is at loggerheads with his father until the wealthy businessman is won over by the enthusiasm of Nicky's crowd at the youth club, who stage a concert to raise £2,000. The cast includes Robert Morley, Carole Young, Richard O'Sullivan, Melvyn Hayes, Teddy Green, Annette Robertson and Sonya Cordeau. *The Young Ones* is directed by Sidney J. Furie and produced by Kenneth Harper, with screenplay by Peter Myers and Ronald Cass.

Meanwhile the press erroneously announce that the 'B' side of the forthcoming 'Young Ones' single will be 'I'll Wake Up Crying'.

■ Making a big splash in the local dive

DECEMBER 10   Cliff appears on 'Sunday Night at the London Palladium', for the first time since 16 October 1960.

DECEMBER 13   *The Young Ones* is premièred at London's Warner Theatre.

DECEMBER 14   *The Young Ones* LP is released.

DECEMBER 19   A clip from *The Young Ones* is screened by BBC TV in 'Picture Parade'.

DECEMBER 20   Cliff appears at Cheshunt Boys Club charity show at the Edmonton Royal.

DECEMBER 22   Cliff has two records in the South African Top 10: 'Tea For Two' (No.8) and 'A Girl Like You' (No.10). 'When The Girl In Your Arms' is No.1 in Norway and 'Now's The Time' is No.4 in India.

DECEMBER 23   Cliff and his mother fly to South Africa to attend *The Young Ones* being premièred at Johannesburg, Cape Town and Durban.

THE CLIFF RICHARD FILE 1961

DECEMBER **26**   The single of 'The Young Ones' is favourably reviewed in a special Boxing Day edition of 'Juke Box Jury'. Hosted by David Jacobs, the panel comprises DJs Peter Murray and Jean Metcalfe, Hayley Mills and Coronation Street star Alan Rothwell.

The same day Cliff tops the bill in ATV's 'All Kinds Of Music' which had been telerecorded the previous Tuesday. The Kaye Sisters appear on the show, but the Shadows are absent due to engagements in Paris.

DECEMBER **31**   Along with Lonnie Donegan, Alma Cogan, Jack Parnell, Vera Lynn, Roy Castle and Bert Weedon, Cliff is showcased in a special 'Sunday Night at the London Palladium' for ATV.

■ Zzzzz . . . . .

19**62**

JANUARY	There are several reports in the national press that Cliff is to marry 17-year-old Valerie Stratford – a claim that Cliff dismisses as 'crazy'.
JANUARY ☐	Cliff's 16th single 'The Young Ones'/'We say yeah' is released. Both tracks are from the film *The Young Ones*.
JANUARY 11	'The Young Ones' goes straight into the chart at No.1 becoming only the fourth single to achieve this feat in Britain. The others being Al Martino's 'Here in my heart' (on the first ever chart) and Elvis Presley's 'Jailhouse Rock' and 'It's now or never'.
JANUARY 11	'The Young Ones' becomes Cliff's 5th chart-topping single, knocking Danny Williams' 'Moon River' off the No.1 spot and staying there for six weeks before being deposed by Elvis Presley's 'Rock-A-Hula Baby'/'Can't Help Falling In Love'.
MARCH 13	At London's Savoy Hotel, Cliff receives an award from the Variety Club of Great Britain as 'Show Business Personality of the Year'.
MARCH ☐	Along with Mike Berry and the Outlaws, Cliff and the Shadows perform at an historic event at the Eton College Missions Youth Club at Hackney Wick. The occasion is attended by Princess Margaret and the Earl of Snowdon, who are given a 15-minute ovation. Afterwards Cliff joins the Royal couple for tea, cakes and a chat. The Princess tells Cliff that she's going to see *The Young Ones* at the weekend, while the Earl of Snowdon starts to chat about his new Mini-Cooper. Cliff chats about *his* new purchase – a black Cadillac – and promises that if he gets passed by their car he'll try not to pull a face! Cliff says after the meeting, 'They're marvellously friendly people!' The occasion, some of which is recorded on film for posterity, features the Shadows playing 'Apache', while handclaps are provided by the Royal couple, Cliff, Arthur Muxlow (the Club's Vice-President), the Bishop of Bath and Wells and the Reverend W.S.Shergold, the Eton College Mission Club's President.
MARCH ☐	Cliff and the Shadows meet Princess Margaret and Lord Snowdon at the Eton College Mission's Youth Club in Hamburg.
MARCH 25	Cliff withdraws from the Spastics Show at Wembley because of laryngitis. His recovery is aided by medicine recommended by Princess Margaret.
MARCH 30	It is announced that John Krish, documentary writer and director, is to direct Cliff's next film *Summer Holiday*, due to be filmed on location in Greece commencing in mid-May. The film was due to be undertaken by Sydney Furie, who directed *The Young Ones*, but he will continue working on a film starring Jess Conrad, *The Boys*, the music for which has been written by the Shadows.
APRIL ☐	Cliff writes an article for the April issue of *Hit Parade* magazine.
APRIL 6	A copy of the film *The Young Ones* is sent to Princess Margaret at Clarence House.
APRIL ☐	*Cliff Richard No.1* EP released.

■ The Young Ones

APRIL 13 The Shadows become the first British group to win a Gold Disc, and Cliff receives one for 'The Young Ones'. Both are presented during a telerecording of the TV show 'Thank Your Lucky Stars'.

APRIL 13 Cliff's producer Norrie Paramor notches up a second hit for himself with 'The Theme from "Z" Cars'. It's Norrie's wife Joan who is responsible for persuading him to release it. On the subject of 'The Young Ones', Norrie says, 'There's been a good deal of discussion about the backing for "The Young Ones". Some people said that when I dubbed on the strings it "made" the record. I don't agree. They add to the effect by all means, and they probably make it sound much nicer.'

APRIL 15 Dressed in a black tuxedo and white frilled shirt, Cliff headlines the annual *NME* Poll Winners' Concert at Wembley, which features among others Adam Faith, Helen Shapiro and Billy Fury. The awards are presented by Brenda Lee and Johnny Burnette. Cliff and the Shadows open with 'Do You Wanna Dance', followed by 'Razzle Dazzle', a selection of numbers from *The Young Ones* including the title track, 'Lessons In Love' and 'Got A Funny Feeling', concluding with 'We Say Yeah'. This is Jet Harris's final appearance with the Shadows.

APRIL 16 The *NME Tenth Anniversary Book* is published and inevitably includes articles on Cliff.
Cliff pays tribute to the Shadows:
'Hank Marvin is one of the nicest people you could ever wish to meet, and

it's virtually impossible to get annoyed or mad with him. Nothing ever seems to bother him and he takes life in his stride without ever a grumble or a moan.

'Bruce Welch is terribly reliable and he's a bit of a taskmaster in as much as he keeps the boys at it during rehearsals until everything is perfect. You see, perfection is Bruce's aim and he spares nothing to achieve his goal. His attitude has won the respect of all of us.

'Jet Harris is a quiet, shy person who's not in the least bit moody. He's a very deep, serious-thinking fellow, but you just can't help liking him. He has a wonderfully dry sense of humour and is without question the greatest animal lover you ever saw.

'Brian Bennett is very honest. When a thing is bad, he'll have no hesitation in saying so. Similarly, if something impresses him, he really lets you know it. When Tony Meehan left the Shadows we immediately thought of Brian for a replacement. We thought he could do it, but we never realised he'd do it so well.'

Cliff also comments on the Shadows' debut album:
'As far as I'm concerned, this is the best LP ever recorded in Britain. I just love it and I play it at every available opportunity.'

In the same publication, Russ Conway talks about a couple of stunts pulled by Cliff. The first was during the London Palladium run:
'Cliff and the cast, which included Des O'Connor, Joan Regan, Edmund Hockridge and Billy Dainty, bought a pile of balloons, blew them all up and put them in my dressing-room. Did I say *pile* of balloons? There were hundreds of them – all colours and all shapes and sizes. From floor to ceiling the room was packed tight with balloons – and when I arrived at the theatre, I just couldn't get in to make-up. It took half an hour before the room was anything like habitable. On another occasion Joan Regan was the victim of a glorious stunt instigated by Cliff. He enlisted the aid of a couple of friends, went off down the road a couple of hours before the show was due to start and bought a big pile of junk. They brought it all back to the theatre and had us sign "Best Wishes" labels which they fixed to the assortment – I recall there were such things as an ancient TV set that didn't work, an old fire and an enormous enamel basin with a hole in it! Then they dumped the lot in Joan's dressing-room. When she opened the door she almost collapsed with laughter. That'll give you some idea of Cliff's fine sense of humour.'

APRIL 22   As Jet Harris leaves the Shadows to pursue a solo career, he is replaced by ex-Krew Kat bass guitarist Brian 'Licorice' Locking, who makes his debut behind Cliff at Blackpool. During the same show, rhythm guitarist Bruce Welch collapses with a septic throat and is replaced for a week by guitarist-songwriter Peter Carter of the original Checkmates.

APRIL 24   Cliff has dinner with the head of EMI, Sir Joseph Lockwood.

APRIL 27   Stanley Black is appointed musical director for Cliff's next film, *Summer Holiday*. The supporting cast is to include Melvyn Hayes, Richard O'Sullivan and Teddy Green, with the Shadows having featured roles.

MAY 2   TV producer Jack Good reckons that Jet Harris will be a serious threat to Cliff Richard as a solo singer.

1962

MAY 4   Cliff's 17th single, 'I'm Looking Out The Window/Do You Wanna Dance', is released. One review says, 'Cliff Richard's most brilliant performance to date'. Comedian Norman Vaughan reveals that his first real break was acting as compère on Cliff's package show.

MAY 5   Cliff and the Shadows appear on TV's 'Thank Your Lucky Stars' along with Joe Brown, Eden Kane and 14-year-old newcomer Candy Sparling. DJ Pete Murray presents Cliff with a Gold Disc for 'The Young Ones' and the Shadows with one for 'Apache'.

MAY 6   Having been recently honoured by the Songwriters' Guild for services to the music industry, Cliff appears at their 'Our Friends the Stars' charity show at London's Victoria Palace with the Shadows, Max Bygraves, Danny Williams, Eden Kane and the John Barry Seven.

MAY ☐   Hits from *The Young Ones* EP released.

MAY 10   Cliff's 17th single release 'I'm Looking Out The Window/Do You Wanna Dance?' enters the Top 10 as a double-sided hit.

MAY 11   Charlie Chaplin's 17-year-old daughter Geraldine is one of many girls tested for the role of Cliff's girl-friend in *Summer Holiday*. It is announced that Peter Yates, until recently working on *The Guns Of Navarone*, is to direct the film.

MAY 14   Along with the Shadows and Norman Vaughan, Cliff appears in a cabaret show for a civic reception for Leyton Orient Football Club.

MAY 14/18   *Summer Holiday* begins to take shape at a gymnasium in Paddington. Cliff's co-star is American actress Laurie Peters who appeared in the Broadway production of *Sound Of Music* and the film *Mr Hobbs Takes a Holiday*, and recently married actor Jon Voight. The story revolves around a group of young mechanics who do up a London Transport double-decker bus and take it across Europe. En route they encounter a girl trio whose car breaks down on their way to a show in Athens, and a young boy stowaway who turns out to be a girl – all of whom end up on the bus. The stowaway is a young starlet desperate to get away from her clinging mother, who ends up chasing the bus across Europe in her car. Despite a few hairy situations, all ends happily with Don (Cliff) and Barbara (co-star Laurie Peters) falling in love. To make the part more realistic, Cliff practises driving a double-decker bus around London: 'I found it unexpectedly easy really; the only thing that fooled me was the length, which I found difficult to manage. Three double-decker buses are already in Europe waiting for us – there's only one bus actually featured in the film, but rather than cart it all round the Continent we've got three dotted about in various places and we shall use them as we come to them!'

MAY 18   Cliff and the Shadows team up with agent Leslie Grade and one of the world's biggest publishers, Aberbach Music, to form a record producing firm which they call Shad-Rich. As well as Leslie Grade, other directors are Aberbach US executive Freddie Bienstock and Cliff and the Shadows' personal manager, Peter Gormley.

On the same day Cliff comments on Elvis Presley's new single 'Good Luck Charm': 'When I first heard it I didn't like it very much, but I found on hearing it a second time I enjoyed it immensely. It's slightly reminiscent of "Teddy Bear" I think, but I rate it fifty times better than "Rock-A-Hula Baby", which I reckon was just about the worst record Elvis has made.'

MAY 19/20   Cliff and the Shadows fly to France for the weekend, to watch Ray Charles in concert at the Paris Olympia, and end up on their feet yelling and shouting enthusiastically. Shadow Bruce Welch says, 'We were screaming right along with the rest of them! It must have been quite a new experience for Cliff to be one of the screamers.'

MAY 25   It's announced that Cliff's management hope he will star in a modern version of an old pantomime at the London Palladium during the next winter season. Also a South African tour – intended to take place in October or November – is set up by the Grade organisation. Kenya's political leader Tom Mboya is promised that Cliff will headline a charity show to aid the country's underprivileged children.

MAY 27   Cliff, the entire cast and film crew fly to Greece to commence shooting *Summer Holiday*.

JUNE 1   Cliff and the Shadows appoint their former drummer, Tony Meehan, as artists' and repertoire chief to take charge of all the recording activities for their newly-formed company Shad-Rich. Since leaving the Shadows, Tony has been working on finding new British talent for Decca Records as well as drumming

THE CLIFF RICHARD FILE **1962**

■ Cliff and his Ford Thunderbird

on records for Jet Harris, John Leyton, Billy Fury and the Vernons Girls among others. Tony comments, 'I do not expect to record any numbers for Shad-Rich until all the initial complications are ironed out and the organisation is running smoothly. This is not expected to be until late summer.'

JUNE ☐   *Cliff Richard No.2* EP released.

JUNE **2**   Columbia label manager Norrie Paramor flies to Greece for talks with Cliff.

JUNE **3**   Norrie is in Greece when the whole cast is given a couple of days off from the gruelling 6am–8pm 7-days-a-week routine: 'A huge party was laid on at one of the hotels and we all had a whale of a time, a lot of fun. The highlight of the evening came when Cliff and the boys decided to recreate the "We've Got A Show" vaudeville routine from *The Young Ones*. They were all a trifle rusty on the words and choreography except Cliff, who was the only one who was able to remember all his lyrics and steps without fault!'

JUNE **4**   Cliff and forty of the cast hire a large cabin cruiser and go for a sea trip to the island of Hydra.

JUNE **9**   Cliff's mother and sisters Jacqueline and Joan fly to Greece for a two-week holiday.

JUNE **16**   The Shadows fly to Greece to film their contribution to *Summer Holiday*.

JULY 20	Cliff reminisces over his four years in show business: 'Sometimes I think my mother will wake me up one morning and I'll find myself back to being plain Harry Rodger Webb, clerk ... I mean, I'm 22 now and when I think that I can't even remember my 14th birthday it gets pretty frightening ... another of my big ambitions is to follow in Jet's footsteps and become a serious actor. Cary Grant is my idol and as I get a bit older I'd like to try and model myself on him.'
AUGUST 3	American TV host Ed Sullivan in an interview about English singers comments '... I think someone like Cliff Richard shouldn't try to put on an Oxford accent when singing a rock 'n' roll song. I know he doesn't and I think his act is all the better for it'.
AUGUST ☐	At Elstree Cliff records Burt Bacharach's 'It's Wonderful To Be Young' especially for the American market.
AUGUST 31	Cliff's 18th single 'It'll Be Me'/'Since I Lost You' is released. The 'A' side is a reworking of the old Jerry Lee Lewis rocker and the 'B' side is a song by Bruce Welch and Hank Marvin.
AUGUST ☐	In Australia, Cliff tops the chart with 'The Young Ones' while 'Do you want to dance?' is at No.6. In Holland 'Do you want to dance?' is No.1, and in Norway 'I'm lookin' out the Window' is No.9.
SEPTEMBER ☐	EMI release Cliff's 32 minutes and 17 seconds LP.
SEPTEMBER 8	Cliff appears on Billy Cotton's TV show.
OCTOBER 2	'It's Wonderful To Be Young' is released in the States as Cliff flies to America for one of the biggest ever campaigns to launch a British artist over there.
OCTOBER ☐	Cliff visits Elvis Presley's home in Memphis at the invitation of Elvis' father Vernon. The American singer is away at the time.

Theatre attendances for Cliff's American tour are low because of the effect of the Cuban crisis.
During his stay in America Cliff meets Nat King Cole, Bobby Darin, Paul Anka and Sal Mineo.

OCTOBER 29	Cliff appears before the Queen on the Royal Variety Show with the Shadows, Helen Shapiro, Andy Stewart, Frank Ifield, Eartha Kitt, Johnny Dankworth and Cleo Laine.
Cliff sings 'The Young Ones', 'I'm On My Way' and 'Do You Want To Dance?'

THE CLIFF RICHARD FILE 1962

NOVEMBER 30   *NME* publish their 1962 poll results:

World Musical Personality

1 Elvis Presley	19,083
2 Duane Eddy	9,825
3 Ray Charles	6,540
4 Cliff Richard	4,392

World Male Singer

1 Elvis Presley	24,243
2 Cliff Richard	7,803
3 Ray Charles	6,291

British Vocal Personality

1 Joe Brown	11,958
2 Cliff Richard	11,334
3 Frank Ifield	11,286

British Male Singer

1 Cliff Richard	18,006
2 Billy Fury	10,977
3 Frank Ifield	10,734

Best British Disc of the Year

1 Frank Ifield	'I Remember You'
2 Tornados	'Telstar'
3 Cliff Richard	'The Young Ones'

■ Cliff meets Bobby Vee

DECEMBER 7   EMI release Cliff's 19th single 'The Next Time'/'Bachelor Boy'. As one review says: 'It is a quiet lazily romantic number with a most pleasing melody.'

DECEMBER 9   Cliff reveals that 'The Next Time' is two separate 'takes' recorded six months apart and subsequently superimposed by producer Norrie Paramor.

DECEMBER □   'The Next Time'/'Bachelor Boy' sells 250,000 copies in one week.

DECEMBER 24/25   Cliff relaxes at home.

DECEMBER 25   Cliff leads an ATV Christmas Day Show 'Christmas Fare' which also features the Mike Cotton Jazzmen and Sheila Southern.

DECEMBER 27   Cliff flies to South Africa.

■ Spot the non Beverley Sister

■ Spot the non Everly Brother

1963

JANUARY 3   The first No.1 of the New Year is 'The Next Time/Bachelor Boy', which stays on top until deposed by 'Dance On' from the Shadows!

JANUARY 3   A complete analysis of the *NME* Top 30 is published (operating on the usual system of 30 points for 1 week at No.1 down to 1 point for 1 week at No.30).

1 Elvis Presley	1,463
2 Cliff Richard	1,131
3 Frank Ifield	817
4 Shadows	723
5 Acker Bilk	702
6 Billy Fury	701
7 Chubby Checker	656
8 Kenny Ball	611
9 Ray Charles	561
10 Del Shannon	555

Cliff is 122 points up on the 1961 table.

JANUARY 3   A letter to the British music papers from Louise Weinstock Jr. of West Lafayette, Indiana is published: 'I am a keen Cliff Richard fan. Many of my friends who have heard the seven Cliff albums which I possess agree that he is better than nine-tenths of our American singers. But the fact is that Cliff has not yet made a record with a really unusual or different sound, and the DJs are reluctant to play what amounts to a run-of-the-mill record by an artist who has had as many comparative flops here as Cliff. What Cliff needs is a disc with a new sound, maybe then he will become a star in America as well as Britain.'

JANUARY 4   Pop singer Kenny Lynch reveals that his favourite single is 'Bachelor Boy'.

JANUARY 7   Along with other acts, Cliff's singles and albums now cost less due to a cut in purchase tax on records. A Cliff single is reduced by 8d to 6s 3d, and an album is to cost 30s 11d instead of 34s 4½d.

JANUARY 10   Cliff's film *Summer Holiday* is premièred simultaneously in South Africa and London, and contains fifteen songs. Cliff, Melvyn Hayes, Teddy Green and Jeremy Bulloch portray a group of London Transport mechanics who 'do up' a double-decker bus and take it across Europe. The cast also includes Una Stubbs, Laurie Peters, Ron Moody and David Kossoff.

    One critic says of *Summer Holiday*: 'I wouldn't have believed that such a first-class musical could have been made in this country – the film will provide all the amenities of a real holiday – with the exception of the tan.'

    Impresario Leslie Grade hosts a post-première party at London's Dorchester Hotel.

JANUARY 11   As the *NME* chart listed 'Bachelor Boy' and 'The Next Time' as entirely

	separate chart entries, Radio Luxembourg ran a competition on its 'Friday Spectacular' inviting listeners to guess which side would go higher in the charts. There were 4000 entries.
JANUARY 16	Cliff and the Shadows begin a tour of South Africa, taking in Port Elizabeth, Johannesburg, Durban, Bulawayo and Salisbury in Rhodesia. Both South African and British newspapers cover the story of amazing fan scenes in Johannesburg and Cape Town.
JANUARY 17	*Daily Express* critic Leonard Mosley says, 'Cliff can't sing.'
JANUARY 18	Cliff admits that he thinks his girl-friend, Jackie Irving, looks like Sophia Loren.
JANUARY 21	The Radio Luxembourg show 'ABC of the Stars' devotes the whole show to Cliff.
JANUARY 24	Elvis's film *Girls, girls, girls* has Elvis playing the part of a fisherman turned part-time entertainer. Despite featured songs like 'Return to Sender' and 'Because of love', the film is compared (inevitably) with *Summer Holiday*, and does not fare too well under the pens of the critics. As one reviewer puts it: 'I'm not praising *Summer Holiday* out of patriotism – it's simply a fact that it has far more freshness and zest than *Girls, girls, girls*!'
JANUARY 25	Danish newspapers reveal that Cliff sold more records than any other artist in Denmark during 1962.
JANUARY 28	Associated British-Pathé executive, Macgregor Scott, is in America discussing the screening of *Summer Holiday* in the US. Most likely distributor is rumoured to be Paramount Pictures, who handled *The Young Ones*.
FEBRUARY 6	In America *The Young Ones* is retitled *Wonderful to be Young* and is reviewed rather cynically by the *San Francisco Chronicle*: 'Richard has all the requisites for idolisation – big brown eyes, wavy hair, a pretty-boy face, a certain magnetism and an undistinguished voice!'

In Holland's *Muzick Expres* poll, Cliff beats Elvis, while the British press refer to North of England dancer Jackie Irving, as 'Cliff's new friend'. |
FEBRUARY 8	Cliff's 20th single, 'Summer Holiday', is released and amongst the rave reviews is one from Keith Fordyce: 'Light-hearted, casual and happy, the mood of this most attractive song is contained in the line "We're going where the sun shines brightly". Top marks to all concerned, including composers Bruce Welch and Brian Bennett.'
FEBRUARY 8	Cliff sends a postcard to the *NME* depicting the Peninsula, which reads: 'Hello there from Africa. Weather great and tour fab. Everything and everyone swinging. This definitely must be the place! Regards, Cliff.'
FEBRUARY 10	Dedicated fans at Stockton queue all night for tickets to see a forthcoming Cliff and the Shadows concert.
FEBRUARY 10	Cliff buys a Chevrolet for his mother, Dorothy Webb.
FEBRUARY 11	Cliff appears in a charity concert for delinquent children in Nairobi which is organised by Kenyan leader, Tom Mboya.
FEBRUARY 15	The single 'Summer Holiday' is officially released.

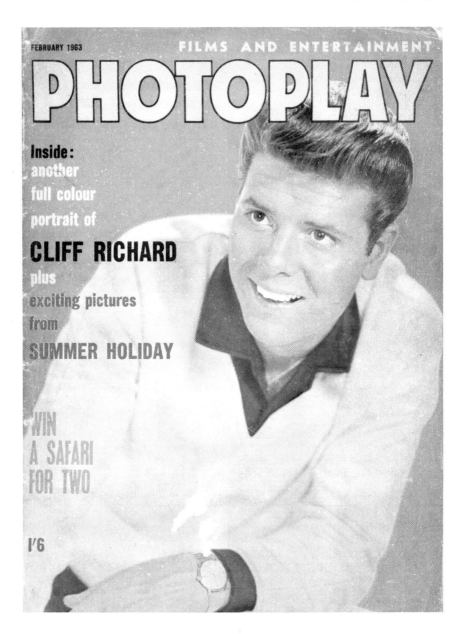

FEBRUARY **18,19,20**	Cliff and the Shadows rehearse for the 'Billy Cotton Band Show'.
FEBRUARY **20**	Cliff talks to the press about his South African tour with the Shadows: 'The whole tour was quite fantastic and we did considerably more business than the last time we were there. The press were very kind to us; of the nineteen shows we played, we only had one bad review, and that was by a Johannesburg critic who thought the whole thing was ridiculous!'

Cliff also spoke about the previous week's *Daily Express* article: 'I agree that I'm not qualified to talk about it, but we did not go to Africa to delve into the racial question. We went there to entertain and perform, but if writers persist in asking me about it I have to make some comment – even if it's only to brush it aside because it's not my territory.'

FEBRUARY 20	Cliff has four titles in the Top 30:
	
	    9 'Summer Holiday'
	  16 'Bachelor Boy'
	  18 'The Next Time'
	  25 'Dancing Shoes'
	
	He becomes the first artist to get four songs from one film (*Summer Holiday*) into the chart.

FEBRUARY 21	Cliff and the Shadows telerecord for the TV programme 'The Billy Cotton Band Show' to be transmitted on 24 February.
FEBRUARY 23	Cliff and the Shadows begin a 41-date 6-week tour of Britain at Cardiff's Sophia Gardens.
FEBRUARY 24	'The Billy Cotton Band Show' is transmitted on TV featuring Cliff and the Shadows, and Cliff and Billy Cotton together in top-hat and tails singing the old Bud Flanagan and Chesney Allen song 'Strollin'.
MARCH 1	It is announced that Cliff and the Shadows will star in their first BBC TV Spectacular in the spring, and they intend spending two weeks recording in Barcelona.
MARCH 1	Cliff is featured in an article in an American journal, *Newsweek*, in which he speaks of his success: 'I got my chance because teenagers have to have an idol, but the new teenagers coming up don't like to take what's left over. But I hope to grow with my audience.'
MARCH □	Among the songs Cliff features in his 41-date tour with the Shadows are: 'Do you Wanna Dance?', 'I Gotta Woman', 'Blueberry Hill' (featuring Hank Marvin on piano), 'The Next Time', 'Baby Face', 'Summer Holiday', 'Spanish Harlem', 'Love Hurts', 'Bachelor Boy', 'Dancing Shoes' and 'We Say Yeah'. The tour also features the Trebletones, xylophone player/comedian Alan Randall, Patsy Ann Noble, the Vernons Girls and Canadian compère Frank Berry.
MARCH □	Bobby Vee covers Cliff's 'Theme for a Dream' on his new album.
MARCH 7	Along with Frank Ifield and Judy Garland, Cliff and the Shadows telerecord in London for America's 'Ed Sullivan Show,' and as they appear the same night at Kingston ABC they have to dash across London from ATV's Wood Green Empire.
MARCH 8	'Summer Holiday' tops the *NME* chart.
MARCH □	Cliff and the Shadows' EP – *Time for Cliff and the Shadows* – is released, containing 'So I've Been Told', 'I'm Walking the Blues', 'When my Dreamboat Comes Home' 'Blueberry Hill' and 'You Don't Know'.
MARCH 14	It is announced that the film *Summer Holiday* will be launched in Canada at Easter, and is to be shown mainly at drive-in movies in Toronto and other major cities. Canadian reaction is to be used as a springboard for the American launch. To coincide with the film, Capitol Records announce that they will release the film sound-track and relevant singles in Canada.
MARCH 15	Arthur Howes, the promoter of Cliff's tour, says: 'This is a record for any of the tours I have ever handled. Every ticket has been sold for every performance at every theatre!' At the same time, Cliff features in the charts of eight countries simultaneously:

'The Next Time'	No.2 in Israel
'The Next Time'	No.6 in France
'The Next Time'	No.10 in Norway
'The Next Time/Bachelor Boy'	No.1 in South Africa
'Bachelor Boy'	No.1 in Holland
'Bachelor Boy'	No.3 in Sweden
'Bachelor Boy'	No.5 in Hong Kong
'Bachelor Boy'	No.26 in Britain
'Summer Holiday'	No.1 in Britain

MARCH 22 It is announced that Cliff will undertake a new film, shooting for which is to commence at the end of his Blackpool summer season, resulting in a cancellation of proposed plans for an Australian tour.

Epic Records reveal that in future they wil be releasing Cliff's records in the United States, while in Britain it is estimated that Cliff may well earn £6,000 composer's royalties for 'Bachelor Boy' which is to be included in a forthcoming *Bachelors* LP.

MARCH 22/28 Cliff appears at Leeds Odeon, Leicester de Montfort Hall, Ipswich Gaumont, Dover ABC, Hastings ABC and Southend Odeon.

MARCH 29 In the *NME* chart points table for the first quarter of 1963, Cliff has taken a strong lead and leads Elvis Presley for the first time since 1960.

1 Cliff Richard	584
2 Frank Ifield	322
3 Shadows	291
4 Tornados	275
5 Jet Harris and Tony Meehan	253
6 Elvis Presley	246
7 Beatles	235
8 Joe Brown	232
9 Bobby Vee	215
10 Springfields	210

■ Cliff and Jet Harris

Of Cliff's points 405 were amassed by 'The Next Time/Bachelor Boy' and the *Summer Holiday* album overtook the consistent *West Side Story* to lead the points table based on the album chart.

MARCH ☐ America's *16* magazine reports that Cliff is becoming a big teenage favourite in the States through the film *Wonderful to be Young*.

MARCH ☐ Cliff and the Shadows say that their nickname for singer Dusty Springfield is 'The White Negress'.

APRIL 1 The 36-page April edition of *Hit Parade* magazine (price 2s.) features an article personally written by Cliff.

APRIL 6 Cliff is featured on the front cover of *Pop Weekly* with Laurie Peters, his *Summer Holiday* co-star, and the St Bernard featured in the film. The magazine also publishes the results of a survey of over-25s as to their favourite artists. The results are as follows :

1 Frank Ifield
2 Cliff Richard
3 Acker Bilk
4 Shirley Bassey
5 Shadows

APRIL ☐		Cliff's current car is a Cadillac, but a new sports car is ordered and on the way.
APRIL ☐		In an interview, Cliff and the Shadows insist that during the summer season at Blackpool they are planning to go to the beach at 8 o'clock each morning 'for exercises and a good long run'.
APRIL ☐		Franklyn Boyd, who played an important part in Cliff's early success, discovers a new singer, 16-year-old Steve Marriott, who releases his first single 'Give Her My Regards'. Steve is eventually to lead the Small Faces and form Humble Pie.
APRIL ☐		Accidental meeting in the M1's Watford Gap Services of Cliff and the Shadows, the Beatles, Tommy Roe and Chris Montez.
APRIL ☐		The Tornados go to watch Cliff and the Shadows on tour, who not only hope to reciprocate by going to see Billy Fury's ex-backing group during their run of shows in Paris, but offer their advice on French audiences, sights to see and places to eat. On Cliff and the Shadows, the Tornados say, 'They're fantastically polished and present a wonderful act, but we wish people would not keep bringing up this question of rivalry. Neither of us is trying to put the other out of business!'
APRIL 12		Cliff and the Shadows send autographed Easter eggs to fans in hospital. In an interview, Cliff reveals that it's his ambition to have three No.1s in a row (his previous two singles both topped the chart – 'Next Time/Bachelor Boy' and 'Summer Holiday'), but is not too optimistic about his chances: 'My last couple of releases were ready-made – in a sense they more or less selected themselves since they came straight from the film. Mind you, we would never have released "Summer Holiday" as a single if it hadn't been featured in a film – frankly, we didn't think it was good enough to stand up on its own!' Cliff also speaks about his songwriting abilities: 'I've always enjoyed writing, but I've never really considered myself a great composer – normally I throw my numbers together very quickly. I get fed up with them after a while. I'm afraid I'm not like Bruce Welch, he can churn 'em out by the dozen!'
APRIL ☐		At Bruce Welch's party guests include Cliff, the Beatles, Patsy Ann Noble and the Vernons Girls. Cliff and the Shadows do a micky-take of the Beatles by singing 'Please Please Me' in exaggerated style – the Beatles reply with a deliberately out-of-tune send-up of Cliff and the Shadows. The two groups play guitars and sing together through the night in Bruce's kitchen, knocking out numbers by the Chiffons, Isley Brothers and Ray Charles. Cliff says of the Beatles: 'The greatest bunch of boys I've met since the Shadows!'
APRIL 13		Cliff checks into EMI's Abbey Road Studios in St John's Wood for an unscheduled recording session to record the songs. The Shadows are to accompany him on all three tracks.
APRIL 13		'Bachelor Boy' enters the Australian charts.
APRIL ☐		Tailor Dougie Millings talks to the press about show-business fashion: 'I've been making Cliff's suits since he used to appear in the 2 I's coffee bar which is practically underneath my premises; that's how I sort of drifted into becoming a show-business tailor. Cliff, in fact, was the first big name I ever made suits for! He's got a very good figure from a tailor's point of view – regular measurements and no faults to cover up. If Cliff needs a suit for stage work, then the most popular material is Italian silk, but it's a bit expensive – about £40.'
APRIL 20		*Kinematograph Weekly* reports that the film in which Cliff made his screen

debut and sang 'Livin' Doll' – *Serious Charge* – is on re-release and doing good business in cinemas around the country.

APRIL 21 Cliff and the Shadows appear at the NME's Poll Winners' Concert at Wembley. The set includes 'Bachelor Boy', 'Do You Wanna Dance', 'Summer Holiday' and 'Dancing Shoes'. The subsequent review sums up the act by saying, 'It's difficult to find words to describe the annual shattering ovation given to the king of popland!'

APRIL 22 Cliff records his own TV Special for BBC.

APRIL 27 R. Hodgetts of Edinburgh has a letter published in *Disc*: 'A lot is said and written about the wonderful artists such as Brenda Lee, Jerry Lee Lewis and Little Eva. Yet I feel the finest stage performance I have seen for some time was given by Cliff and the Shadows on their recent tour.'

APRIL 27 The Shadows earn their seventh Silver Disc for the single taken from *Summer Holiday* – 'Foot-tapper', and Cliff's 21st single is released – 'Lucky Lips', written by the legendary songwriting team Leiber and Stoller, and previously released by Alma Cogan in March 1957 on the 'B' side of 'Whatever Lola Wants'!

APRIL 28 Cliff's BBC TV Spectacular is screened on Sunday night. Included in the show are the new single, tracks from the forthcoming *Holiday Carnival* EP with Cliff and the Shadows combining with the Rooftop Singers, 'Walk Right In', and a folk medley comprising 'Greensleeves', 'All Through the Night' and 'Cockles and Mussels'. Cliff also duets with Sid James and Millicent Martin.

APRIL ☐ 'Lucky Lips' is reviewed and as one record critic puts it: '"Lucky Lips" is not a new song. It has been tried on record before but never to the sort of success it is going to get from now on. Cliff takes the Leiber-Stoller shuffler and eases it onto your feet. Accompanied by the Shadows, he makes this a happy and extremely infectious release. It'll take him high in the Top 10 once more. 'I Wonder' (the 'B' side), accompanied by the Norrie Paramor Strings, is a song written by Cliff and Hank Marvin. Attractive little Latin ballad.'

MAY ☐ Cliff's *Holiday Carnival* EP is released, featuring 'Carnival', 'Moonlight Bay', 'Some of These Days' and 'For You, For Me'.

MAY 11 Misses B. Davis and M. Richardson from Christchurch in Hampshire write to the music press: 'We wish to thank everybody connected with *Summer Holiday* for making such a wonderful film. Most people think we are mad because we have seen *Summer Holiday* fifteen times!'

Another letter on the subject of Cliff is published the same week: 'Recently, I purchased a good seat to see Cliff and the Shadows at a concert. I'd have done better to buy an LP! Why do the screamers go to these shows? Cliff and Co. tried, but it was five against the crowd. I thought it was gross bad manners on the part of the screaming three-quarters of the audience. Friends with me said, "Never again!", and I know what they mean.' (Mrs. B. Ruston, Bracken Edge, Leeds 8.)

MAY 12 BBC TV screen the Ivor Novello Awards, which include the Tornados, Matt Monro, Acker Bilk – and a clip of *Summer Holiday* as Cliff is unable to attend owing to a holiday in Spain, where he also records before starting rehearsals for the Blackpool summer season.

MAY 14   Cliff and the Shadows broadcast from the Paris Olympia – topping the bill on the 'Europe One' radio show.

MAY □   A typical day for Cliff and the Shadows holidaying in Sitges, 23 miles from Barcelona :

9.00-1.00	Rehearsals in the music room at the hotel in Sitges.
1.00-4.00	Break.
4.30	Bus to Barcelona (23 miles of bumpy roads with lots of steep climbs and hair-raising descents).
6.00-10.00	Recording.
10.30	Bus back to the hotel, stopping at a transport café on the way.
1.00	Bed!

Cliff records several numbers in Spanish including 'Perfidia' and 'Que sera sera', 'Frenesi', 'Amor' and 'Perhaps, Perhaps, Perhaps'. After work Cliff and the boys either relax in a small restaurant on the sea-front, where fish soup and asparagus is a definite favourite, or play the juke-box in Ricky's Bar. Cliff and the Shadows are given instruction in the art of bullfighting by an aged toreador using baby bulls, and are presented with diplomas stating that they have proved their mettle in the bull-ring. They are also talked into attending a real bullfight, where despite initial apprehension Hank films all seven fights. Cliff is not wildly impressed: 'You certainly wouldn't call it a sport – I'm glad I went, but I wouldn't want to go to another!'

MAY 18   J. Helm of Downes Place, London SE15 has the following letter published in the music press: 'Is Cliff Richard superhuman? Is he *never* off form? Does he *ever* muff his lines or forget the words of a song? All his records are reviewed in such glowing terms. His every appearance on TV or radio is acclaimed as "brilliant". His films are guaranteed to be "the biggest thing on the British musical scene" practically before they are started. He is one of the best-dressed men. And now we are informed by his tailor that his figure is faultless! Frankly, I'm becoming a little bored with such perfection.'

MAY 18   In the Hong Kong charts Cliff's 'Summer Holiday' is No.2 and 'Bachelor Boy' is No.6. In Norway 'Summer Holiday' is No.1, while in South Africa he has three in the Top 10 – 'Bachelor Boy' at No.3, 'Dancing Shoes' at No.4 and 'Summer Holiday' at No.10.

MAY ☐   Cliff and the Shadows rehearse a routine for their summer season, for which they promise 'an entirely new type of presentation'.

MAY 31   Prior to the public opening the following day, Cliff and the Shadows are the star attractions at the opening of Blackpool's £400,000 ABC Theatre before an invited audience of 2,000 and the Mayor of Blackpool.

MAY 31   *Life with Cliff Richard* is published – available from all good newsagents at 3s.6d. a copy. It claims to 'paint a vivid portrait of the sincere, homely boy behind the glittering star legend ...!'

JUNE 1   Cliff and the Shadows' opening night at Blackpool ABC. The show (seats from 6s.6d. to 9s.6d.) features colour film back-projection and includes a scene where Cliff, Hank and Bruce are in a speeded-up hair-raising race through London's traffic, only to end up crashing into the gates of Harrow School. The scenes range from Paris to Majorca, Hollywood, Lake Tahoe and Las Vegas, while the girls range from Cliff's *Young Ones* co-star Carole Gray to the girl with whom he is linked romantically by the press, Jackie Irving. Other artists appearing include Jim Dailey and Terry Wayne, and ventriloquist Arthur Worsley with his dummy Charlie Brown. As well as the usual numbers expected from him, Cliff also includes 'Moonlight Bay', Sophie Tucker's 'Some of these Days', 'Strangers in Town' and 'Carnival'. Four hundred people attend the opening night supper party.

JUNE ☐   *Hits from Summer Holiday* EP is released, featuring 'The Next Time', 'Summer Holiday', 'Dancing Shoes' and 'Bachelor Boy'.

JUNE 1   *Disc* magazine sounds out various artists on the subject of legendary singer Ray Charles. Cliff says: 'It was so great, I'm going again! I wasn't expecting the same from Ray on stage as on his records, but he doesn't lose one bit from appearing in person. When one realises that the man is blind, and he can't of course move around on stage but just sits at the piano, he is absolutely fantastic!'

JUNE ☐   'Lucky Lips' peaks at No.4 in the record retailer chart and No.3 in the disc chart.

JUNE 7   Elstree Music publish *Cliff Richard and the Shadows Special Souvenir Album*, price 6s.

JUNE 8   Cliff and the Shadows reveal that they plan to carry out midnight recording sessions during their summer season.

JUNE ☐   Bruce Welch hosts a small party for Cliff in Blackpool. The Beatles are among the guests and Cliff, the Shadows and John, Paul, George and Ringo end up singing and playing together half the night.

JUNE ☐   Cliff stays at Lytham St Annes (5 miles south of Blackpool) for the summer season, and spends his spare time indulging in his favourite hobby – cine-photography. 'The Shadows and I are working on some comedy films with ourselves as the "stars" – you've never seen anything like it in your life! Also, I've had to move house once already; my address got out and I woke up one morning and found 150 fans outside. It wasn't that *I* minded, but it would have disturbed the neighbours if that had gone on all season, so I moved.'

JUNE ☐   Cliff's mother and two of his sisters join him in Blackpool, and he now drives a new 160-mph Corvette which he exchanged for his red Thunderbird.

JUNE 14   In a letter to the music press, Jennifer Haines of Bournemouth writes: 'For goodness sake, Cliff fans, pull your socks up! Are you going to let Britain's King of Talent be beaten by a flash-in-the-pan group like the Beatles?'

JUNE 14   Stanley Matthews Jnr, son of legendary footballer Stanley Matthews, reveals that he's a big Cliff fan. Meanwhile, on the London Record label, similarly-named Cliff Rivers releases his first British single.

JUNE 15   Producer of Cliff's forthcoming film, Kenneth Harper, announces that filming for the new movie will be based at ABC Studies in Elstree, with location shooting in Mexico and South America: Sidney Furie will direct. Peter Myers and Ronald Cass are signed to write the screenplay, as they have previously for *The Young Ones* and *Summer Holiday*.

JUNE 21   Cliff's 'Life Lines', first featured in the *New Musical Express* on November 14 1958, is the subject of a half-page in the June 21 issue and includes:

First public appearance:	Youth Fellowship dance in Cheshunt, 1954.
Dislikes:	Insincere people; putting on a false smile for photographers; smoking.
Favourite food:	Indian curry and rice.
Favourite drink:	Tizer with ice cream.
Favourite guitarists:	Duane Eddy, Al Casey, Hank Marvin.
Favourite band:	Glenn Miller.
Favourite female singers:	Connie Francis, Julie London, Helen Shapiro.
Favourite male singers:	Elvis Presley, Rick Nelson, Ray Charles, the Beatles.
Hobbies:	Collecting Elvis records; playing badminton.
Greatest ambition:	To meet Elvis.
Musical education:	Taught guitar by his father.
Former job:	Office clerk.
Educated:	Stanley Park Road School, Carshalton. Cheshunt Secondary Modern.
Sisters:	Donella, Jacqueline and Joan.

THE CLIFF RICHARD FILE 1963

JUNE 22 Bill Edge from Howard Street, Salford 5, Lancashire writes to the music papers on the subject of Cliff's current single: 'I think that it is a crying shame that such a great artist as Cliff Richard should have to go on stage and sing a song ['Lucky Lips'] which sounds like Elvis six years ago. I think that he should get some new songwriters. I could do better than this myself.'

JUNE 25 'Lucky Lips' is released in the US with 'The Next Time' on the 'B' side.

JUNE 28 The *NME* publish their points chart for the first half of 1963 (30 points for No.1 to one point for No.30).

1 Cliff Richard	877
2 The Beatles	577
3 Frank Ifield	548
4 The Shadows	522
5 Jet Harris and Tony Meehan	492

JUNE 29 Cliff announces the postponement of a projected Australasian tour the following February, and the intention of starting on the new film in November, followed by a British tour in March and April. A possible tour of Israel is also hinted at.

JUNE 29 Screenplay writers for *The Young Ones*, *Summer Holiday* and the forthcoming film, Peter Myers and Ronald Cass, chat to the press about Cliff. '... if Cliff had to give up singing, he could always make a living as a dancer ...', '... he has a natural acting ability ...', '... really, you can say he is part writer of some of the songs – but he doesn't get any of our royalties!', '... there is never any display of temperament ...'. Ronald Cass concludes the interview with the following tribute: 'I have a little boy of three – if he grows up to behave like Cliff, then I shall be happy.'

■ Cliff shows off his new antlered shoes to the Tiller Girls

JULY 1   From today, along with other EMI artists, Cliff's singles cost fivepence more. His albums go up from £1 10s.11d. to £1 12s.0d. and EPs are also affected, going up 8d. to 10s.9d.

JULY 1   Cliff is deposed as 'Best-Dressed Show Business Personality of the Year' when the British Federation of Clothing Manufacturers award the title to Adam Faith.

JULY ☐   *Cliff's Hit Album* is released, containing 14 tracks ranging from 'Move It' to 'Do You Wanna Dance?'.

JULY 5   Actress/singer Millicent Martin reveals that Cliff is her favourite TV personality.

JULY ☐   Wink Martindale covers 'The Next Time' in the States, while Cliff's former manager Tito Burns announces that he's handling new Liverpool group the Searchers, who have a Top 10 hit with 'Sweets for My Sweet'.

JULY 6   Other music papers adopt the *NME*'s chart system (30 points for a No.1 to 1 point for No.30) to gauge artists' success in relation to each other. *Disc*'s half-yearly analysis looked like this:

1 Cliff Richard	722
2 Beatles	583
3 Shadows	538
4 Frank Ifield	535
5 Jet Harris & Tony Meehan	475
6 Gerry & the Pacemakers	450
7 Springfields	448
8 Billy Fury	392
9 Del Shannon	375
10 Roy Orbison	342

JULY 7   Cliff and the Shadows travel down from Blackpool to undertake a Sunday evening recording from 7.00 to 10.00 at EMI's Abbey Road studios. They record four titles despite producer Norrie Paramor suffering from a slipped disc.

JULY ☐   Cliff confesses that as an avid film fan he shows movies during the day just for friends at the ABC Blackpool. Some of the silver screen epics shown at the private viewings are Doris Day's *Calamity Jane*, Frank Sinatra's *Guys and Dolls* and Westerns *Shane*, *High Noon* and *The Magnificent Seven*. Cliff's all-time favourite, it seems, is *West Side Story*. 'I think it is the best film ever made – it has everything, a great story, fabulous songs and dancing that's out of this world.'

JULY 8   Cliff dashes from Blackpool to London to record English lyrics to five songs he recorded in Spain with the Shadows back in April.

JULY 10   Cliff and the Shadows' producer, Norrie Paramor, talks about future recordings: 'I found, when I worked with the boys in Spain, that we can really get down to it and experiment a good deal more when the time factor is not so pressing, and it is so much easier on Cliff if we get together on the backing first. We can also come up with some new ideas – try out experiments with trumpets, strings and so forth. This has brought criticism from some quarters, but I am all for trying out something new.'

JULY 20   'Lucky Lips', coupled with 'The Next Time', is poised outside the American Top 100 at No.116 just a few days after its release.

JULY ☐	Cliff's producer, Columbia A & R man Norrie Paramor, launches a search for new talent and starts by signing six Birmingham acts: Danny King and the Royals, Carl and the Cheetahs, Mike Sheridan and the Nightriders, The Rockin' Jaymen, Pat Wayne and Keith Powell and the Valets.
JULY 20	Frank Ifield's road manager, Fred Derry, talks to the press about Cliff: 'During my ten years in show business, I have met plenty of big stars, and with some of them their heads are as big as their billing, but this is certainly not true of the biggest of them all. Cliff's phenomenal success has not spoiled him one bit – he is charming and completely unaffected. He treats everyone the same, from the humblest fan to the most influential person in the business. I don't know anyone who gets more presents from his admirers – they bombard him with knitted sweaters, ties and socks! Off-stage he likes nothing more than to relax with a book – he's a great reader of science-fiction space stories! He and the Shadows have a zany sense of humour – they sent a telegram to Frank Ifield when he opened in a Birmingham panto which read: "Just heard you're doing three matinees on Christmas Day!"'
JULY 20	'Lucky Lips' is No.1 in South Africa, No.3 in Israel and No.9 in Hong Kong, also in the Swedish Top 10.
JULY 26	In a letter to the music papers, Ron Dennison writes from Ottawa, Canada: 'Cliff Richard has at last broken through in Canada! "Bachelor Boy" was No.1 in most Canadian cities, including five unchallenged weeks here in Ottawa, and currently "Summer Holiday" is the best-selling LP in the country. In fact, he is now so popular over here that several groups are modelling themselves on Cliff and the Shadows.'
JULY 27	Plans for top American TV host, Ed Sullivan, to record a show in Blackpool starring Cliff and the Shadows fall through, due to lack of suitable locations for filming.

Cliff's Hit Album is released. As one reviewer, Nigel Hunter, puts it: 'You can trace Cliff's pop progress as the album plays. The earlier items are noticeably simple and straightforward in content and accompaniment, but songs, performance and backings gain in depth and imagination as time goes by.' |
JULY ☐	The Shadows reveal that they are taking riding lessons – which they hint may give some clue as to what might be seen in Cliff's next film.
JULY ☐	American magazine *16* runs the headline: 'Can Cliff Richard be the next Elvis?'
JULY 29	US composer Roy Bennett (who writes with Sid Tepper), flies to London with some new songs written with Cliff in mind: 'His very first epic title, "Lucky Lips", shows signs of breaking as a big hit, so we'd be delighted if he'd consider using more songs by us, remembering that he has featured our songs in the past – "Travellin' Light", "When the Girl In Your Arms", "The Young Ones" and "'D' In Love" amongst others.
AUGUST 2	Cliff wins his first-ever American poll honour when he is voted 'Most Promising Singer' in a nation-wide ballot by the leading US teenage magazine *16*.
AUGUST 2	Cliff enters *Billboard*'s Hot 100 with 'Lucky Lips' – his first American hit since 'Livin' Doll'.
AUGUST ☐	Cliff is reported as having taken up golf.

AUGUST 9	'Lucky Lips' simultaneously tops the charts in six different countries: Norway, Israel, South Africa, Hong Kong, Sweden and Holland. In America's *Billboard* chart, the same track climbs from No.95 to No.89.
AUGUST 10	During the 100th edition of ABC TV's 'Thank Your Lucky Stars', Cliff receives a Gold Disc for a million sales of 'Bachelor Boy/The Next Time'. Viewers see him singing, 'Your Eyes Tell On You' and the new single 'It's All In The Game'. Also appearing on the programme are Billy J. Kramer and the Dakotas, the Searchers and Brian Poole and the Tremeloes.
AUGUST 16	For his 22nd single, Cliff releases 'It's All In The Game', a song which Tommy Edwards took to No.1 in the British charts in 1958. The tune, originally entitled 'Melody in A major,' was written in 1912 by Chicago banker General Charles Gates Dawes, who later became Vice-President of the USA.
AUGUST 16	'Lucky Lips' continues to climb the American charts – a thirteen-place climb takes it to No 76.
AUGUST ☐	In an interview with *Evening News* reporter James Green, Cliff admits that dancer Jackie Irving is his 'steady date'!
AUGUST 23	'Lucky Lips' rises to No 69 in the *Billboard* chart.
AUGUST 23	American TV host Ed Sullivan announces that he's booked Cliff for his coast-to-coast TV show in October.
AUGUST 23	Susan Goodall from Birmingham has an anti-gossip column letter published by the *NME*: 'I wish *NME*'s "Alley Cat" would stop writing about Cliff Richard and Jackie Irving going steady. What if they are? I think it's about time that Cliff was given a little private life – he's only human, you know.'
AUGUST 30	In an *NME* feature 'Tribute to Cliff and the Shadows' fifth anniversary in show business', Cliff answers questions about his love-life and career:

Q. How do you envisage the next five years?

A. I think things will slow down tremendously ... success is all very well, but it becomes pointless if one is unable to secure and solidify that position. From the recording point of view, there's very little else I can hope to do – apart from continuing to please the public to the best possible extent.

Q. When you started out as a rock 'n' roller five years ago, did you plan to try and develop your career in this way?

A. No, I most certainly didn't. My attitude in those days was to live for the present, to exploit my latest record and to get as many bookings as I could.

Q. How do you feel about your film career? Do you think it might ultimately become the most important aspect of your career?

A. If by that you are suggesting that I might eventually give up touring, TV and recording in order to concentrate on films, the answer is definitely no! Sooner or later I hope that I shall be able to make a film without any singing at all. My great ambition is to play Heathcliff in *Wuthering Heights*.

Q. Exactly four years ago, you declared that you had no intention of marrying before you were 27. Do you still feel the same way?

A. I've always thought I would marry at 27 simply because I regard it as the most suitable age for a man to marry. However, the situation doesn't arise at the moment because there are no prospects in view.

Q. Do you enjoy being a star or do you sometimes wish that you were just an ordinary bloke?

A. I very rarely have any complaints. I like the life very much indeed. You sometimes hear it said that it's a lonely life at the top, but I can assure you it isn't. It depends entirely on what you make of it yourself.

AUGUST 30   It is announced that *Summer Holiday* is to be released in America at the end of October.

AUGUST ☐   Cliff telerecords a guest appearance for the ATV Midlands children's 'Tingha and Tucker', in which he is seen in a non-singing role as Uncle Cliff on Blackpool beach.

SEPTEMBER 6   Esther L.M. Chamberlaine writes to the *NME* from Leighton Buzzard: 'Cliff Richard has had five years in show business – so what? The Everly Brothers have clocked up eight and they are the world's greatest. So why not a tribute to them – they deserve one.'

SEPTEMBER 7   Bobby Vee reveals that he is going to include Cliff's 'Theme for a Dream' on his next LP, and Pat Boone confesses that he prefers Cliff's new version of 'It's All In The Game' to the original.

SEPTEMBER 13   Cliff trots out his ten all-time-favourite records:
1 'Rock Around The Clock' – Bill Haley and the Comets.
'"Rock Around The Clock" remains the most exciting side with the most authentic sound that rock and roll has ever produced.'
2 'Heartbreak Hotel' – Elvis Presley.
'It is to me the most dynamic Presley performance ever committed to wax.'
3 'Dum-Dum' – Brenda Lee.
'Despite her many successes as a ballad singer, I happen to prefer Brenda as a rock and roll singer. She has a perfect rock voice.'
4 'Maria' – Andy Williams.
'Taken from Andy's *Moon River* LP, this ballad has established itself in my mind as just about the most touching song based on someone's name ever written.'
5 'There's A Place' – the Kestrels.
'This group is outstanding among the comparatively few British vocal groups which simply sing instead of playing instruments as well.'
6 'My Colouring Book' – Andy Williams.
'"My Colouring Book" may usually be considered more of a girl singer's number, after its US chart entries by both Kitty Kallen and Sandy Stewart, but I've chosen Andy Williams again.'
7 'Drown In My Own Tears' – Ray Charles.
'When he turns to the blues, Ray Charles can tug at my heartstrings without fail. This fairly long track, taken from a 1959 concert, can be found on either of two LPs: *Ray Charles In Person* or *Ray Charles' Story (Vol.2)*.'
8 'Guess Who I Saw Today' – Nancy Wilson.
'She is neither a pop artist nor particularly commercial sounding in the "quality" field, but such a professional voice should be heard much, much more in Britain.'
9 'Woe Is Me' – Helen Shapiro.
'Having been recorded in Nashville, Tennessee, this could be thought of as

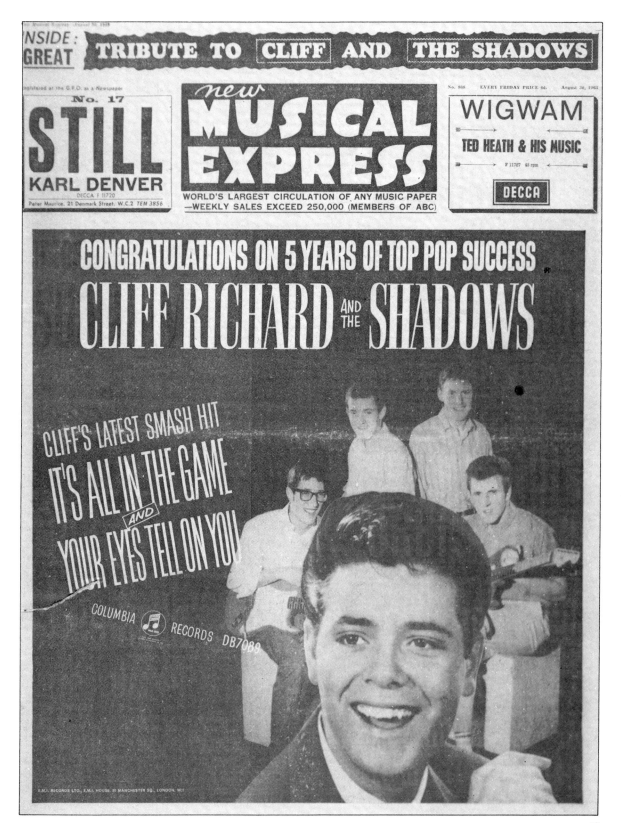

an American side, I guess. Even so, as a British produced and British sung offering, "Woe is Me" rates as something for us to be conspicuously proud of.'
10 'FBI' – the Shadows.
'My favourite group! As soon as I heard this number on tape before release, I thought, "this has got to be a single!"'

SEPTEMBER 13   The Shadows are booked to top ATV's 'Sunday Night at the London Palladium' for the second time in three months, thus delaying by a day their recording of the Ed Sullivan Show with Cliff.

SEPTEMBER 14   Newspapers report the likelihood of Robert Morley (who played Cliff's father in *The Young Ones*) appearing in the new film.

SEPTEMBER 20   Bruce Welch announces that he's leaving the Shadows due to health reasons, after visiting a Harley Street specialist who recommends a complete rest: 'It is terribly unfortunate and the last thing in the world I want to do, but if the doctor says it's the best thing, I have to listen to him.'

Cliff pays tribute to Bruce's contribution to the Cliff and the Shadows success story, 'It's going to be a terrible wrench for all of us after five years of close harmony, but you can't argue with your health. The main consolation is that we shall still be in a close contact as Bruce will be looking after our publishing interests and continuing his songwriting.'

SEPTEMBER 22   Bruce Welch's 'farewell' TV appearance on 'Sunday Night at the London Palladium'.

SEPTEMBER 24   Cliff speaks out about the way certain factions of the national press have been commenting on his relationship with dancer Jack Irving: 'I get the impression they're trying to marry me off – they're certainly creating a romance where none exists. They must enjoy playing Cupid – or perhaps they're just short of news. It's true that I've taken Jackie out more than any other girl, but then being placed as I am, it's only natural that I should take out girls I know rather than those I don't know. Jackie and I have been thrown together professionally quite a lot and I've grown to know her pretty well. I enjoy her company very much, but I can assure you that we've never even discussed the possibility of marriage – except perhaps to the contrary. Jackie's a good pal and we're the best of friends, but the chances are that now the Blackpool season is over, I shan't see her again for a few months, and that hardly indicates romance, does it?'

SEPTEMBER 24   Having led the *NME* chart table by over 300 points from the Beatles at the year's half-way stage, Cliff's lead has now been narrowed down to 50 points. When asked if the prospect of being overhauled worries him, he replies: 'I'm not too worried about it because it's happened so often before. I actually won the points table on one occasion when Elvis was in the Army, but otherwise I've always been second to him. So I'm used to being runner-up, but if the Beatles win the points table, I'll have nothing but praise for them because they're a great group.'

SEPTEMBER 26   Cliff and the Shadows leave for a two-week tour of Israel – they are greeted there by enormous crowds.

SEPTEMBER ☐   Rome record label boss, François Minchin, urges Norrie Paramor to record Cliff in Italian.

SEPTEMBER 29	Huge crowds bring traffic to a standstill as Cliff and the Shadows open their tour of Israel in Tel Aviv.
OCTOBER 1	Singer Heinz chooses his all-time Top 10, which includes Cliff's 'It's All In The Game': 'To my mind no Top 10 would be complete without Cliff being represented – and I sincerely believe this is one of his all-time best. It's a superb interpretation and a fine arrangement. I've long been an admirer of Cliff and this really does him credit.'
OCTOBER 5	Cliff telephones England from Israel and chats to the Light Programme's 'Saturday Club' compère, Brian Matthew, as part of the programme's fifth birthday celebrations.
OCTOBER ☐	The ex-president of Cliff's Swedish fan club marries Spotniks member, Bob Lander.
OCTOBER ☐	Cliff talks about 'My Own Taste in Music' in the October edition of *Hit Parade* (2s.).
OCTOBER 9	Cliff and the Shadows return from Israel, whereupon manager Peter Gormley comments on Bruce's resignation: 'When they get back from the French tour, Bruce will seek medical advice on whether his health will allow him to go to the Canary Islands to film there early in December.' Cliff raves in the press about the Israel tour: 'I honestly think it's the most enjoyable overseas tour we've ever done, although over there they show their appreciation by giving you the slow handclap!' Among the numbers in the acts, 'Bachelor Boy', 'Lucky Lips' and even 'Move It' and 'We Say Yeah' were included by huge demand.
OCTOBER 13	Cliff records 'Don't Talk To Him' at EMI's Abbey Road Studios.
OCTOBER 15	Cliff and Peter Gormley fly to the States to record for the Ed Sullivan Show. Whilst in New York, Cliff buys records by John Hammond, Aretha Franklin, Nancy Wilson and Dakota Staton, six slim-jim ties and two pairs of cufflinks. He also goes to see Dakota Staton live in Greenwich Village, John Hammond at Folk City and *Lord of the Flies*, about which he says, 'It's a weird film – but great!' During the flying visit, he also meets American hit-maker Mitch Miller, and Britain's *Oliver* star Georgia Brown.
OCTOBER ☐	A company called J.B. Walker of Yorkshire advertises Cliff biros for 2s.6d, Cliff stationery for the same price (24 sheets of notepaper and 12 envelopes!) and a set of four pencils, also for 2s.6d., bearing the inscription, 'I Like Cliff!'
OCTOBER 18	Cliff's *Lucky Lips* EP is released, containing the title track 'It's All In The Game', 'Your Eyes Tell On You' and 'I Wonder'.
OCTOBER 18	Before leaving for a tour of France, Shadow Bruce Welch says he's now hopeful that, following more consultation with a specialist, he may be able to stay permanently with Cliff and the Shadows.
OCTOBER 19	A major announcement about Cliff's new film *Wonderful Life* discloses that it will be shot in the Canary Islands, commencing early in December. The musical score will include six pop-songs, two Shadows instrumentals and nine production routines. Susan Hampshire (who appeared with Cliff in *Expresso Bongo*) is to play the leading lady alongside Melvyn Hayes, Una Stubbs and Richard O'Sullivan. Actors Dennis Price and Robert Morley are *not* now to appear on the film.
OCTOBER ☐	Radio Luxembourg's *Book of Record Stars* is published, and includes a six-page interview and photograph section devoted to Cliff. The article is

headed 'Cliff says "Be yourself and be different!"' and contains advice on how to be popular, what kind of guys girls like and ways of doing something useful with your spare time: '... popularity isn't a matter of taking. It's a matter of giving and you win friends by offering your friendship, your help, not by standing around waiting for others to drop it into your lap ...', '... maybe one reason for your seeming unpopularity is that you're in the wrong crowd ...', '... one thing for sure, the girl who tries to win popularity by the necking route is heading for disaster. Boys who know that a chick is an easy "make" will take her out all night, but it won't be where anybody can see her ...', 'all boys aren't angels, but most of them are looking for one.'

OCTOBER 19   Cliff's new co-star, Susan Hampshire, appears on BBC TV's 'Juke Box Jury' with Dusty Springfield and 'Z Cars' actor Terence Edmond.

OCTOBER 30   Cliff and the Shadows pre-record 'Thank Your Lucky Stars' for November.

NOVEMBER 1   Cliff's new single, his 23rd, 'Don't Talk To Him', is reviewed in the music press: 'Here's another facet of Cliff Richard's many talents. In sharp contrast to "All In The Game" comes a haunting melody in slow cha-cha tempo, written by Bruce Welch and Cliff himself. Don't see how Cliff can go wrong here, 'cos it's ideal for dancing and makes easy-on-the-ear listening.'

NOVEMBER 3   Cliff and the Shadows top the bill on 'Sunday Night at the London Palladium'. It is Shadows' bass player 'Licorice' Locking's final live TV appearance with the Shadows, as he dramatically and suddenly announces his intention to leave the group to devote more time to being a Jehovah's Witness. Cliff pays tribute to him: 'We shall certainly miss "Lick" terribly, he's been a good friend to all of us and I'm thankful that Bruce has decided to stay!'

NOVEMBER ☐   The press hint that Cliff may be joined on his spring tour of Britain by Bob Miller and the Millermen, which would enable him to present full recording arrangements of ballads on stage. The suggestion apparently comes from Cliff after working with them on 'Parade of the Pops'.

NOVEMBER 8   Cliff talks about his new single: 'Bruce brought me the melody and asked if I could think of a lyric – which I did. So this marks the birth of a new Rodgers and Hammerstein partnership!'

NOVEMBER 8   *NME* reader C.A. Armstrong of Co. Durham, makes a prediction in the letters column of the paper: 'In five years' time, the Beatles will have settled down to steady jobs, Cliff Richard will still be getting world-wide hits (including America) and Elvis Presley will have made a non-singing film.'

NOVEMBER ☐   Cliff and the Shadows send the Beatles a 'Good Luck' telegram before their appearance on the Royal Variety Show.

NOVEMBER 8   In America's *16* magazine, Cliff names Carole Gray as his favourite girl.

NOVEMBER 15   Cliff talks about the discovery by fans of his new £30,000 six-bedroom Tudor-style 11-acre mansion in Upper Nazeing, Essex: 'We thought we could keep our new home secret, but now that it is known there is nothing we can do about it. Don't think I'm trying to hide from my fans, I'm not. Neighbours resented fans standing outside my last house and I don't blame them.'

The national papers also carry a story about a guard with dogs and a gun. Cliff comments: 'That's a lot of rubbish, specially about the Alsatians. We've only got a poodle! It was just my chauffeur's way of being funny, but on that day he had a bad scriptwriter.'

NOVEMBER 24	Cliff records two songs with Hank Marvin, Bruce Welch and Brian Bennett, with producer Norrie Paramor on piano: 'I'm The Lonely One' and 'Watch What You Do With My Baby!'
NOVEMBER 30	Cliff and the Shadows appear on 'Thank Your Lucky Stars'.
NOVEMBER 31	Cliff conducts an interview from the snooker room of his house with pop writer Derek Johnson, who afterwards says: 'I experienced some difficulty in getting to the front door owing to the large number of fans who had congregated outside the house, and later in the day police had to be called to disperse crowds which had smashed down Cliff's fence.' During the interview, Cliff discusses the musical content of the forthcoming film *Wonderful Life*: 'I honestly think the pop songs are better than those in *Summer Holiday*. Bruce has written an absolutely fantastic ballad called "In A Matter Of Moments". I imagine it will be coupled with a light-hearted piece titled "On the Beach" which I have written with Hank and Bruce.'
DECEMBER ☐	Popic Figures of Nottingham advertise a life-like 5⅝-inches-high figurine of Cliff in Denby Pottery for 19s.6d.
DECEMBER 13	*NME* publish their poll results: **World's Most Outstanding Singer:** 1 Cliff Richard 2 Elvis Presley **World's Outstanding Musical Personality:** 1 Elvis Presley 2 Cliff Richard **British Male Singer:** 1 Cliff Richard 2 Billy Fury **British Vocal Personality:** 1 Joe Brown 2 Cliff Richard
DECEMBER ☐	Radio Luxembourg Top 20 Show DJ, Barry Alldis, selects his favourite twenty records of 1963. Top of the list is 'Bachelor Boy'.
DECEMBER 25	Cliff hosts an hour-long record show on the BBC Light Programme between 12.30 and 1.30pm. He also introduces the Shadows and plays some of his favourite records.
DECEMBER 25	Cliff and the Shadows (marking the debut of new Shadow bass player, John Rostill) star in an hour-long ATV Spectacular. The show is entitled 'Sounds and Sweet Airs'. Both the radio and TV shows were recorded before Cliff leaves for the Canary Isles, where he spends Christmas.

1964

JANUARY □

Cliff's *Top Pops* book is published, in which he writes about other artists:
Elvis Presley – Round the world, thousands copied him. Some simply grew Elvis sideburns, some styled their hair the Presley way and others sold their bicycles and put down a deposit on a guitar.
Adam Faith – Even a six-figure win on the pools wouldn't give you the satisfaction, adventure and the thrill of living that has come the way of Adam and me.
Billy Fury – Off-stage he doesn't strike one as furious at all. He talks quietly and laughs quietly – on-stage it's different.
Frank Sinatra – I spent an afternoon with him at Northwood, Middlesex, when he visited the British blind children. They flocked around him feeling for his hands. 'Oi, Sinarcher' cried one blind Cockney boy of six, 'come an' see the sandpit!'
The Everly Brothers – They produce a sound that is as ear-catching in Tokyo as it is in Tooting or Texas, and I see no reason why they should ever stop ...!

| JANUARY 3 | *NME* publish the final chart points places for 1963 – 30 points for every week at No.1, down to 1 point for No.30. |

1 Beatles	1,741
2 Cliff Richard	1,323
3 Shadows	899
4 Gerry and the Pacemakers	894
5 Frank Ifield	838
6 Roy Orbison	772
7 Billy J. Kramer & the Dakotas	680
9 Billy Fury	623
10 Freddie and the Dreamers	584

| JANUARY 3 | In a survey by *Billboard* magazine using the sales charts of 34 countries outside America, Cliff emerges as world champion with Elvis second and the Shadows and Frank Ifield third and fourth respectively. |

| JANUARY ☐ | Cliff reveals his hopes for the new year to reporter Alan Smith: 'I hope for a year of peace and prosperity for all mankind, and for the betterment of international relations and understanding. If in some small way the Shadows and I can help the spread of British goodwill abroad, then I shall be very happy.'

And on the music scene: 'I hope that the Beatles and their contemporaries go from strength to strength, because their achievements are acting as a tremendous shot in the arm to the music business as a whole. |

| JANUARY 10 | On the set of *Wonderful Life* Cliff talks about his acting career: 'I can't wait to get older – with a few wrinkles and some grey hairs I might get offered some full-length character roles.' He also gives a few tips on riding a camel: 'Don't imagine it's like riding a horse, that would be fatal. What you have to do is watch his droopy eyes, get ready for grunts and then hang on like grim death because it's rougher than a roller-coaster ride!' |

■ Cliff on the set of *Wonderful Life*

THE CLIFF RICHARD FILE 1964

JANUARY ☐   Dave Clark of the Dave Clark Five includes Cliff's 'Do You Want To Dance?' in his all-time Top 10. 'This is my personal choice. The old rocking-type tune is treated with a solid beat which all adds up to being first class to dance to.'

JANUARY ☐   New York *Motion Picture Herald*'s survey, using 2,300 British cinemas, puts Cliff at No.1 most popular film star in Britain for 1963, with Peter Sellers and Elvis Presley in second and third places respectively.

JANUARY 17   Bad weather in the Canaries delays the shooting of *Wonderful Life*.

JANUARY 24   One of the scenes in *Wonderful Life* is dubbed 'controversial' by some people on the set. The shot in question is the mickey-take of the beach scene between Sean Connery and Ursula Andress in the James Bond film *Dr No*. As 'Ursula', Susan Hampshire emerges from the waters of a tropical lagoon clad in a figure-revealing bikini, Cliff, as James Bond, is waiting on the beach and a passionate clinch ensues! Says Susan, 'After the kisses, I was going round bumping into furniture for hours.' Cliff comments: 'I kept telling the director I was ready for more and more takes!'

Cliff's 24th single is released, the 'A' side, 'I'm The Lonely One', is a song written by Viscounts member Gordon Mills. The 'B' side, 'Watch What You Do With My Baby', is a number from one of Elvis's songwriters, Bill Giant.

JANUARY ☐   Cliff buys a holiday home in Albufeira on the Atlantic coast of Portugal, where Frank Ifield, Shadow Bruce Welch and Cliff's manager Peter Gormley already have houses.

JANUARY ☐   Among the reviews for Cliff's new single is one from Derek Johnson: 'This is the type of number that Cliff used to record years ago, but today it's well in keeping with teenage demand. A distinct r & b flavour and a melody slightly reminiscent of "What'd I Say".'

JANUARY ☐   Holidaying in the Canaries, Max Bygraves watches Cliff filming *Wonderful Life*.

JANUARY 31   Ralph G. Evans writes to the music press: 'Why did Cliff Richard and the Shadows have to sink so low and go all r & b on their latest record? On this disc, they lose all claim to originality.'

'It's All In The Game' starts to climb the American charts.

FEBRUARY ☐   Cliff's *When in France* EP is released, featuring 'La Mer', 'Boum', 'J'attendrai' and 'C'est si bon!'

FEBRUARY ☐   *Rave* magazine is launched and includes a colour portrait of Cliff and a feature 'On location in the Canaries'.

FEBRUARY 7   The press reports that Cliff is not seeing dancer Jackie Irving any more.

FEBRUARY 11   On his return to Britain, 'I'm The Lonely One' enters the Top 20. Says Cliff: 'Actually, it wasn't originally planned as a single. I usually include a couple of rockers on my albums, and this song was cut with that in view, but the beat craze changed our plans!'

FEBRUARY 16   Cliff headlines at the London Palladium and among other songs sings, 'Maria' from *West Side Story*.

FEBRUARY ☐   'It's All in the Game' peaks at No.25 in America's *Billboard* chart.

FEBRUARY 17   Talking to the press on board the former presidential yacht *Potomac* at Long Beach, California, Elvis Presley reveals, 'I like Cliff Richard's work.'

FEBRUARY ☐	Cliff's former girl-friend, Jackie Irving, joins the Lionel Blair Dancers.
FEBRUARY/MARCH ☐	Cliff and the Shadows shoot interior shots for *Wonderful Life* at Elstree Studios.
MARCH **6**	In an interview, Shadow Hank Marvin says: 'We were very annoyed when we read some of the comments on our backing to Cliff's "I'm The Lonely One". A couple of writers suggested that we were simulating the Mersey sound. Frankly, I've never read such rubbish!'
MARCH ☐	Beatles manager Brian Epstein declines offer for his protégée, Cilla Black, to appear on Cliff's forthcoming tour.
MARCH ☐	*Cliff Sings Don't Talk To Him* EP is released, featuring 'Don't Talk To Him', 'Say You're Mine', 'Who Are We To Say', 'Spanish Harlem' and 'Falling In Love With Love'.
MARCH **13**	Interviewed on the Elstree set of *Wonderful Life*, Cliff says: 'This film has got to be twice as good as the last one to be half as good! People judge you by what they hold to be your personal best. People still say I've never made a record as good as "Livin' Doll".'

MARCH ☐	For one scene of the film within *Wonderful Life* (entitled *The Daughter of the Sheik*) director Sidney Furie plans to take down the advertisements for the current film showing at the Warner Cinema in Leicester Square, and replace them with neons for a make-believe première.
MARCH ☐	Police refuse permission to shoot the scenes for *Wonderful Life* in Leicester Square.
MARCH ☐	Cliff's latest American LP includes a version of 'Secret Love'.
MARCH 28	Cliff and the Shadows, augmented by Bob Miller and the Millermen, commence a 3-week British tour opening at the ABC Southampton.
MARCH 28	Cliff and the Shadows appear with the Hollies on the BBC Light Programme's 'Saturday Club'.
MARCH ☐	EMI chief Joseph Lockwood presents Cliff and the Shadows with a Gold Disc for one million worldwide sales of 'Lucky Lips'.
APRIL ☐	On tour, Cliff opens his 35-minute act with 'I Wanna Know', followed by 'Come To Me', '24 Hours From Tulsa', 'Da-do-ron-ron', 'It's All In The Game', 'Maria', 'You Don't Know', 'Constantly', 'Bachelor Boy', 'Whole Lotta Shakin', ending with 'What'd I Say'.
APRIL 10	'I'm The Lonely One' enters America's *Billboard* magazine chart at No.92.
APRIL 10	Millie, riding high in the charts with 'My Boy Lollipop', names Cliff as her favourite singer.
APRIL 17	Cliff's new single 'Constantly' is reviewed. As one reviewer puts it: 'A captivating rock-a-ballad with an exotic Latin lift – this must rank as one of Cliff's best and most polished discs to date.'
APRIL 24	Cliff's 25th single 'Constantly' is released. Adapted from the Italian hit song 'L'Edera', it was recorded in the Canaries the previous December and is backed with a composition written by Shadow Bruce Welch, 'True True Lovin'.
APRIL 24	Cliff's agent Leslie Grade reveals that he has turned down offers for him to appear at The Sands and the Desert Inn in Las Vegas, the Beirut Casino and the Australian Chevron Hilton.
APRIL 25	Cliff appears on 'Thank Your Lucky Stars'.
APRIL 26	Along with the Beatles, Rolling Stones, Manfred Mann, Gerry and the Pacemakers, the Dave Clark Five and other *NME* poll winners, Cliff and the Shadows appear at the annual concert staged by the music paper. Cliff sings Ray Charles' 'I Wanna Know', his hit from the previous Christmas 'Don't Talk To Him', 'Whole Lotta Shakin' Goin' On', 'Bachelor Boy' and 'I'm The Lonely One'.
MAY 1	Epic Records in America invite Cliff to record an album in the US without the Shadows.
MAY ☐	It is announced that Cliff will visit Los Angeles in July to discuss starring in both a Hollywood musical and a Hollywood picture.
MAY 3	*NME*'s poll concert is televised.
MAY 5	Cliff and the Shadows fly to Amsterdam to begin a continental tour.
MAY 8	*Photoplay* magazine features an exclusive article on Cliff: 'Is Cliff heading for marriage – his next step could be right up to the altar!'

THE CLIFF RICHARD FILE **1964**

MAY ☐ *Cliff's Palladium Successes* EP is released. The tracks are, 'I'm The Lonely One', 'Watch What You Do With My Baby', 'Perhaps, Perhaps, Perhaps' and 'Frenesi'.

MAY 12 Cliff records a programme for German TV in Munich.

MAY 22 Cliff is interviewed while he and the Shadows are playing at the Paris Olympia: 'It's really marvellous here in Paris; it's a fantastic city and the audience couldn't be bettered anywhere in the world. They have this admirable knack of remaining perfectly quiet during each number, then suddenly bursting into a volume of applause when it ends. In Belgium, Holland and Germany, we were playing different towns every day. Sometimes we'd have an afternoon show, then boat and train for a couple of hours and give an evening performance in another city miles away.' For the Paris shows Cliff learns 'La Mer' and 'Boum' in French: 'That wasn't as tricky as "Lucky Lips" and "I'm The Lonely One", which I had to learn phonetically in German. I've also been singing a couple of Spanish songs on the tour, so altogether I've been working in four languages.'

MAY 27 Two-week tour of Scandinavia begins.

MAY ☐ In *Rave* magazine, astrologer Maurice Woodruff predicts that Cliff will fall in love.

END OF MAY ☐ 'Constantly' peaks at No.4 in the charts.

JUNE ☐ Leslie Grade appoints sports writer Bob Ferrier as publicity agent for Cliff and the Shadows.

JUNE 12 The July edition of *Photoplay* features Cliff and Susan Hampshire on the front cover in a scene from *Wonderful Life*.

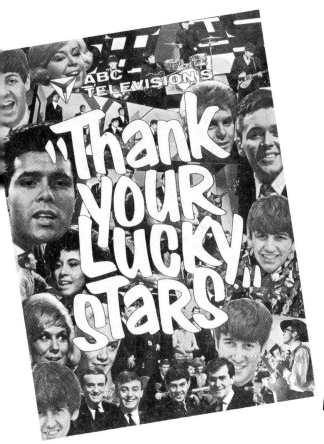

JUNE 12	In an interview with the London *Evening News*, Cliff says: 'People think I must be a millionaire. I'm not. Nowhere near it. I have to ask my accountant if I can afford it before making a big purchase.'
JUNE 19	Cliff's new single 'On The Beach/In A Matter Of Moments' is reviewed: '"On The Beach" is a medium-fast happy-go-lucky twister, and the soothing dreamy ballad "In A Matter Of Moments" is one of Bruce Welch's best compositions.'
JUNE 22, 23, 24	Cliff records at EMI's Abbey Road Studios with the Norrie Paramor Orchestra.
JUNE 26	Cliff's 26th single, 'On The Beach/In A Matter Of Moments' is released.
JUNE 30	Cliff telerecords a Spectacular for the following day for ATV, featuring the Shadows and guest star Liza Minnelli.
JULY 1	ATV Spectacular is postponed owing to an ITV strike.
JULY ☐	At the halfway mark in the *NME* annual points survey, Cliff is eleventh with fewer than half the points he had amassed by the same time the previous year.

1 Beatles	710
2 Bachelors	647
3 Dave Clark Five	529
4 Cilla Black	467
5 Hollies	458
6 Rolling Stones	448
7 Searchers	441
8 Gerry and the Pacemakers	412
9 Swinging Blue Jeans	391
10 Jim Reeves	352
11 Cliff Richard	344

JULY 2	Princess Alexandra and her husband, Angus Ogilvy, attend the première of *Wonderful Life* at the Leicester Square Empire in London. Proceeds of the event go to the National Association of Youth Clubs. Of the film, one critic says: 'No one will be able to say they haven't had their money's worth, there's everything in it but the kitchen sink.' And another comments: 'He [Cliff] improves with every picture he makes. Not only is his acting much more convincing, but he also displays considerable talent as a light comedian and impressionist.'
JULY ☐	Plans for Cliff and the Shadows to write the music for – and star in – *Aladdin* at the London Palladium next Christmas are hinted at in the press. It is also rumoured that Robert Morley is likely to be cast as Abanazer.
JULY 12	Cliff guests on BBC2's 'The Best of Both Worlds' with the Stanley Black Orchestra.
JULY ☐	*Rave* magazine reveals the location of Cliff's holiday home in Portugal and publishes pictures of Cliff and his sisters at their new home in Upper Nazeing, Essex.
JULY ☐	*Wonderful Life* LP is released.
JULY 15	Cliff's postponed ATV Spectacular is screened, replacing the scheduled documentary about Beatlemania, 'Fans, fans, fans'.
JULY ☐	*Go* magazine publishes *Cliff and his Wonderful Life* book for 3s.6d.

■ Wise guise! Cliff and Richard O'Sullivan

JULY ☐	As the film *Wonderful Life* is released in forty different cities, Cliff speaks about the picture: 'I've yet to see it properly – I've sat through it three or four times, but all I've seen is me and my mistakes!' He also comments on his recording career: 'We have been toying with the idea of releasing "Maria" as a single, but we may just do a *West Side Story* EP on which it would be one of the tracks.'
	In addition, Cliff reveals that he will be recording in New York and Nashville: 'I would also love to record in Chicago. That's the home of that great writer Curtis Mayfield, and that superb group the Impressions. Nothing would make me happier than to record a Mayfield song with the Impressions backing me!'
AUGUST ☐	EMI release *Wonderful Life No.1* EP, containing four tracks from the film.
AUGUST 19-21	Cliff records in New York, planning to record in Nashville and Chicago later in August.
AUGUST ☐	During his stay in America, Cliff goes to see Barbara Streisand's *Funny Girl* on Broadway and watches several live artists including Buddy Greco, Kay Starr and Della Reese.
AUGUST 28	It is announced that Una Stubbs and Arthur Askey will appear with Cliff in *Aladdin* at the London Palladium later in the year.
SEPTEMBER 5	Cliff flies to Portugal for a holiday on the Algarve.
SEPTEMBER ☐	Cliff's *A Forever Kind Of Love* EP is released.
SEPTEMBER 23	Cliff's 27th single, 'The Twelfth Of Never', is released and reviewed: 'Cliff reverts to his more romantic approach with his revival of the Johnny Mathis song – the captivating lilt is ideal for cheek-to-cheek dancing.'
SEPTEMBER 25	It is announced in the press that advance bookings for the London Palladium pantomime starring Cliff and the Shadows are the highest in the history of the theatre.

THE CLIFF RICHARD FILE 1964

OCTOBER ☐		Norrie Paramor produces new songs for Cliff in Portugal.
OCTOBER 9		Choosing his all-time Top 10 records for the *NME*, singer P.J. Proby includes Cliff's 'Constantly': 'This is the first disc of Cliff's I've liked – before I thought he was an atrocious singer!'
OCTOBER 16		*NME* publish a letter from an 'indignant Cliff fan' from Hull: 'How dare P.J. Proby call Cliff an atrocious singer? Until a few months ago, P.J. Proby was unknown, whereas Cliff is already world famous.'
OCTOBER ☐		Cliff and the Shadows tour Britain. Cliff kicks off his act with 'We Say Yeah' which he follows with 'A Matter Of Moments', 'Constantly', 'The Twelfth Of Never', 'Da-doo-ron-ron', '24 Hours From Tulsa', a medley of 'The Young Ones', 'Livin Doll', 'Lucky Lips' and 'Bachelor Boy', finishing with 'What'd I Say'.
OCTOBER 30		On a fashion note, one critic reflects on Cliff's new short hair-cut: 'It's a fascinating thought that at a time when most pop idols are competing against each other to see who can grow the longest locks, one of our tip-top stars defies the trend by having his hair cut.'
OCTOBER ☐		*Wonderful Life No.2* EP released.
NOVEMBER 2		Cliff and the Shadows perform at the Royal Variety Show in front of H.M. the Queen. Also appearing are Cilla Black, Brenda Lee, Kathy Kirby, Millicent Martin, Jimmy Tarbuck, David Jacobs, the Bachelors, Bob Newhart, Gracie Fields, Lena Horne, Morecambe and Wise and Tommy Cooper. Cliff sings 'Wonderful Life' accompanied by the entire London Palladium orchestra, conducted by Norrie Paramor, followed by 'The Twelfth Of Never', ending with a version of the Supremes' 'Where Did Our Love Go'.
NOVEMBER 20		Cliff and the Shadows' forthcoming LP *Aladdin and his Wonderful Lamp* is reviewed.
NOVEMBER 27		Cliff's 28th single is released, both sides coming from the pantomime *Aladdin*: 'I Could Easily (fall in love with you)/I'm In Love with You'.
NOVEMBER 27		Cliff agent Leslie Grade announces that Cliff and the Shadows are to star in a screen version of *Aladdin*: 'A complete new screenplay will be written and the film will have a very big budget. We haven't yet decided which company we will let make it; there have been many offers since I registered the title for film rights.'
NOVEMBER ☐		In a popularity poll run by the *Muzick Expres*, which covers Holland, Belgium and parts of Germany, Cliff is voted top male singer with 39% of the votes, ahead of Sicilian-born Belgian singer Adamo with 17%, Elvis with 13% and Roy Orbison 7%.
NOVEMBER ☐		Over £100,000 in advance booking money for *Aladdin* taken by the London Palladium.
DECEMBER ☐		As leading lady in *Aladdin*, Una Stubbs talks about Cliff: 'Cliff is a marvellous person. I owe an awful lot to him – he gave me my first opportunity in show business. When I did my screen test for *Summer Holiday*, he told the producer that he thought I'd be right for the part.'
DECEMBER ☐		In Michael Braun's newly published book on the Beatles, *Love Me Do*, he attributes this quote to John Lennon – 'We hate Cliff Richard's records.'
DECEMBER ☐		*Hits from Wonderful Life* EP released.
DECEMBER 11		The *NME* annual poll results are published:

World Male Singer
1 Elvis Presley	5,861
2 Roy Orbison	4,638
3 Cliff Richard	3,987

World Musical Personality
1 Elvis Presley	4,010
2 Roy Orbison	2,837
3 Cliff Richard	2,528

British Male Singer
1 Cliff Richard	6,269
2 Billy Fury	2,516
3 Mick Jagger	2,472

British Vocal Personality
1 Cliff Richard	5,785
2 John Lennon	4,613
3 Dusty Springfield	3,408

DECEMBER 22   Cliff and the Shadows open in *Aladdin* at the London Palladium with Una Stubbs and Arthur Askey. It is scheduled to run for 3½ months.

Souvenir Brochure

at the famous LONDON PALLADIUM

LESLIE A. MACDONNELL & LESLIE GRADE in assoc. with BERNARD DELFONT present

ALADDIN and his WONDERFUL LAMP

1965

Cliff hits new heights!
Just wait till he spots the Beatles on the other end of the wire!

JANUARY 1 — The *NME* annual points table for 1964 is published – 30 points for a No.1 down to 1 point for a No.30 record.

1	Beatles	1232
2	Bachelors	1035
3	Rolling Stones	1005
4	Jim Reeves	958
5	Roy Orbison	824
6	Searchers	749
7	Cliff Richard	747
8	Manfred Mann	676
9	Cilla Black	618
10	The Hollies	610

Cliff reveals his New Year hopes for 1965: 'I trust that my next film is well-liked. It won't be a musical really, you see, as there's only about four songs in it. I don't think I want to undertake any tours this year. The panto doesn't finish until May 10th and we start filming soon after that. And on top of that I might possibly be making a film of *Aladdin* in 1965 too.'

JANUARY 12 — Cliff sends a 'Good Luck' telegram to the Beatles for their London show.

JANUARY 13 — Cliff's and Frank Ifield's private companies are taken over by Constellation Investments, bringing them £474,000. The *Daily Express* comments: 'Most of the money is likely to go to 24-year-old Cliff Richard, which almost certainly establishes him as a millionaire.'

JANUARY 15 — Twenty-one-year-old Freddy Self, former lead singer with Liverpool group the Trends and Cliff's understudy in *Aladdin*, releases a single 'Don't Cry'.

JANUARY 15 — 'I Could Easily Fall' is in the Top 10 in Britain, Sweden and Holland.

JANUARY ☐ — The Shadows' 32-minute film *Rhythm and Greens* goes on release, featuring Cliff as King Canute.

JANUARY ☐ — Actress Leslie Caron goes to see Cliff in *Aladdin* at the Palladium.

JANUARY 22 — Cliff reveals that his current favourite single is Little Anthony and the Imperials' 'Goin' Out of My Head'.

JANUARY ☐ — Cliff replies to press suggestions that he intends to retire and settle in Portugal: 'The truth is that sooner or later I do hope to retire from the business. Let's face it, that's the ultimate ambition of most entertainers. After all, we realise we can't go on for ever and the time must come when we have to quit. I would much rather leave while I am at the top than wait for the public to turn its back on me, and the obvious place for me to retire to when the time comes is Portugal.'

FEBRUARY ☐ — Columbia release the *Why Don't They Understand* EP.

FEBRUARY ☐ — It is reported that Cliff has formed his own film production company, Inter-State Films.

MARCH ☐ — *Hits From Aladdin And His Wonderful Lamp* EP released.

MARCH 5 — Cliff's 29th single (recorded in Nashville), 'The Minute You're Gone/Just Another Guy' is released and reviewed: ' "The Minute You're Gone" is unlike anything we've heard Cliff perform before. The tune is catchy, simply constructed and easily memorised.'

MARCH 5 — Edward Nunn of London N16 writes to the music press pointing out the facial similarity between Cliff and actor Dirk Bogarde.

MARCH ☐ — 'I Could Easily Fall' is in the Top 10 in Israel, the Lebanon, Hong Kong, Finland and Holland. In Malaysia it's No.1 with 'Twelfth Of Never' at No.3.

MARCH 14 — On 'Sunday Night at the London Palladium', Cliff receives his NME trophy for being voted Top British Singer (for the sixth time).

MARCH 19 — Norbert Langerbeins of Cologne writes to the music press, asking which is Cliff's favourite of all the songs he's recorded. Cliff replies: 'There's no doubt about my answer to this question – "The Twelfth Of Never". For years and years it was my favourite song ever since I heard it sung by Johnny Mathis, and I was really happy when I recorded it and it was issued as a single. An absolutely beautiful number!'

MARCH ☐ — Herman's Hermits record 'Travellin' Light' (a 1959 hit for Cliff) for their new LP.

APRIL ☐ — Cliff's 'Havin' Fun' is in the Top 10 in Israel.

APRIL 9 — In a retrospective look at the pantomime run, Cliff says: 'I haven't been bored once during the entire run. Each show has been interesting, mainly because something has happened at each performance.'

THE CLIFF RICHARD FILE 1965

APRIL 15	Columbia release the LP *Cliff Richard* which includes tracks recorded in London, New York, Nashville and Barcelona.
APRIL 15	'The Minute You're Gone' knocks Unit Four Plus Two's 'Concrete And Clay' off the No.1 spot in the charts.
APRIL ☐	Cliff and the Shadows telerecord three hour-long Spectaculars for ATV to be screened in June.
APRIL 21	In the *NME*, 'Alley-cat' comments: 'In the next poll, Tom Jones could give Cliff Richard stiff opposition!'
APRIL 22	'The Minute You're Gone' is deposed at the top of the chart by the Beatles' 'Ticket To Ride'.
APRIL ☐	Cliff holidays on the Norfolk Broads with the Young Crusaders group from Finchley.
APRIL 30	In reply to *NME*'s 'Alley-cat' comment the previous week, 'Alley-cat' fan writes: 'So "Alley-cat" thinks Cliff has to fear Tom Jones. Never! I saw Tom Jones on the Palladium when he "murdered" "I Believe" – he's rough.'
MAY ☐	Cliff records twenty songs in EMI's Lisbon studios with Norrie Paramor – six in English and fourteen in Italian. 'I'm having to write out all fourteen songs phonetically, so when it comes to the actual sessions, I shan't have the faintest idea what I am singing!'
MAY 18	The *Daily Mirror* reports: 'Cliff Richard and Frank Ifield have made £256,000 profit on paper on the Stock Exchange in four months – last night Constellation shares went up to 10s. making Cliff's and Frank's shares worth £730,000.'
MAY ☐	*Look In My Eyes, Maria* EP released.
MAY ☐	In an interview with *Disco* magazine, Cliff says that he does not know what happens to the greater part of his money: 'I leave it to the businessmen. All I've asked is that they tell me six months before I go broke so that I can get out.'
JUNE 4	Cliff's 30th single is released and reviewed – 'On My Word' (recorded in the US) and 'Just A Little Bit Too Late': 'It's set to a shuffle rhythm with a subtle Latin flavour, plus brass and chirping girls – Cliff sings in huskily appealing low register which contrasts effectively with the bounding beat.'
JUNE 13	Cliff and the Shadows appear on 'Sunday Night at the London Palladium'.
JUNE 18	Cliff admits that he actually buys the Beatles records but not the Rolling Stones, and that of the current groups around he thinks the two likely to stay the course are the Beatles and the Searchers.
JUNE ☐	The *NME* publish their points chart for the first six months of 1965 (30 points for a No.1 down to 1 point for the No.30 position):

1 Seekers	552
2 Sandie Shaw	481
3 Beatles	367
4 Cliff Richard	359
5 Rolling Stones	342
6 Animals	330
7 Kinks	317
8 Them	312
9 Marianne Faithfull	310
10 Herman's Hermits	309

JULY 8 — Cliff and the Shadows fly to Scandinavia.

JULY 9 — Cliff and the Shadows open their six-city tour with two dates in Copenhagen. Four thousand people, average age 15 years, attend the two appearances to hear Cliff sing numbers like 'Don't Talk To Him', 'Constantly', 'Angel', 'Bachelor Boy', 'Do You Wanna Dance?', 'On The Beach' and 'Hi-heel Sneakers'. The Shadows also do their own set, as do supporting Danish acts the Defenders and the Rocking Ghosts.

JULY ☐ — Cliff appears on the front cover of *Rave* magazine.

JULY ☐ — Cliff's *Aladdin* understudy, singer Freddie Self, changes his name to Freddie Ryder – chosen through a Radio Caroline competition.

JULY 16 — Cliff at No.1 in Malaysia with 'The Minute You're Gone'.

JULY 23 — Cliff is at No.2 in the Israeli chart with his version of 'Sway'.

JULY 25 — In an interview with *Disc* magazine, Cliff reveals: 'I never eat lunch, apart from something like cheese and biscuits. I don't even have breakfast or a good meal when I get home in the evening – I've got to look after my weight.'

JULY 26 — Cliff and the Shadows appear for half a week at Southend Odeon with Des O'Connor.

AUGUST ☐ — The music papers pose the question, 'Why has Cliff Richard *never* been on the TV show "Ready Steady Go"?'

AUGUST 6 — Cliff and the Shadows fly out to Bahrain to begin a tour of Spain, France and Switzerland, taking in Vienna, Marseilles, Casablanca, Zurich and Geneva.

AUGUST 13 — Cliff's 31st single is released: 'The Time In Between/Look Before You Love'. Derek Johnson of the *NME* writes: 'Back again with the Shadows after two American recorded singles, this is a French song with a new English lyric which the Shadows were originally going to record.' Says Shadow Hank Marvin: 'We were thinking of cutting "The Time In Between" but when Cliff heard it he was so enthusiastic about it that we passed it over to him.'

AUGUST ☐ — A plethora of artists are in the South of France at the same time as Cliff and the Shadows – Dionne Warwick, Françoise Hardy, Rolling Stone Keith Richard, and Paul McCartney's brother Mike McGear.

AUGUST ☐ — Columbia release Cliff's *When In Rome* LP.

AUGUST ☐ — In an interview with *Disc* magazine, Cliff says: 'I would like to get married very much eventually ... I've no one particular in mind at present. There's been a couple of false alarms which I wouldn't want to happen again.'

AUGUST ☐ — It is revealed that Cliff's next film will go into production on 1 November. Cliff's manager, Pete Gormley, describes it as 'altogether more sophisticated than his last pictures'.

SEPTEMBER 2 — Cliff performs at the ABC Northampton at a charity show in aid of a Milton Keynes church rebuilding fund.

SEPTEMBER 15 — First of three ATV Cliff Richard and the Shadows Specials shown on ITV.

SEPTEMBER 22 — Second ATV Cliff and the Shadows Special screened.
Cliff films US TV show for Ed Sullivan.

SEPTEMBER 24 — Mary Langley of Barnsley has this letter published in the *NME*: 'Wasn't "Time In Between" a waste of time? Please, Cliff, stop making lovey-dovey records. Don't you realise that most of your fans are adults now? I often hear records

	that I wish you'd made. Sorry, I know you don't really like critics but I see so many artists get to the top with trash, and I do so want you to show them that you're the best.'
SEPTEMBER 24-26	One-night stands in Britain.
SEPTEMBER 29	Third ATV Cliff and the Shadows Special shown on ITV.
OCTOBER 1-3	One-night stands in Britain.
OCTOBER 1	Cliff is pictured sporting a fringe.
OCTOBER ☐	Columbia release Cliff's *Take Four* EP.
OCTOBER 10	Cliff and the Shadows fly to Warsaw to play two concerts at the Roma theatre in the Polish capital, organised by the Polish government.
OCTOBER 13	Cliff and the Shadows fly back to London.
OCTOBER 14	Cliff celebrates his 25th birthday as he and the Shadows fly to the Lebanon to play concerts in Beirut.
OCTOBER 21	The BBC's Light Programme presents 'The Cliff Richard Story', written and produced by Peter Noble.
OCTOBER ☐	Cliff's 'Angel' in the Hong Kong Top 10.
OCTOBER 28	Cliff and the Shadows become the first British artists to play at the French film industry's Gala Concert. It is staged at the Paris Marigny Theatre and they play in the presence of Princess Grace of Monaco. Cliff and the Shadows then go on to play a week of one-nighters in France.
OCTOBER ☐	Ronnie Gabay of Jerusalem has a letter published in the *NME* which proclaims, amongst other things, that 'Cliff is still the most popular artist in Israel.'
OCTOBER 29	Rolling Stone Keith Richard reveals that he and Mick Jagger have written a song called 'Blue Turns To Grey' which Cliff Richard is going to record.
OCTOBER 29	Cliff's 32nd single 'Wind Me Up (let me go)'/'The Night' is released. One reviewer says: 'It was recorded in Nashville, like his No.1 "The Minute You're Gone", though I don't think it'll be such a big hit as that. Slight suggestion of sweet corn.'
NOVEMBER 5	Cliff appears on TV's 'Thank Your Lucky Stars' with the Animals, Ian Whitcomb and Danny Williams.
NOVEMBER 12	Following mediocre receptions for 'Wind Me Up' by DJs, record reviewers and the 'Juke Box Jury' panel on television, Cliff replies to the critics both with a Top 20 chart entry and verbally: 'It just shows that you have to take adverse criticism with a pinch of salt. Frankly, I've given up worrying – it's impossible to please everyone. Actually, it was Bruce Welch's brainwave to release "Wind Me Up" as a single, and it was his suggestion that we released "It's All In The Game" and "The Twelfth Of Never" as singles.'

On the film front, Cliff comments: 'The last news to be announced was that we would make this film together and later start work on the screen adaptation of *Aladdin* some time in 1966. Now all that has changed and *Aladdin* is definitely going to be the next film. We have already returned the script three or four times for various alterations – for one thing, I wanted a bit more swashbuckling and less drama sequences.'

THE CLIFF RICHARD FILE **1965**

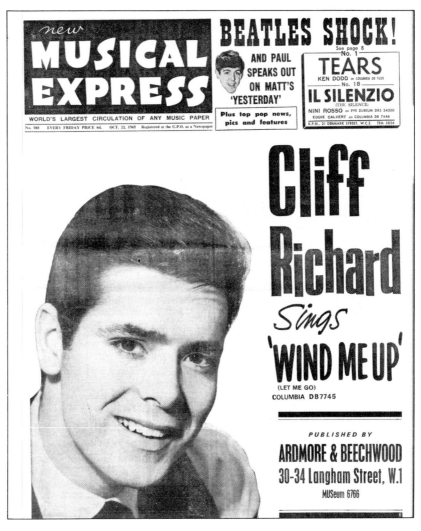

NOVEMBER ☐	Cliff's *Love is Forever* LP is released.
LATE NOVEMBER ☐	Various one-night stands around the country.
NOVEMBER 24	In an interview with the *Daily Express*, Cliff reveals: 'I now arrange my work to have weekends free for youth activities. All my closest friends are teachers.'
DECEMBER ☐	Cliff reveals that neither he nor the Shadows have managerial contracts with Peter Gormley.
DECEMBER 3	Cliff talks to journalist Alan Smith about new recordings: 'One song we've just completed is called "Kinda Latin" and another is "Sing A Song of Disney" with numbers from Disney films like "Chim-Chim Cheree". I used to write a lot, but just lately I haven't been able to get the inspiration. I think I've lost my contact. I don't do the same kind of songs I used to because I've had to change as the years have gone by. I can't stay for seven years what I was at 17. If I did, it would be bad for my career and bad for my ego.'
DECEMBER 4	Cliff and the Shadows headline a charity concert at his old school, Cheshunt Boys' School, with Mark Wynter, Unit Four Plus Two, Al Saxon and Elkie Brooks.

DECEMBER 10   The *NME* publish their 1965 poll results:

World Male Singer
1 Elvis Presley	6,002
2 Cliff Richard	4,848
3 Gene Pitney	3,526

World Music Personality
1 Elvis Presley	4,197
2 John Lennon	2,656
3 Bob Dylan	2,548
4 Cliff Richard	2,423

British Male Singer
1 Cliff Richard	6,599
2 Paul McCartney	2,892
3 Mick Jagger	2,736

British Vocal Personality
1 John Lennon	5,631
2 Cliff Richard	5,407
3 Mick Jagger	3,002

Best New Disc of the Year
1 Rolling Stones – 'Satisfaction'
2 Beatles – 'Help'
3 Rolling Stones – 'Get Off My Cloud'
4 Paul McCartney – 'Yesterday'
5 Cliff Richard – 'The Minute You're Gone'

Cliff comments on his success in the *NME*: 'I regard myself as a very fortunate person, for this is the eighth time you have bestowed poll honours on me – the first in 1958 was as "Best New Singer". I want you to know that I value it deeply.'

DECEMBER 25   'Cliff Richard's Christmas Cheer' is shown on BBC TV from 2.15 to 3.00pm. It stars Cliff, the Shadows and Frank Ifield.

DECEMBER 31   The *NME* annual points championship results are published (30 points for a No.1 down to 1 point for a No.30):

1 Rolling Stones	836
2 Seekers	813
3 Beatles	760
4 Animals	656
5 Sandie Shaw	649
6 Cliff Richard	631
7 Ken Dodd	617
8 Yardbirds	607
9 Manfred Mann	569
10 Hollies	567

DECEMBER 31   G.J. Howard of Leicester has a letter published in the music press: 'Cliff Richard need not in any way feel surprised at being voted Top British Male Singer for the seventh year. For sheer professionalism there is no one who comes anywhere near him. Unless some miracle occurs during the next five years, he should still be on top for a long, long time.'

DECEMBER ☐   In an interview with the London *Evening Standard*, Cliff reveals that two of his sisters have become Jehovah's Witnesses.

1966

JANUARY 1 — In an interview with *Disc* magazine, Cliff says, 'As far as I'm concerned, long resident shows and long provincial one-nighters spoil my social life – something I've begun to enjoy more than anything else.'

JANUARY 17 — Cliff talks about his forthcoming cabaret debut: 'I had a meeting last week with my manager Pete Gormley and ex-Shadow Tony Meehan who is helping me prepare my act. We decided it'd be wrong to attempt something entirely different – after all, I don't consider myself as a Buddy Greco.'

'I've come across an old Frank Sinatra number which I like immensely called "My One And Only Love", and we're going to put that in, and I shall also be doing "My Colouring Book" – we also decided to include one out-and-out raver to represent the rock n' roll phase of my career – "Dizzie Miss Lizzie".'

Cliff also talks about Tony Meehan's involvement in his career: 'He's helping me to select material as well as to routine it and shape the backings – and he's also assisting me in working out my "Talk of the Town" act.'

JANUARY 17 — Cliff records at Abbey Road Studios under Tony Meehan's supervision.
JANUARY ☐ — Cliff's recording manager Norrie Paramor is appointed director of the music publishers Ardmore and Beechwood.

JANUARY 28 — An *NME* chart survey covering the last five years is published (using their usual points system).

1	Cliff Richard	4,841
2	Elvis Presley	4,344
3	Beatles	3,737
4	Shadows	3,107
5	Billy Fury	2,458

JANUARY 31 — Cliff and the Shadows make their cabaret debut at London's 'Talk of the Town', as Columbia Records reveal that during the four-week tour the act may be recorded for future release as an LP. In the audience on the opening night are Cilla Black, Frank Ifield, 'Ready-Steady-Go' compère Cathy McGowan, Sid James and Tony Meehan. After the Shadows' 25-minute stint, Cliff sings fourteen numbers plus a medley, including '24 Hours From Tulsa' and 'The Girl From Ipanema', as well as several of his hits.

FEBRUARY 11 — It is announced that Cliff's cabaret season at 'Talk of the Town' is to be extended by two weeks to 12 March, and that plans to record a live LP have been scrapped.

FEBRUARY 28 — In line with other EMI records, Cliff singles go up 7d to 7/3d.
FEBRUARY ☐ — The long list of stars who go to see Cliff in cabaret include: Paul McCartney, Jane Asher, Petula Clark, Pat Boone, Tony Hatch, Jackie Trent, Paul and Barry Ryan, Cilla Black, Russ Conway, Wee Willie Harris and BBC producer Bill Cotton Jnr.

FEBRUARY ☐ — Columbia release Cliff's EP *Wind Me Up*.

THE CLIFF RICHARD FILE **1966**

MARCH **6**   Cliff's new single is reviewed: 'The prospect of Cliff Richard handling a Jagger-Richard song is one of the most intriguing I've come across for some time – and I'm glad to see that Cliff has adapted it to his own style rather than following in the footsteps of the Stones.'

MARCH **18** Cliff's 33rd single, 'Blue Turns To Grey/Somebody Loses' is released.
MARCH □   In an interview with *Disc* weekly, Cliff announces that he is planning to leave show business to become a teacher.

A Time of DECISION

THE CLIFF RICHARD FILE 1966

MARCH ☐   It is reported that Cliff's next film may not be *Aladdin* after all. Several supporting artists are not available.

MARCH 22   Cliff appears on 'Pop Inn' with Harry Secombe, Roy Orbison, Cilla Black and Crispian St Peters.

MARCH 26   Cliff and the Shadows appear on ABC TV's 'Thank Your Lucky Stars' with Dusty Springfield, Dave Dee, Dozy, Beaky, Mick and Tich, and Billy Joe Royal.

MARCH 28   Cliff and the Shadows top the bill on the BBC Light Programme's Monday lunch-time radio show.

APRIL 1   *NME*'s 'Alley-cat' says that Cliff and the Shadows look dated on 'Thank Your Lucky Stars'.

APRIL 3   Cliff and the Shadows appear at the *Daily Express* Record Star Show at the Empire Pool, Wembley in aid of the Spastics Society.

APRIL ☐   *When in Rome* EP is released.

APRIL ☐   At the invitation of the Bishop of Coventry, Cliff participates in a service at the Albert Hall to mark the 25th Anniversary of the Abbey Christian Community.

APRIL ☐   Cliff talks to the press:
On films:
'*Aladdin* has now been postponed.'
On his new LP:
'Do you know what's given me the greatest kick in the preparation of the LP "Kinda Latin"? It's the fact that the sleeve is going to feature a picture of my sister which I took myself.'
On holidays:
'I plan to go camping in Cornwall for a fortnight with the Crusader Union, and then I hope to have two or three weeks at my villa in Portugal.'
And on his future:
'It's perfectly true that I would like to take up teaching at some time in the future. After all, I have to be sensible and think ahead, because I can't expect to remain a star for the rest of my life. If I do eventually decide to retire, it's more likely to be in the region of five years' time.'

APRIL 8   BBC TV screens the 'Stars Organisation for Spastics Special Star Show', starring Cliff and the Shadows, Manfred Mann, the Fortunes, Sandie Shaw, Georgie Fame, Adam Faith, Wayne Fontana, Paul and Barry Ryan, Chris Andrews, Kenny Ball and Jackie Trent.

APRIL 15   Cliff's 1966 Christmas plans are revealed. He is to play Buttons in the Palladium production of *Cinderella*, scheduled to open a few days before Christmas and run until Easter 1967.

APRIL 30   Cliff and the Shadows feature in ABC TV's tenth anniversary programme 'The ABC of ABC' with the Vernons Girls and Valerie Mountain.

APRIL 30   Cliff and the Shadows appear at the *NME* Poll Winners' Concert. Among the other artists appearing are the Beatles, Rolling Stones, Walker Bros., Small Faces, Yardbirds, Herman's Hermits and Roy Orbison. Cliff sings 'Blue Turns To Grey', 'The Minute You're Gone' and 'Bachelor Boy'.

MAY ☐   It is reported that Cliff's former girl-friend, Jackie Irving, is currently seeing Adam Faith.

THE CLIFF RICHARD FILE 1966

MAY 8 — The first half of the *NME* poll concert featuring Cliff is screened.

MAY 9 — Cliff and the Shadows co-star with Tom Jones and the Squires in a BBC Light Programme 2-hour special, 'Let the Good Times Roll!' Also on the programme are the Hollies, Lulu and compère Ray Orchard.

MAY ☐ — Cliff Richard Ltd is formed.

MAY 9-13 — Final auditions to select supporting artists for Cliff's new film take place.

MAY 27 — Cliff's fifth film, *Finders Keepers*, starts production at Pinewood Studios. The picture is a light-hearted musical comedy about a nuclear bomb which is lost in the sea off the coast of Spain; the supporting cast includes the Shadows, Robert Morley, Peggy Mount and Graham Stark. George Brown, who conceived the story, is the producer.

JUNE 3 — Marlon Brando's girl-friend, 20-year-old South American actress Viviane Ventura, is named as Cliff's leading lady in *Finders Keepers*.

JUNE 3 — In a letter to the music press, Mary Maynard of Richmond in Surrey says: 'Although I admire much of Cliff Richard's work, I can only deplore the proposed story for his next film. The lost nuclear bomb is hardly a suitable story for a "light-hearted musical comedy". Surely Mr Richard realises that this serious and dangerous situation is not fitting for any kind of frivolity. Nuclear bombings are no laughing matter.'

JUNE ☐ — It is announced that Terry Scott will appear at the London Palladium in Cliff and the Shadows' Christmas pantomime.

JUNE 4 — Cliff and the Shadows appear on the 400th edition of the BBC's 'Saturday Club' with Billy Fury and Marianne Faithfull.

JUNE 16 — Cliff takes the stage at a Billy Graham Crusade meeting at London's Earls Court to sing 'It's No Secret' and announces that he is a Christian to an audience of 25,000. He also declares his intention to embark on a three-year divinity course when his pantomime finishes in April 1967.

JUNE 18 — Cliff's mother, Dorothy, marries East End undertaker and their former chauffeur, Derek Bodkin. Says Cliff: 'I didn't know until this morning when they phoned me. I bought some wine and arrived for the celebrations after the ceremony.'

JUNE ☐ — Cliff talks to the press about various topics:

Finders Keepers
'I think this is going to come out okay. We do about nine weeks in the studio and then go to the South Coast for some exteriors, and we have doubles in Spain doing other exteriors. I like all the songs in the picture, but think that "This Day" and "Time Drags By" are sort of stand-outs.'

His Christian activities
'Someone suggested it is sissy to proclaim your Christian beliefs, but I don't think it is; I feel great all the time and know it is because of my beliefs. I've felt this way for two years now and it has relieved me of the petty jealousy one gets in show business and helped me to help others. I did a Billy Graham study course of about five weeks and found it stimulating; then I had a letter asking me if I would speak at a meeting. I was petrified. There was a desk in front of me and I put my arms on it as I spoke. Then, when I sang, I put my arms to my sides and had terrible pins and needles. I tried to raise my arms to emphasise the words in the song, but I couldn't, and at the end I walked off with my arms

still pinned to my sides!' Cliff also discussed the song he had performed at Earls Court, 'It's No Secret (what God can do)' and said that, although he liked Elvis Presley's version from the LP *Peace in the Valley* and was aware of versions by Pat Boone, Lonnie Donegan and Jo Stafford, he would not be recording it.

His mother's marriage

'It's her life – I hope she and Derek (I can't call him Dad!) will be very happy. I'll be buying them a house as a wedding present and they'll be going to my place in Portugal. I'll also buy a house for my sisters if they want one, and one for my aunt and two teenage cousins who have been living with us. Then I'll probably sell the big house I have and get a flat.'

JUNE ☐ The *Daily Express* reports that Cliff has given former Shadow Jet Harris a wedding present of a £700 guitar and amplifiers, so that he can get back into the music business.

JUNE 19 Granada TV announce that they plan to film a 45-minute Special focused on Soho's 2 Is coffee bar, to be screened in September – the tenth anniversary of Tommy Steele being discovered there. Granada hope to include Cliff and the Shadows, Lionel Bart, Terry Dene, Wee Willie Harris and record producer Micke Most.

JUNE 24 In the *NME*'s chart points table for the first half of the year, Cliff does not even figure in the Top 20.

JUNE ☐ Cliff's nine-year-old 42,000-strong Fan Club announce they will be closing down the following April. Club secretary, 22-year-old Jan Vane, says: 'I am relinquishing the job and have already started winding up the Club's affairs.'

JUNE ☐ Viviane Ventura, Cliff's leading lady in *Finders Keepers*, says: 'Cliff's so happy he makes me happy. When we have a romantic scene, we go into a corner to work things out. He is so open to suggestions and has so many good ideas himself that it's a joy to be in a picture with him – I'm a lucky girl.'

JULY 3 Cliff makes the Week's Good Cause appeal on the BBC Home Service on behalf of the Westminster Homes for Elderly People.

JULY 15 'Visions', Cliff's 34th single, is reviewed: 'Cliff's at his most appealing in this subdued, wistful and sentimental number. Bernard Ebbinghouse's delicate accompaniment is unobtrusive, with a rippling guitar figure, softly chanting group and the suggestion of a Latin lilt.' The flip side is a Hank Marvin-Bruce Welch song, 'What Would I Do'.

JULY 21 'Visions' enters the charts.

JULY ☐ Another delay is announced on the commencement of shooting for the film adaptation of *Aladdin*. The projected date for work to start is now spring 1967, which will mean postponement of plans for Cliff's divinity course.

JULY ☐ Cliff sells his house, 'Rookswood', in Nazeing, Essex, for a reported £43,500.

AUGUST 5 Having previously been heralded in the press as Marlon Brando's girlfriend, it is revealed that Cliff's leading lady in *Finders Keepers*, Viviane Ventura, is engaged to Frank Duggan.

AUGUST ☐ Pauline Harris from Stockton writes in *Fabulous 208* magazine's letters page: 'In my opinion "Visions" is the best thing that Cliff has recorded for ages.' The magazine replies that the song was written by actor Paul Ferris (currently appearing in Harry Secombe's revue at the London Palladium) of the Paul Ferris-Nicky Henson songwriting team.

AUGUST 13	*Finders Keepers* leading lady, Viviane Ventura, appears on BBC TV's 'Juke Box Jury' with Simon Dee, actor Anthony Booth and singer Sheila Southern.
AUGUST 19	Cliff reveals that it is still one of his ambitions to film *Wuthering Heights*.
AUGUST 20	The papers publish news of Cliff buying a house for his mother at Highfield Drive, Broxbourne, another for his sisters nearby and a third for his aunt.
AUGUST ☐	Cliff holidays in Portugal after finishing filming for *Finders Keepers*.
SEPTEMBER 2	A 'Cliff Crossword' compiled by D.R. Stanford of Birmingham is published in the *New Musical Express*.
SEPTEMBER 10	Cliff talks to *Fabulous 208* magazine: 'I'm more ambitious now. The more success you have, the more you want. What's the use of feeling suicidal if you don't get what you want? Another way I've changed is that I have learned to take criticism. But you've got to be discerning about criticism – you must know what you've done wrong and be prepared for someone else to tell you about it.' And on his active interest in the Church: 'It's made so much difference to me. I'm a much happier person and I've never felt so refreshed before. My whole life has changed because of a healthier state of mind. I believe there's only one way to live and that is by the Bible. It's the only source which is completely reliable and I set my own life on this. If you've got a focal point in your life, you can't fail. The Church has been the biggest influence in my life. I think young people are a bit self-conscious about religion. I don't care what anybody thinks, I always go ahead and do the thing I think is right – regardless!'
SEPTEMBER 12	A Birmingham group called Finders Keepers release a single, 'Light', which is produced by Scott Walker. They insist that they didn't copy the name from Cliff's film.
SEPTEMBER 12-16	Cliff and the Shadows record new songs at EMI's Abbey Road Studios.
SEPTEMBER ☐	*Daily Express* columnist Judith Simons forecasts that Tom Jones will take over from Cliff as Britain's No.1 solo singing idol.
OCTOBER 4	Cliff appears on 'Pop Inn' with Diana Dors and Herman's Hermits.
OCTOBER 7	One review of Cliff's 35th single, 'Time Drags By', says: 'This is an easygoing jog-trotter with a happy-go-lucky approach. The beat's pretty solid with tambourine and harmonica.'
OCTOBER 7	Paul McCartney raves about 'Time Drags By'.
OCTOBER 9	Cliff tops the bill and also compères live the first 'Sunday Night at the London Palladium' show of the 1966/67 season. He is presented with a petition organised by May Clifford of Islington and signed by 10,000 fans, begging him not to leave show business.
OCTOBER 14	Cliff celebrates his 26th birthday.
OCTOBER 22	Cliff joins the Archbishop of York and the Bishop of Coventry on stage at the Albert Hall to mark the 21st anniversary of the Lee Abbey evangelical training centre. Cliff, who sings two gospel songs at the event, says: 'As a Christian, I feel it is my duty to take every opportunity to profess I am a Christian and that I personally was saved by Jesus Christ.'
OCTOBER 24	In an interview with the *Sunday Mirror*, Cliff reveals that he has been invited to appear in Russia, Czechoslovakia, Yugoslavia and Bulgaria: 'The money just

	about covers expenses but, so what? I just love new, exciting experiences.'
OCTOBER 28	'Visions' is at No.5 in Poland.
OCTOBER 29	Cliff appears at a Christian meeting at the Liverpool Empire. He arrives with two clergymen, but needs a dozen bodyguards to control the fans. Cliff sings 'Sinner Man', a re-vamped version of Bob Dylan's 'Blowin' In The Wind' and 'It's No Secret' and talks to the audience from the stage: 'People do not realise how easy it is to become a Christian – and I hope that whether you are Christians or not your ears have been opened to Christianity.'
NOVEMBER ☐	Cliff's *La la la la la* EP is released and, along with the title track, includes Neil Diamond's 'Solitary Man', the Beatles' 'Things We Said Today' and 'Never Knew What Love Could Do'.
NOVEMBER 4	Columbia issues *Thunderbirds Are Go* EP containing three Shadows tracks and a vocal ('Shooting Star') from Cliff. It is announced that a film of the same name in which puppet figures of Cliff and the Shadows perform to the sound-track will be premièred some time in December.
NOVEMBER 11	It is announced that Cliff is unlikely to make any personal appearances in 1967 apart from one or two summer concerts. It is also revealed that he will almost certainly have a leading dramatic role in a religious picture being made by an evangelical company, for which production is expected to begin in May. In the film, Cliff will play an atheist who becomes converted to Christianity.
NOVEMBER 13	The *Sunday Express* reports that Cliff is to be confirmed as a member of the Church of England, and that he has recently lunched with Canon Frederic Hood, Chancellor of St Paul's Cathedral.

1967

JANUARY 14 — Cliff speaks out in an interview with *NME*: 'I'm not being self-righteous, I just want to get out of this business because I feel I have to. When I leave depends on the results of my Religious Instruction 'O' level examination. Don't think I regard everybody in show business as sinful, I love the atmosphere and the life. If I didn't want to teach religious instruction in a secondary school, I'd stay in it till Domesday. When I give up this life, it's not going to be a complete break; I don't think people realise that I'll still be making records. I just want to be an ordinary teacher in an ordinary secondary school. I don't care if some people do think I'm a phoney, they're entitled to their opinions.'

JANUARY ☐ — Cliff records at EMI's Abbey Road Studios with arranger Mike Leander, and includes a new version of 'Move It' and 'Good Golly, Miss Molly'.

JANUARY ☐ — EMI release the *Cinderella* LP.

JANUARY ☐ — Cliff appears on the BBC Light Programme's 'Five to Ten' religious programme: 'I've found I can mix both my Christian life and my show-biz life because I treat my show-biz life, as we are biblically told, as a job that we're going to give to God.'

JANUARY 21 — In an in-depth article on the subject, 'Are films a jinx for pop stars?', journalist Derek Johnson comments: 'Most people regard *Finders Keepers* as Cliff Richard's worst film to date. This is an opinion that I do not share, but as I appear to be in the minority one can only say that it must be due to the hurried hotch-potch fashion in which it was put together. A pity, for Cliff had previously set an all-time high in the standard of British film musicals.'

JANUARY 28 — Following the publicity surrounding his recent Christian activities, the 'Alleycat' column of the *NME* suggests that Cliff should record a 'long-praying LP!'

JANUARY ☐ — Cliff's 'Blue Turns To Grey' is in the Polish Top 10.

JANUARY ☐ — Raymond Smith, from Dartford in Kent, writes to the music press on the subject of Cliff's beliefs: 'I have never really been a fan of Cliff Richard's, but I was thrilled to see how Cliff has stood out for what he believes to be right. I am sure he has not found it easy to stick to his Christian principles ... If becoming a religious instruction teacher is what he believes God wants him to do, then I hope nothing will stand in his way. He certainly seems to be a young person who knows where he is going and that is more than can be said for a lot of people nowadays.'

FEBRUARY ☐ — The readers of *Disc and Music Echo* vote Cliff the best-dressed male star.

FEBRUARY ☐ — Cliff finishes work on his new LP with arranger Mike Leander. Tracks include Little Richard's 'Dizzy Miss Lizzy', the Beatles' 'I Saw Her Standing There', Buddy Holly's 'Heartbeat' and Simon and Garfunkel's 'Homeward Bound'.

MARCH 11 — Cliff's 37th single, 'It's All Over', is released – a song orignally recorded by the Everly Brothers and written by Don Everly. One reviewer says: 'One of those sentimental husky-voiced ballads that Cliff always handles with conviction ... although I don't rate this as one of Cliff's best discs.' The 'B' side, 'Why Wasn't I Born Rich', is a Shadows' composition from the *Cinderella* pantomime.

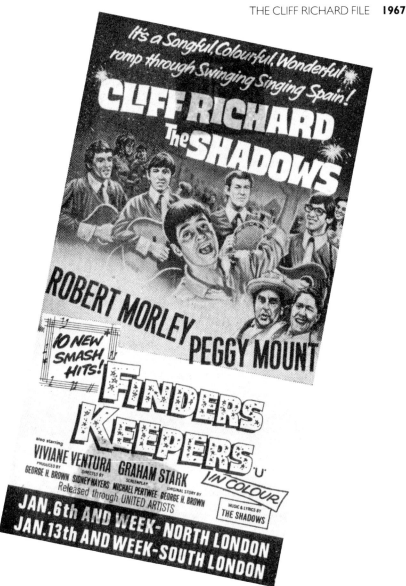

MARCH 18 Miss P. Grossmith of Liverpool has a letter about Cliff published in the music press: 'If anyone is to be given credit for consistency, surely it must be Cliff Richard. His career began in 1957 before the Beatles, Stones and the Monkees were even thought of. Now, ten years later, Cliff is still chalking up hit after hit. I wonder if the Monkees will still be doing likewise in 1976?'

MARCH □ Cliff speaks out about plans for a new, as yet untitled, film: 'The story will be about moral issues. Four songs will be featured, but the movie won't be a musical by any means. We don't intend to play up the comedy angle as we did with the H-Bomb in *Finders Keepers*. I particularly want to make a war story. I hope it will be a believable production showing how a group of young people can become easily involved in warfare, even though they do not want to be. The movie will not actually be *about* Vietnam, but it has been inspired by it and will project a similar situation.'

MARCH □ In the Ivor Novello Awards, presented annually by the Songwriters' Guild of Great Britain, 'Time Drags By' – sung by Cliff in *Finders Keepers* – is runner-up to 'Born Free' in the 'Film Song of the Year' category.

THE CLIFF RICHARD FILE 1967

APRIL 1 — Cliff talks about his music: 'Ballads have been my stepping-stone. I like singing "raw" as I did at the start with numbers like "Move It" – but if I hadn't changed, I couldn't have performed at all. Now I think it's time for a change again. I can't plug the Everly Brothers' LP enough, its fantastic. And I can't understand why the Evs. threw "It's All Over" away on an LP. They should have released it as a single ages ago.' He goes on to talk about public reaction to his beliefs: 'The main reason I couldn't go on as I am now is simple enough; the public gets fed-up with a pop singer talking about religion. It's getting like that already. People are saying, "Oh no, not Cliff Richard spouting about religion again!" They're building up a resistance. If I become a teacher it means I shall have to go into a training school for at least three years. After that the novelty will have worn off and I don't think the children I teach would be distracted.'

APRIL ☐ — Cliff turns down an offer to head the 'Sunday Night at the London Palladium' show, as he says that with performances in *Cinderella* six nights a week, Sunday is his only day off.

APRIL 8 — *Don't Stop Me Now* LP is released.

APRIL ☐ — The national press report that Cliff and the Shadows are to split.

APRIL 22 — Cliff's manager, Peter Gormley, answers the rumours that Cliff and the Shadows are going their separate ways: 'The misunderstanding has arisen because the Shadows will be touring abroad while Cliff is making his religious film – which starts shooting in June and continues into July. They will get together again in September to work on the dramatic film inspired by the Vietnam war, and we are now planning another picture which will go into production early in 1968. This will be a musical spectacular in the pattern of Cliff and the Shadows' previous film successes. At the end of the year, they will make several TV appearances which will probably include a Christmas Day show and a short series of six half-hour programmes.'

APRIL 27 — In an interview with *Disc and Music Echo*, Cliff says: 'When I quit, I'll keep "Cliff" because I can't stand the name Harry, but I'll add "Webb" on the end because the "Richard" thing has got to go.'

MAY ☐ — An EP from *Cinderella* is released.

MAY 7 — Cliff appears at the *NME* Pollwinners' Concert at Wembley with the Beach Boys, Small Faces, Troggs, Move, Cat Stevens, Dusty Springfield, Georgie Fame, the Cream and compères Jimmy Savile and Simon Dee. Cliff sings 'Out In the Country', 'It's All Over', 'Move It' and 'Shout'. His trophy for the Best British Male Vocalist is presented to him by John Maus of the Walker Brothers. Beatles manager Brian Epstein is seen in the audience enthusiastically applauding Cliff's act.

MAY 6 — Cliff appears with Georgie Fame, the Troggs and the Searchers on the BBC Light Programme's 450th edition of 'Saturday Club'. Cliff is backed on the show by the Mike Leander Orchestra.

MAY 13 — Cliff appears on BBC TV's 'Juke Box Jury' with fellow panellists Anita Harris, Roy Hudd and actress Leila Tasha.

MAY ☐ — Cliff begins recording his first religious album with arranger Mike Leander, which is to contain gospel songs, spirituals and hymns.

MAY 24 — Cliff stars in a one-hour ATV Spectacular.

JUNE **3**   William Brown from Manchester writes to the press: 'Let's have no more nonsense about Cliff Richard and Elvis Presley being the world's No.1 singers – they should both listen to Frank Sinatra, who has been at the top for 25 years!'

JUNE **3**   Cliff's 38th single is released – 'I'll Come Runnin'/I Get The Feelin'. Both sides are Neil Diamond songs. One reviewer comments: '... it explodes into a pulsating chorus with blaring brass, chirping girls and Cliff in his most rhythmic mood.'

JUNE ☐   Cliff (playing the part of an art student) films *Two a Penny* for evangelist Billy Graham, with all the proceeds going to charity. The film, with a £150,000 budget, includes three songs written by Cliff – who is also seen singing 'Twist and Shout' – and co-stars Avril Angers and Dora Bryan as Cliff's mother.

JUNE **18**   Cliff (as an Anglican) chats with Cathy McGowan (Roman Catholic) and Hugh Lloyd (Methodist) about their beliefs in a religious discussion programme on the BBC Home Service.

1967

JULY 1 — The *NME* publish their half-yearly chart table based on the points system of 30 points for a week at No.1 to 1 point for a week at No.30. The top five positions are:

1	Engelbert Humperdinck	554
2	Monkees	546
3	Tom Jones	453
4	Tremeloes	426
5	Jimi Hendrix	408

Cliff comes 18th with 248 points, equal with the Supremes.

JULY ☐ — Cliff's former bass player, ex-Shadow Jet Harris, effects a comeback signing for Fontana Records, and has his new material produced by ex-Shadow Tony Meehan.

JULY 9 — Cliff and Billy Graham appear on ABC TV's religious programme 'Looking For An Answer'.

JULY ☐ — Cliff writes the three songs which he will feature in the film *Two A Penny* being made by Worldwide Productions for the Billy Graham organisation.

JULY 16 — Cliff and self-confessed atheist, Paul Jones, take part in the BBC's controversial religious discussion programme 'Looking For An Answer'. The programme includes scenes from Paul's film *Privilege* – some of which parody Christianity – and scenes from a Billy Graham religious film.

AUGUST 5 — Cliff's 39th single is released – 'The Day I Met Marie'/'Our Story Book' and is described by one reviewer as 'a hauntingly tender ballad with a strong folk flavour ... in the chorus it explodes into a jaunty martial beat with oom-pah trombones, tambourines and chanting girls.' The song is written by Hank Marvin and arranged by Mike Leander.

AUGUST 12 — Cliff flies to Portugal for a three-week holiday prior to beginning work with the Shadows on 'A musical with a war background'.

AUGUST 19 — Jackie Irving, a former girl-friend of Cliff's, marries Adam Faith at Caxton Hall. Cliff's manager Peter Gormley is at the reception at Upper Court in Cobham, Surrey, along with Lionel Blair and TV producer Mike Mansfield.

AUGUST 30 — Cliff returns from holiday in Portugal.

SEPTEMBER 2 — Strong rumours that Cliff and the Shadows will no longer work together are dispelled by the announcement that they will not only star together in a French TV Spectacular, but also undertake major TV dates later in the year. Their joint agent Michael Grade says: 'We are also working on plans for two or three big TV shows in this country.'

SEPTEMBER 16 — In an interview, Cliff recalls a conversation with John Lennon in which they were chatting about their favourite artists. 'I've always liked Ray Charles,' Cliff told John. 'Well, I used to until everyone else started liking him,' replied Lennon. Cliff says that he always remembered that odd attitude. 'When John Lennon told me that, I was shocked. I don't know if he still has the same views nowadays, but I thought it was dreadful that anyone should change their opinions just to be different from everyone else. I'm all in favour of non-conformists, but I certainly don't agree with people not conforming just to be different.'

CLIFF RICHARD'S 'The Day I Met Marie'

Imagine a still summer's day
When nothing is moving—least of all me
I lay on my back in the hay
The warm sun is soothing—it made me feel good
The day I met Marie.
The sound of a whispered "Hello"
Came tiptoeing softly into my head
I opened my eyes kind-a slow
And there she was smiling—it made me feel good
The day I met Marie
With the laughing eyes
She tossed her hair and tantalised,
She came she touched me,
Then, she'd gone,
Just like a summer breeze.
I remember her kiss so soft on my brow,
And the way that she said
Baby—go to sleep now
Baby—go to sleep now.
I woke with a chill in the air
The warm sun no longer hung in the sky
I reached out but she was not there
She'd gone where she came from—but I still feel good
To think I've known Marie
With the laughing eyes
She tossed her hair and tantalised
She came she touched me,
Then, she'd gone,
Just like a summer breeze.

© 1967 by Shadows Music Limited, 17 Savile Row, London, W.1.

Words and music by Shadow HANK MARVIN

SEPTEMBER ☐   Cliff performs, 'The Day I Met Marie' on 'Top Of The Pops', hosted by Jimmy Savile, and is mobbed by fans. Cliff comments: 'I'm really surprised, I thought those days were over now.'

SEPTEMBER ☐   Cliff reveals that when he made the film *Two A Penny*, Equity – the actors' union – would not allow him to work for nothing; they insisted on a payment of £40 a week.

■ Jamie Hopkins (Cliff) attacks Fitch (Geoffrey Bayldon) in *Two a Penny*

SEPTEMBER ☐   Cliff says of the Beatles and the Maharishi: 'I think they are searching along the wrong track – the Beatles have said they are searching for God. There's only one way to find him – that's through Jesus Christ.' On the subject of transcendental meditation, Cliff comments: 'Meditation, like an LSD trip, is only a temporary thing. Christianity is something which is with you all the time.'

SEPTEMBER 23	Cliff's manager Peter Gormley announces that the projected film is to be delayed until 1968. He denies that Cliff is to star in the film adaptation of Keith West and Mark Wirtz's *Teenage Opera*: 'We were asked if we were interested and we said we would be. In this case, though, I imagine that shooting would clash with Cliff's own film with the Shadows.'
SEPTEMBER 23	*Melody Maker* readers vote Cliff 'Top Male Singer', a title he regains from Tom Jones who captured the title from Cliff in 1966!
OCTOBER ☐	Cliff records songs in Italian and German for the continental market at Abbey Road Studios.
OCTOBER 14	On his 27th birthday, Cliff flies to Tokyo to star in two concerts and a TV Spectacular with Norrie Paramor and a Japanese orchestra.
OCTOBER ☐	It is announced that Cliff is to be Britain's representative in the 1968 Eurovision Song Contest.
OCTOBER ☐	David Winter's book on Cliff – *New Singer, New Song* – is published.
OCTOBER 21	Cliff's *Good News* album is released and includes 'The 23rd Psalm', 'When I Survey The Wondrous Cross', 'The King Of Love My Shepherd Is' and 'What A Friend We Have in Jesus'.
OCTOBER 29	The *Daily Mirror* reproduces part of an address given by Cliff to a congregation at Cuffley Free Church in Hertfordshire: 'People who sleep around make the most unhappy marriages – pre-marital sex is unhealthy to the mind.'
NOVEMBER 4	Cliff's 40th single 'All My Love'/'Sweet Little Jesus Boy' is released. One reviewer claims: 'The with-it set will probably regard it as a retrogressive step for Cliff Richard because he's abandoned the zestful, refreshing style of "Marie" in favour of a sugary, sentimental ballad.'
NOVEMBER 25	Cliff talks about his sight problem. 'About a year ago, I got some contact lenses and I just couldn't wear them. Recently I was told that some German lenses were the best in the world, so last week I went to Germany and had them fitted. I find the strain affects my nose and makes me sneeze. I don't see people when I haven't got glasses or contact lenses – I see vague blurs!'
NOVEMBER ☐	Cliff and the Shadows announce the likelihood of a spring tour together, but reveal that not all the members of the group are keen to be in the new film, which is put back yet again – this time to June 1968.
DECEMBER 6	Cliff is confirmed by the Bishop of Willesden, Graham Leonard, at St Paul's, Finchley, in North London.
DECEMBER 9	The *NME* poll results are published:

World Male Singer

1 Elvis Presley	4,632
2 Tom Jones	4,410
3 Cliff Richard	3,863

World Musical Personality

1 Elvis Presley	4,273
2 John Lennon	3,333
3 Cliff Richard	3,206

British Vocal Personality

1 Cliff Richard	4,700
2 John Lennon	4,019
3 Tom Jones	3,261

British Male Singer

1 Tom Jones	5,785
2 Cliff Richard	5,121
3 Engelbert Humperdinck	2,654

In the 'Best British Disc of the Year' category, Cliff's 'The Day I Met Marie' comes fourth behind Procul Harum's 'A Whiter Shade Of Pale', the Beatles' 'All You Need Is Love' and the Bee Gees' 'Massachusetts'.

DECEMBER ☐   It is announced that Cliff is to star in a dramatic play to be recorded for ATV in February, in which he plays the part of a young gang leader who plots to steal a famous jewel collection. Cliff admits that he may not now start work on a new film in the summer, as none of the scripts submitted has been up to standard.

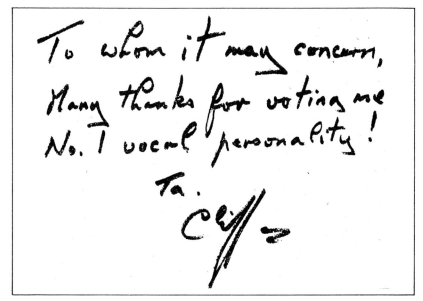

To whom it may concern, Many thanks for voting me No. 1 vocal personality! Ta. Cliff

1968

JANUARY **8-12**   Cliff is featured on David Symonds' Radio 1 show every evening.

JANUARY ☐   *NME* publish their 1967 points table (30 points for No. 1, down to 1 point for No. 30). Cliff comes 7th.

1 Engelbert Humperdinck	1218
2 Monkees	916
3 Tom Jones	890
4 Beatles	695
5 Tremeloes	633
6 Diana Ross & the Supremes	544
7 Cliff Richard	529
8 Dave Dee, Dozy, Beaky, Mick & Tich	489
9 Move	487
10 Traffic	479

The paper points out that not one of Cliff's releases has ever missed the chart, and that chart-wise he has definitely taken over the title of 'King of Consistency' from Elvis.

JANUARY **13**   Shadow Hank Marvin releases 'London's Not Too Far' – a song he originally wrote for Cliff.

JANUARY ☐   Along with Sandie Shaw, Cliff attends the launch of Southern TV's pop series 'New Release'.

JANUARY ☐   Cliff sends Engelbert Humperdinck a 'Good Luck' telegram for the opening of his pantomime.

JANUARY **16**   During their 'Talk Of The Town' season, Shadows drummer Brian Bennett is taken ill with appendicitis, resulting in Cliff sitting in on the drums for one night only until former Shadows drummer Tony Meehan takes over.

JANUARY **27**   DJ Keith Skues selects his list of all-time Top 10 records which includes Cliff's 'Summer Holiday'.

JANUARY **28**   In an interview with the *Sunday Times*, Cliff says: 'I've lived for years with people saying I'm a poof, but I don't give a damn. My best friends know me and that's all that matters. Even before I became a Christian, I wasn't going to lay chicks to prove myself . . .'

FEBRUARY ☐   Cliff accepts an invitation to preach three sermons on the Christian faith and its relation to the world of show business at Notting Hill's Kensington Temple in May.

FEBURARY ☐   Cliff shoots the ATV play *A Matter Of Diamonds*.

FEBRUARY ☐   The results of the *Disc & Music Echo* poll are published.

         Top Male Singer (*British*)
         1 Tom Jones
         2 Cliff Richard
         3 Scott Walker (*American*)

THE CLIFF RICHARD FILE 1968

Top Male Singer (*World*)
1 Scott Walker
2 Tom Jones
3 Cliff Richard

Mr Valentine – 1968
1 Scott Walker
2 Cliff Richard
3 Dave Clark

Best-Dressed Male Star
1 Cliff Richard
2 Tom Jones
3 Engelbert Humperdinck

Top TV Artist (*Male*)
1 Simon Dee
2 Tom Jones
3 Cliff Richard

FEBRUARY 17   The six Eurovision Song Contest contenders that Cliff is to sing in BBC TV's series 'Cilla' are announced.

Congratulations	by Bill Martin & Phil Coulter
Wonderful World	by Guy Fletcher & Doug Flett
High and Dry	by David and Jonathan
Do You Remember	by Tommy Scott
Sound of the Candyman's Trumpet	by Tony Hazzard
Little Rag Doll	by Mike Leander

FEBRUARY 24   Lynne Grossmith from Liverpool has a letter about Cliff published in the music press: 'Many people fail to realise that Cliff was responsible for introducing pop into places like "Talk Of The Town" that formerly would only have considered the Sinatras, Bennetts and Lena Hornes of the entertainment world.'

■ Cliff with evangelist Billy Graham

MARCH 9   Cliff's sister Joan is given away by Cliff when she marries Colin Phipps at Hoddesdon, Hertfordshire.

MARCH 12   On the 'Cilla Black Show', viewers vote for 'the Song for Europe'. The winning number, to be sung by Cliff on the Eurovision Song Contest, is 'Congratulations', which polls 171,000 of the 250,000 votes.

MARCH 23   Cliff's 41st single, 'Congratulations', is released with 'High 'n' Dry' on the 'B' side. Reviewed as being 'in the same bubbling effervescent style as "Puppet On A String"' it's also written by the same songwriters – Bill Martin and Phil Coulter. The 'B' side is a Roger Cooke and Roger Greenaway (David & Jonathan) song. The backing vocals on 'Congratulations' are by the Ladybirds.

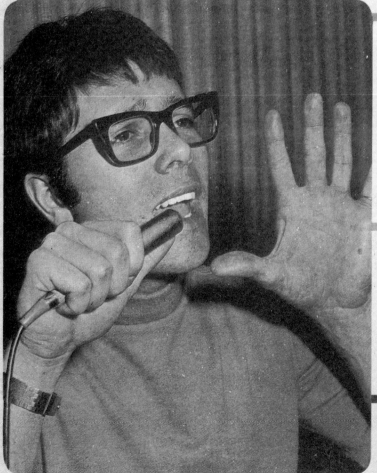

THE CLIFF RICHARD FILE 1968

MARCH ☐   It is announced that Cliff is to star in three major continental gospel concerts with the Settlers, in aid of local charities.

MARCH 24   Cliff appears on Simon Dee's BBC TV show 'DeeTime' with Adam Faith, Joe Brown, the Paper Dolls, the Easybeats and Lois Lane, but doesn't sing due to a sore throat.

MARCH ☐   In *Disc and Music Echo*, Bob Farmer reviews and comments on Cliff's book *The Way I See It*: 'Cliff Richard, whether you consider him nutty as a fruitcake or, as he really is, as nice as pie, is unquestionably doing a splendid job for his Saviour . . . he can communicate. The church's biggest failing in the present-day society is its failure to communicate with the layman at large . . .'

For his part, Cliff turns the teachings of Christ into amiable coffee-bar banter: 'He was a man like us . . . his mother was a woman, a human. His father is God. What a person! You really ought to get to know "him" and I must admit I still get knocked out when God answers my prayers.' Farmer goes on to say that, 'He writes – and talks – with the same enthusiasm as if he were a teenybopper raving about a pop-star, or a youngster boasting about his favourite football team. Cliff makes Christ a person to chat about easily and without embarrassment; the Church made him a forebidding figure, about whom it is indecent to talk above a whisper.'

MARCH 25   Cliff takes part in a photo-session with stable-mate John Rowles to celebrate both his hit – 'If I Only Had Time' – and his 21st birthday.

APRIL 1   *A Matter of Diamonds*, in which Cliff portrays a young crook, is shown on television.

APRIL 6   The Eurovision Song Contest is staged at London's Albert Hall and is screened in seventeen countries to 200 million viewers. Final placings are:

1	Spain	Massiel	'La La La'
2	UK	Cliff Richard	'Congratulations'
3	France	Isabelle Aubret	'The Spring'

After losing, Cliff says: 'Of course I'm disappointed, but it was so close, I don't consider it any disgrace.'

THE CLIFF RICHARD FILE **1968**

APRIL ☐ It is announced that fifty-six versions of 'Congratulations' are being released around the world and that Cliff has personally recorded the song for release in nearly every country in Europe. Co-writer Bill Martin comments: 'The ironic thing is that Germany, whose votes lost us the contest, have placed a 150,000 advance order!'

APRIL 6 Cliff's role in *A Matter Of Diamonds* is reviewed by David Hughes: 'Normally I never fail to feel embarrassed at the sight of a pop-star attempting to become a serious actor, but Cliff has at last bridged the gap, and although "Riley Walker" was not the most taxing of roles, he coped competently. But let this not be a signal for an avalanche of new pop-stars to turn actors. Cliff has mildly embarrassed in at least four films before he found the conviction of his acting ability.'

APRIL 13 Hollies drummer Bobby Elliott comments on Cliff's new single: 'I hate "Congratulations" and I hate the whole atmosphere that surrounds the Eurovision Song Contest. This gives me a sickly feeling inside.'

APRIL ☐ Singer John Rowles visits Cliff's clairvoyant, who tells him he will marry twice, have a son and own a house by the sea in the USA.

APRIL ☐ Cliff holidays on the Norfolk Broads with the Crusader Union. The days are spent boating and the evenings are taken up with Bible classes and discussions. Someone suggests that as the Maharishi is to the Beatles, so Billy Graham is to Cliff. Cliff replies: 'The relationship is as wide apart as anything could be. I just admire what Billy Graham says and does – the Maharishi maintains he can do something for the Beatles. Billy Graham can't do anything for me in that way.'

APRIL ☐ Cliff announces that he plans to star in a West End stage play for a seven-week season in the autumn.

APRIL ☐ Cliff appears on an all-star Easter 'Top Of The Pops' with the Hollies and Lulu.

APRIL 24 Cliff raves about the new Shadows single, 'Dear Old Mrs Bell': 'I think it's a great song – it's fantastic. The kind of record I'd buy.'

APRIL 25 Cliff flies to Sweden to start what is dubbed as a 'mini-Eurovangelism tour', taking in Stockholm, Rotterdam and Zagreb. His co-stars on the three-country tour are the Settlers, Cindy Kent, John Fyffe and Mike Jones.

APRIL ☐ American versions of Cliff's 'Congratulations' are released by Perry Como and Bobby Vinton.

MAY 2 All over Europe, Cliff's Eurovision single 'Congratulations' is outselling the actual winner by Massiel.

MAY 4 Cliff appears on the BBC's 500th edition of the radio programme 'Saturday Club' with the Bee Gees, the Hollies, the Tremeloes and the Seekers.

MAY 5 Cliff stars with the Bonzo Dog Doo-Dah Band and Lulu in ATV's 'The Big Show'.

MAY 12 Cliff appears on the 16th *NME* Poll Winners' Concert at Wembley's Empire Pool in front of a 10,000-strong audience. He performs 'In the Country', 'Shout', 'The Day I Met Marie' and 'Congratulations'. He is presented with his award for 'Top British Vocal Personality' by American singer Robert Knight. The bill also includes Status Quo, Love Affair, Don Partridge, the Association, the Shadows, Amen Corner, the Herd, the Tremeloes, the Move, Dusty

THE CLIFF RICHARD FILE 1968

MAY □	Springfield, Scott Walker, Dave Dee, Dozy, Beaky, Mick and Tich and the Rolling Stones. 'Congratulations' hits the top of the charts in Holland, Denmark, Belgium, Sweden and Norway, as it had the previous month in Britain. It also moves into the Top Ten in Spain, France, Germany and New Zealand.
MAY 12	Cliff's season at London's 'Talk of the Town' opens. He includes songs like 'Ain't Nothing But A Houseparty' and 'Girl, You'll Be a Woman Soon'. He tells the opening night audience: 'I'm not becoming a monk and I'm not becoming a nun either, and I have no stained-glass windows in my "E-type".'
MAY 18	Cliff announces that he wants to be the first British pop star on the 'Rock Revival Bandwagon': 'I don't think rock ever died, it's always been around. The Beatles have proved this with a lot of songs. I'd like to have "Move It" out again – it would be good for me.' Cliff also speaks out about his lack of success in America: 'It just won't happen for me there and I won't change my career to make it. There was a time when things were pro-British over there and anything that was big in the chart here, automatically got away. I was somehow left behind. We decided about five years ago that we couldn't gear our career to the States – yes, the Shads and I are very tiny in America!'
MAY □	In preparation for the Bratislava Song Festival in which he is to appear in June, Cliff is given a lesson or two by Czechoslavakian actress Olinka Berova.
JUNE □	'Congratulations' peaks at No. 99 in the American Billboard Hot 100.
JUNE □	Cliff and the Shadows star in a 50-minute Rediffusion TV Special 'After Ten Fellas – Ten!' This is a look-back over their ten years in show business.
JUNE 13-18	Along with Julie Driscoll and Brian Auger, Cliff is due to represent Britain in the Czechoslovakian Festival of Pop Songs – Bratislava, Lyra, '68. Gene Pitney represents the USA, Massiel represents Spain, and the Commonwealth is represented by the Easybeats. Due to an upset stomach, Cliff pulls out of the festival. Rumours are rife that (a) he has been killed in a car crash and (b) he is suffering from appendicitis.
JUNE 20	Cliff attends the première of Billy Graham's production *Two A Penny* in London. The film co-stars Dora Bryan and Avril Angers.
JUNE 21	Cliff's 42nd single, 'I'll Love You Forever Today/Girl, You'll Be a Woman Soon' is released. The 'A' side is featured in his film *Two A Penny*.
JUNE 22	Cliff appears on BBC TV's 'Billy Cotton Band Show'.
JUNE 22	Critic Alan Smith reviews *Two A Penny*: 'Attempted rape, the seduction of a young man by an older woman . . . drug trafficking . . . and Billy Graham with the word of God. In some respects it's the best film Cliff's ever made – as he says himself, he's no Sir Laurence, but at least he gets the chance to act in a serious and straightforward story. Rave versions by Cliff of "Twist and Shout" plus three catchy numbers "Two A Penny", "Love You Forever Today" and "Questions".'
JUNE 22	In *Disc* magazine, Penny Valentine reviews Cliff's new single, 'I'll Love You Forever Today': '. . . probably the most boring song Cliff's ever recorded. It's a shame really, because with his nice inoffensive way of singing, he has usually managed to lift even the most trivial of songs to a slightly higher commercial plane. But it would take a coal-heaver to do anything with this one – and he's certainly not that.'

JUNE 28   Cliff's one-man TV show, 'Cliff Richard at the Talk of the Town', is screened by BBC2.
JUNE 29   In the *NME* half-yearly look at the chart points table, Cliff is equal 15th with the Monkees.
JULY ☐   'Congratulations' earns Cliff his first Gold Disc for five years.
JULY ☐   Cliff's recording manager Norrie Paramor and his wife Joan celebrate their silver wedding, which is attended by Cliff's mother Dorothy and the Shadows.
JULY 17   Cliff appears on BBC TV's 'Juke Box Jury'.

JULY 22	Cliff flies to America for a six-week stay: five weeks on a private visit and one week with manager Peter Gormley for discussions with film companies.
JULY ☐	John Rowles reveals that his hit 'If I Only Had Time' had previously been turned down by both Cliff Richard and Engelbert Humperdinck.
AUGUST 10	It is reported that the Shadows will officially 'break up' at Christmas.
AUGUST 11	Tenth anniversary of Cliff's first official engagement – a 20-day season at Butlins Holiday Camp, Clacton.
AUGUST ☐	In an interview, Shadow Hank Marvin talks about Cliff ten years on: 'He's much more mature of course, but he appears to be just as ambitious as he was then – perhaps more so. He's giving more and more of his time to helping others through his Crusader work and this is a change in him – taking time off when he could be earning money, to work for something that brings him no cash return. He was a young enthusiastic lad – and this he hasn't lost. He'd rave about some clothes he'd seen or a song, a film or a girl, and it's still exactly the same. Before, he revelled in the first glories of fame, whereas now his natural enthusiasm is tempered with awareness.'
AUGUST ☐	Cliff and four friends holiday in the USA, taking in Sunset Strip, Disneyland, Santa Barbara, Las Vegas, San Francisco and Hollywood. While there, Cliff reflects that despite being on his fourth American label and having performed on seven Ed Sullivan shows, he still hasn't really cracked it in the States. When asked about groupies, Cliff says: 'I didn't know you called them groupies, but that's a good word. There are a dozen or so girls who are always around – I see them everywhere. I couldn't say what the perfect girl is as far as hair colour and so on. I know I'd like her to be reserved, because I like to make the first move. A good dress sense is nice, and if she can cook corn on the cob ...! I think American girls are more attractive on the whole because everyone looks so healthy here. English girls have that pasty look.'
AUGUST 31	Cliff announces that he will play gospel concerts with the Settlers at Coventry Cathedral and London's Royal Albert Hall later on in the year.
AUGUST ☐	Billy Graham works on German and Japanese versions of Cliff's film *Two A Penny*.
AUGUST ☐	On the subject of the Beatles, Cliff says: 'They felt they had to say clever things in front of the press, but when John Lennon, for example, came about with that quote about the Beatles being more popular than Jesus Christ, I regarded it as the height of childishness for a supposed adult cynic – I just feel the Beatles are too ready to rush on to new sounds ... But as people, they've risen in my estimation because they try so hard to find something worthwhile out of life and when they find it's not the answer, they have the guts to say so – like with LSD and then with the Maharishi. If only they gave Christianity the same gusto – boy, they'd find what they were seeking.'
SEPTEMBER ☐	The *NME* adds a special tenth anniversary 'Cliff and the Shadows' supplement as a tribute to their decade in show business: '... he has won every major award Britain has to offer – World Male Singer, Top British Male Singer (on 8 occasions), Personality of the Year, Best-Dressed Young Man, Artist who's the Greatest Credit to Show Business etc.'
SEPTEMBER ☐	Cliff discusses his forthcoming 'A' level in religious instruction and the 'O' level he passed 3 years before: 'I was 25 – I went to Lewes in Sussex for a hush-hush exam. I was put into a room all alone and about five masters of the school took turns to watch that I didn't cheat! Imagine me cheating while doing a religious instruction exam!'

SEPTEMBER ☐   Cliff continues to live in his Georgian house in Highgate with his friend, teacher Bill Latham (an ex-boyfriend of his sister Jacqueline) and Bill's mother. Cliff and Bill spend most Tuesday nights playing badminton at the church hall and discussing ways of making money for charity. On Sunday afternoons, Cliff is the assistant leader in the Crusaders Union – an inter-denominational religious group to teach boys of 8-18.

SEPTEMBER 14   Cliff's sister Jackie marries 19-year-old landscape gardener Peter Harrison at Hoddesdon Register Office.

SEPTEMBER 19   Cliff's 'Autumn Show' commences a 12½-week run at the London Palladium. He is supported for the first two weeks by the Chris Barber Band, after which the Shadows take over on completion of their Danish tour.

SEPTEMBER 21   Cliff and the Shadows appear in a London Weekend TV Special 'Cliff Richard at the Movies'.

SEPTEMBER 22   Cliff attends Coventry 'Call to Mission' meeting.
SEPTEMBER ☐   EMI release a special LP *Established 1958*, to mark Cliff and the Shadows' tenth year in show business.

SEPTEMBER 28   The critics slate Cliff's London Palladium show, but not his performance. The general consensus of opinion is that Cliff's fans don't want to sit through acts by comedian Mike Yarwood, the Palladium Orchestra and Chris Barber's Traditional Jazz Band for two hours before the person they came to see even sings a note. Cliff includes, 'When I'm 64', 'Shout' and 'If Ever I Should Leave

You'. One critic comments: 'It was a sad night – Cliff's return to the Palladium for his autumn season – sad, because it marked beyond all shadow of doubt that the era of Cliff, the teenage idol, has finally departed.'

OCTOBER 2   Cliff is interviewed by Keith Skues for the BBC's 'Saturday Club'.

SEPTEMBER ☐   Cliff's 43rd single is released – 'Marianne/Mr Nice'.

OCTOBER ☐   Cliff performs at the London Palladium throughout October, while the press report that a weak supporting bill is not helping mediocre audience figures.

NOVEMBER ☐   It is announced that Cliff and Anita Harris will star in ATV's 'Bruce Forsyth Show' on Christmas Eve.

NOVEMBER 5   Cliff records for BBC's radio programme 'Off The Record', choosing and discussing eight of his favourite records.

NOVEMBER 9   It is revealed that Cliff is to star in his own mini-TV series for Tyne Tees in 1969 – six weekly religious shows with the Settlers, in which Cliff will not only perform alone and with the group but also in religious sketches.

NOVEMBER 16   Cliff's 44th single 'Don't Forget To Catch Me' is released and reviewed by journalist Penny Valentine: 'Presumably because he's celebrating his tenth anniversary in pop – though I hardly find this a good enough excuse – they have issued this track from Cliff's LP *Established 1958*. I find it a bit pointless and sad. Lately, Cliff surprised me by coming up with some quite good records – "Marianne" being one of the best – and it's a shame that this is reverting back to the corny, boring stuff of years gone by. A waste of time, talent and people's ears.'

NOVEMBER 23   Reviewer Derek Johnson goes into print with nothing but praise for Cliff's new single: 'I've got a feeling that this could give him his highest chart place since "Congratulations", because the material is more closely allied to the dictate of the hit parade than were his last two releases.'

On the same day, Cliff duets with French singer Mireille Mathieu on her ITV show.

DECEMBER 1   Cliff introduces 'Songs of Praise' from Manchester's Holy Trinity Church.

DECEMBER 4   Cliff takes part in the cutting of a 650lb-Christmas pudding for the Mental Health Trust at London's Carlton Towers Hotel.

DECEMBER 7   The NME Annual Poll results are published:

World Male Singer
1 Elvis Presley
2 Tom Jones
3 Cliff Richard

World Musical Personality
1 Elvis Presley
2 Jimi Hendrix
3 Cliff Richard

British Vocal Personality
1 Cliff Richard
2 Tom Jones
3 Paul McCartney

British Male Singer
1 Tom Jones
2 Cliff Richard
3 Scott Walker (*American*)

Cliff's 'Congratulations' is voted 4th best British Disc of the Year behind the Beatles' 'Hey Jude' (1), Mary Hopkin's 'Those Were The Days' (2) and the Rolling Stones' 'Jumping Jack Flash' (3).

DECEMBER 7 *Disc and Music Echo* publish a letter from Harry Morrison of Greenock, Renfrewshire: 'Having seen Cliff Richard, I am convinced he's going to reach the class and status of Frank Sinatra.'

DECEMBER 14 Following the partial retirement of the Shadows, reports appear in the press that the Settlers will be Cliff's support group for many dates in 1969, as well as their recording a single together. Cliff says: 'I first saw them at a two-hour concert in London's Festival Hall and was immediately impressed. We'll make a record together and see how the public react to it – if it goes well, then obviously we'll record together much more.'

DECEMBER ☐ Cliff rejects reports that his recent Palladium season had been a box office disappointment: 'I was told 90% of West End theatres would have liked to have done our business, but it was a bad time of year – there's no money and no people in November.'

DECEMBER ☐ Cliff hits out at people's changing attitudes towards Christmas. 'Christmas is turning. People don't celebrate Christmas for the right reasons any more. To too many, Christmas is just a holiday – a booze-up time – although I've got nothing against boozing. They forget the fact that the only reason we celebrate is because it is Christ's birthday. They really don't know why they have these few days off from work. There is so much apathy in the land towards religion that it must follow, in time, they will forget what everything's about. The only aspect of commerciality at Christmas of which I disapprove is the case of the people who take advantage. The toymakers who up the price of toys at Christmas time from 30 shillings to £2.00. That's sharp practice and deplorable.'

DECEMBER ☐ Following a gospel concert at Manchester Palace with the Settlers, a critic in the *Guardian* newspaper writes that the concert was 'old-fashioned' and adds, 'The devil *still* has the best songs.'

DECEMBER 21 Cliff reveals his plans for 1969: 'I'm not letting up. I'm doing another film for the Billy Graham organisation, only this time it'll be on location in Israel and I'll play a guy adopted by a Jewish couple. I'll be recording again soon, but there's also the show I'm doing for Scottish TV in colour, which is being made with the Golden Rose of Montreux in mind and is a bit of technical genius in which there are marvellous camera angles and effects and things. It's called "Cliff in Scotland" and yes, I do wear a kilt!'

DECEMBER 25 Cliff sings 'Congratulations' on BBC TV's 'Top of the Pops'. Also appearing are Manfred Mann, Esther and Abi Ofarim, Love Affair, Georgie Fame, the Beatles and the Rolling Stones.

DECEMBER 25 Cliff appears on the 'Morecambe and Wise Christmas Show' with Lulu, Petula Clark, Nana Mouskouri, the Seekers and Louis Armstrong.

DECEMBER 25 On Radio 1, Cliff presents an hour of his favourite tracks from seasonal LPs.

DECEMBER 27 Cliff flies off with friends for a four-day holiday.

1969

JANUARY 4   In the *NME*'s 1968 points table based on chart positions during the year (30 points for 1 week at No. 1, to 1 point for 1 week at No. 30), Cliff appears in 22nd position with 308 points between Hugo Montenegro and Otis Redding. Tom Jones heads the table with 708 points.

JANUARY 13-17   Cliff and the Norrie Paramor Orchestra are featured daily on Radio 1's 'Dave Cash Programme'.

JANUARY 15-16   Cliff and the Settlers perform at London's Albert Hall in aid of the homeless starving refugees of Biafra. Tickets for the concerts – advertised as 'A Gospel Folk-Beat-Blues Evening' – range from 3/6d to 19/6d.

> **A gospel folk-beat-blues evening with –**
> **Cliff Richard & the Settlers**
> **The Royal Albert Hall 7·30 pm Jan 15th & 16th**
> A Concert in aid of refugees, homeless and starving people.
> Tickets: 19/6, 14/6, 9/6, 7/6, 3/6 from the Royal Albert Hall and usual agents

FEBRUARY 8   Cliff agrees to take part in a 12-minute colour film titled *Give Us This Day* – a short documentary about the John Groom Childrens' Homes in Kent. Cliff is to sing a song called 'Thank You' in the picture, which is to be available free of charge to schools, clubs and voluntary organisations.

FEBRUARY 19   Cliff appears on Cilla Black's TV show singing 'Good Times' and 'Don't Forget'.

FEBRUARY ☐   The pop music paper, *Disc and Music Echo*, publishes the results of its annual poll.

        Top Male Singer (British)
        1 Tom Jones
        2 Scott Walker (*American*)
        3 Cliff Richard

        Mr Valentine – 1969
        1 Scott Walker
        2 Cliff Richard
        3 Johnnie Walker (Radio DJ)

        Top TV Artist / Male
        1 Scott Walker
        2 Cliff Richard
        3 Simon Dee

Best-Dressed Male Star
1 Cliff Richard
2 Scott Walker
3 Tom Jones

Cliff was voted 5th best male singer in the world behind Scott Walker, Tom Jones, Otis Redding and Elvis Presley.

FEBRUARY ☐ Having been voted 'Best-Dressed Star', Cliff talks about fashion during rehearsals at West Finchley Methodist Church Hall: 'I've got nothing against outrageous clothing – in fact, if I'm invited to a party where they say "informal clothes", I think it's a great excuse to wear something extravagant like a pink frilly shirt!' Cliff reveals that as well as sporting 50-guinea-plus suits from his Savile Row tailor Robert Valentine, he also has some wilder gear like a jacket that's made out of 'Black Watch tartan material'.

FEBRUARY 22 Cliff's 45th single, 'Good Times (Better Times)/Occasional Rain', is released. One reviewer comments: 'A happy light-hearted and immensely danceable disc – though I don't rate the material as particularly memorable even though it was written by the joint talents of Jerry Lordan, Roger Cook and Roger Greenaway.' Another writes: 'Here's someone else who seems to simply float through recording sessions, pack his bag at the end of one "take", smile "thank you, fellas" and go home. Cliff's records are always simple, uncluttered, uncomplicated and as a result are often boring.'

FEBRUARY ☐ Cliff spends ten days at EMI's Abbey Road Studios recording, 'Don't Forget To Catch Me' in Italian, German and French.

THE CLIFF RICHARD FILE 1969

FEBRUARY 27	Cliff appears on 'Top of the Pops' with Sandie Shaw, Donald Peers, the Hollies, Cilla Black, Peter Sarstedt, Glenn Campbell and Marvin Gaye – the show is hosted by Stuart Henry.
MARCH 1	Cliff flies to Germany to guest in the German equivalent of British TV's 'The Golden Shot'.
MARCH 3	Cliff flies to Rumania for five days to guest in a televised song festival.
MARCH 8	Cliff appears on BBC TV's 'Rolf Harris Show' which has been pre-recorded.
MARCH 9-12	Cliff undertakes appearances in Italy.
MARCH 15	Ernest Fullman from Coventry has a letter about Cliff published in the press: 'Since his smash hit "Congratulations", his records have been dull and wearing ... buck up your ideas, Cliff, or you will be in the same boat as Elvis.'
MARCH 19	Cliff appears on 'Top of the Pops' with the Tremeloes, Love Affair, Tony Blackburn, Marvin Gaye, the Hollies, Sandie Shaw and Peter Sarstedt. The show is hosted by Pete Murray.
MARCH 21-22	Cliff undertakes appearances in Holland.
MARCH 26	Cliff appears on Liberace's TV show.
APRIL 5	Discussing more rumours that he intends giving up the music business to pursue his religious activities, Cliff comments: 'I realised that if I quit, it would be like a rat deserting a sinking ship. There are other active Christians in show business, and it was partly due to some of them that I decided to stay in the business. There is nothing immoral or sordid about entertainment, providing you don't allow yourself to be carried away by the glamour and financial rewards. I am a hundred per cent Christian and everything I do is done with my religion in mind. I don't mean I have to walk around all day with God on my mind, but everything I do is motivated by my Christian beliefs. Unfortunately, even in religious activities, you find unscrupulous people. I was asked if I would talk to some young men and women in Scotland; at the time, I was busy filming and I told the person that if I could possibly make it, I would arrive. But he had big posters printed saying I was going to speak – naturally, he was selling tickets and making a lot of money out of it.'
APRIL ☐	Cliff reveals: 'Minority religious groups like the Jehovah's Witnesses and the Exclusive Brethren take things so literally they lose all the Bible's meaning – groups like the Exclusive Brethren really scare me. By cutting themselves off from the rest of the people, they are destroying the whole essence of Christianity, that of fellowship and spreading the gospel.'
APRIL 3	Cliff appears on 'Top of the Pops' with the Hollies, the Marbles, the Beach Boys, Lulu, Joe South, Mary Hopkin, the Foundations and Marvin Gaye. The show is hosted by Alan Freeman.
APRIL 5	Cliff reveals that his first big thrill in show business was when he was impersonated on television by Benny Hill.
APRIL 8	In the *Daily Express*, Cliff complains that he's always had to be a 'larger-than-life' Cliff Richard in all his films. 'What I want is a tiny little nothing part opposite Albert Finney ... no one takes me seriously. I have an unfortunate image.'

APRIL ☐	Cliff talks on the subject of earnings, having revealed that he collects £15 in cash every Friday to see him through the week. 'Friday was *always* pay-day for me and I think that unless you are paid in hard cash and actually see your money being spent, you can lose all sense of its value. My father raised our whole family on £11 per week... If I thought my money could convert anyone to my beliefs, then I would give it away. But money doesn't change anything. John Lennon could never be converted because of my money.'
APRIL ☐	It is announced that later in the year, Cliff will speak at a Billy Graham religious crusade in the Holy Land.
APRIL 12	Cliff's first show-biz tailor, Dougie Millings, talks about his early days designing for Cliff: '... I made him a white sharkskin suit, with a black satin shirt and tie. He's kept coming back to me over the years and there was one time when he was in Glasgow and I was in London and we agreed to meet up at Carlisle, where I fitted him for a new suit on the station platform at midnight!'
APRIL ☐	Hank Marvin and Cliff are approached to do a tour of Japan, Hong Kong, Singapore and Australia in September.
APRIL ☐	Scottish TV's 'Cliff in Scotland' in entered for the Montreux Film Festival.
MAY ☐	The Settlers release a new single, 'Love Is More Than Words', which Cliff has co-written.
MAY 11	Cliff closes the first half of the *NME* Poll Winners' Concert at Wembley where he appears along with Bob and Earl, Desmond Dekker, Scaffold, Marmalade, Move, Tremeloes, Lulu, Hank Marvin, Amen Corner, Love Sculpture and Peter Sarstedt. The concert is compèred by Jimmy Savile and Tony Blackburn. Cliff sings 'Move It', 'Good Times', 'La La La, La, La,', and 'Congratulations'.
MAY 17	Cilla Black and Hank Marvin guest on BBC1's Saturday night 'Cliff Richard Show'.
MAY ☐	The *NME* reviews Cliff's concert appearance: 'His voice is wild, screaming with soul. This is Cliff on his greatest form, literally destroying any contention that his religious beliefs make him tame and goody-goody. There is no doubt that Cliff Richard is a phenomenon of British pop...'
MAY ☐	Estranged Bee-Gee Robin Gibb is invited to write a song for Cliff.
MAY ☐	In Totteridge, Hertfordshire, singer Frank Ifield becomes a neighbour of Cliff's – as are Hank Marvin, Bruce Forsyth and Frankie Vaughan.
MAY 23	Cliff's 46th single 'Big Ship/She's Leaving You', is released and gets the thumbs-up from the critics: 'Cliff Richard has never suffered the indignity of a chart failure... I have every confidence this will maintain his unbroken run of successes.' Another reviewer writes; 'I'd go so far as to say it's the best thing he's done. Raymond Froggatt wrote the song, which is a cross between a very stray immediate melody line and an almost gospel chorus.'
MAY 24	Cliff's former personal assistant Mike Conlin announces the release of a single ('200 Weeks') by a solo Australian vocalist whom he manages. The singer, Terry Britten, who was formerly with the Twilights, has already had four songs recorded by Cliff. On the same day, Cliff flies to America for discussions on his forthcoming film for Billy Graham, the follow-up to *Two A Penny*. Cliff is helping to write the music for the score.
MAY 26	Comedian Peter Kaye is praised by the press for his impersonation of Cliff on BBC TV.

THE CLIFF RICHARD FILE   1969

JUNE ☐	Cliff's 'Congratulations' wins him two Ivor Novello Awards for the most performed work and as 'International Song of the Year'.
JUNE 7	Cliff appears on Radio 1's 'Pete's Saturday People' with the Flirtations and Raymond Froggatt.
JUNE 8	Cliff appears on 'Top of the Pops' with Jethro Tull, Tommy Roe and Chicken Shack.
JUNE 9	Having appeared with Jethro Tull on the previous week's 'Top of the Pops', Cliff enthuses: 'I think Jethro Tull are fantastic. They have so much talent. But the term "Underground" still baffles me – I think of it as meaning a group without a hit.'
JUNE 14	Cliff appears on 'Top of the Pops' with the Ohio Express, Des O'Connor, Amen Corner, Edwin Hawkins Singers, Scott Walker and the Beatles. The show is hosted by Pete Murray.
JUNE 21	Singer Peter Sarstedt says of Cliff's current hit 'Big Ship': '... just another formula song. I don't know why he does that – I don't like any of his recent songs. With this, everything is arranged to sell with a huge "S".'
JUNE 28	Former Shadow Hank Marvin comments on Cliff's show business longevity: 'Much of the credit for Cliff's staying power must go to the way in which his career has been guided by Pete Gormley, his manager, who stays so much in the shadows. He has the knack of bringing out the best in his artists and building them up in an aura of prestige and stardom. Yet Peter himself hates personal publicity. He finds it all a bit of a drag; he never goes to premières and things like that. His enjoyment is in having artists with a talent and doing his best for them.'
JULY 12	In the *NME* half-yearly chart table (30 points for a No.1, 1 point for No.30), Cliff is 28th with 190 points. Leaders are Fleetwood Mac with 479 points, followed by the Beatles with 389 and Herman's Hermits with 340.
AUGUST 23	The BBC announce plans for a TV series starring Cliff, scheduled to begin early in 1970. Hank Marvin and actress Una Stubbs will be co-starring.
AUGUST/SEPTEMBER ☐	Cliff holidays in Portugal and then with the Crusader camp on Herm in the Channel Islands.
SEPTEMBER 4	Cliff is interviewed on BBC Radio 1's programme 'Scene and Heard'. On the same day, Cliff and Hank appear on 'Top of the Pops' along with Humble Pie.
SEPTEMBER 6	Cliff's new single (his 47th) is a duet with Hank Marvin, who wrote the 'A' side 'Throw Down A Line'. The 'B' side is 'Reflections'. Among the reviewers' comments: 'Cliff's back to blues ...' 'The lyric is intense, almost bitter ...' 'Cliff throws off years of boredom ... it proves that Cliff has suddenly plonked himself right in the middle of the music scene of today ...' 'A Number One'.
SEPTEMBER ☐	On the subject of lyrics, Cliff comments: '... when I do forget lyrics, it's not usually new songs, but things like "Livin' Doll". I guess it's because I've sung it so many times, I don't bother to read the words and then my mind goes blank.'
SEPTEMBER 13	Cliff admits, 'Television still frightens me a little. "Top of the Pops" doesn't bother me because it's such a casual show. But I always have the feeling of all those unseen viewers.'

SEPTEMBER ☐   It's rumoured that Cliff's next single may be another Hank Marvin song – 'Love's Truth and Emily Stone'.

SEPTEMBER 25   Jimmy Savile introduces 'Top of the Pops' which includes Cliff and Hank, Oliver, Fat Mattress, Bobby Gentry and Creedance Clearwater Revival.

SEPTEMBER 27   Radio 1 DJ David Symonds makes his feelings felt on 'Throw Down A Line': 'Cliff and Hank's record is very undignified. I think it falls between two kinds of thought and Cliff is basically at his best singing commercial pop-songs. This is out of character – he's a good clean-cut lad. They're climbing on to a band-wagon and I don't think Cliff's personal commitments fit the scene.'

THE CLIFF RICHARD FILE 1969

SEPTEMBER 29	Cliff guests on Pete Murray's 'Open House' radio show for the BBC.
OCTOBER 14	Cliff is 29.
OCTOBER ☐	The Shadows re-form to back Cliff on a Japanese tour. Hank Marvin, Brian Bennet and John Rostill add keyboard player Alan Hawkshaw to their line-up. Cliff comments on the Japanese fans: '... they don't understand the lyrics too well, and to them it's just a sound, so providing the melody is strong and simple, you're in with a chance.'
NOVEMBER 5	Cliff and the Shadows commence a short British tour. Marcie and the Cookies are also on the bill.
NOVEMBER ☐	Several tour dates are cancelled, due to Cliff's laryngitis.
NOVEMBER 15	Cliff's 48th single, 'With The Eyes Of A Child/So Long' is released. The critics comment: '... an enchanting ballad with a philosophical lyric pleading for universal brotherhood...' '... a tender quasi-protest song with Cliff pleading for a more beautiful world in which kids can grow up'.
NOVEMBER ☐	Cliff talks about actress Una Stubbs: 'She'd be my own personal Miss World. One of the most underestimated artists in the whole world too. We first met in *Summer Holiday*. She's a very experienced girl and the sort you can talk to quite easily and really open yourself up to her ... a very wordly person.'
NOVEMBER 28	Cliff sings 'Throw Down A Line' and 'With The Eyes Of A Child' on French television.
DECEMBER ☐	Cliff is tipped to top the list of Britain's 'Best Bespectacled Gentleman' poll prepared by the Birmingham Opthalmic Council. He was third in 1965 and 11th in 1968. All his spectacles are supplied by Scruvers in London's Regent Street.
DECEMBER ☐	Cliff tops the chart in Japan with a cover of Vanity Fayre's 'Early In The Morning'.
DECEMBER 20	It's announced by the Bromley Theatre Trust that Cliff will star in a stage version of a ten-year-old West End play *Five Finger Exercise*, and also – along with the Shadows – will do a stage musical version of *Pinnochio* for Christmas 1970.
DECEMBER 23	Cliff goes carol-singing with the Crusaders to raise money for Fegan's Homes, for which they collect about £20.00.
DECEMBER 24	Cliff attends the Christmas Eve Carol Service at his church in Finchley.
DECEMBER 24	Cliff appears on the 'Cilla Black Show' with Dusty Springfield. Kenny Everett also guests, with a look-back at the music scene of 1969.
DECEMBER 24	'Christmas With Cliff' on Radio 1 and Radio 2. He features as disc jockey, playing an hour of his favourite records.
DECEMBER 25	Cliff stars in 'Let's Go With Cliff' on Radio 4, in which his guests are Salena Jones, Los Paraguayos and the Norrie Paramor Orchestra.
DECEMBER 27	LWTV screens *The Young Ones*.
DECEMBER 31	Jimmy Savile introduces a 75-minute BBC1 TV show 'Pop Go The Sixties', which includes Cliff and the Shadows performing their 1962 hit 'Bachelor Boy'. The show also includes Adam Faith, Helen Shapiro, the Rolling Stones, Sandie Shaw, the Tremeloes, the Who, the Bachelors, Lulu, Dusty Springfield and a film of the Beatles.

1970

JANUARY ☐ BBC1's 13-week TV series, 'It's Cliff Richard', begins.

JANUARY ☐ Talking at the BBC theatre at Shepherd's Bush, Cliff says: 'I think my acting is the direction my career must improve in ... I can't see my voice improving any more, and if I didn't have anything else, nothing more to strive for, I might be in danger of getting stale.'

JANUARY ☐ Cliff sticks up for the much criticised Kenny Rogers single, 'Ruby, Don't Take Your Love To Town', by replying to all the people who said it was a sick record: 'All those people who said that it sounded like a bunch of old women ... it was a hard-hitting record, but hardly sick. There must have been lots of them who came back from a war and found themselves in that position. The record is a statement of true fact and as unpalatable as that may be, it cannot be sick and distasteful.'

JANUARY 10 The *NME* publish their annual chart table based on 30 points for a week at No.1 to 1 point for a week at No.30. Cliff is fifteenth in the table with 372 points between the Isley Brothers and Peter Sarstedt. Table leaders are Fleetwood Mac with 728 points.

JANUARY ☐ Comments appear in the press about comedy sketches spoiling Cliff's new series.

JANUARY 17 The *NME* publish the results of a points survey based on the Top 30 over the past decade:

1 Cliff Richard	7,913
2 Elvis Presley	6,438
3 Beatles	6,394
4 Shadows	3,790
5 Rolling Stones	3,126
6 Roy Orbison	3,103
7 Adam Faith	2,965
8 Hollies	2,863

JANUARY ☐ On his TV show, Cliff does impressions of Tiny Tim and Ken Dodd.

JANUARY 24 The *NME* poll results are published.

British Male Singer
1 Tom Jones	5,332
2 Cliff Richard	4,667
3 Mick Jagger	2,378

British Vocal Personality
1 Cliff Richard	3,839
2 Tom Jones	3,695
3 John Lennon	1,776

World Male Singer
1 Elvis Presley	5,727
2 Tom Jones	3,816
3 Cliff Richard	2,925

THE CLIFF RICHARD FILE 1970

Cliff is voted fourth most popular 'World Musical Personality' behind Elvis Presley (1), John Lennon (2), and Eric Clapton (3). Cliff and Hank's 'Throw Down A Line' is voted 5th best single of the year.

JANUARY ☐   Korea votes Cliff their most popular star.

JANUARY ☐   Cliff receives an award from the Songwriters' Guild of Great Britain for 'The Most Outstanding Service to Music in 1969'.

FEBRUARY 7   Cliff's 49th single, 'The Joy Of Living' (with Hank Marvin), also features Hank's 'Boogatoo' and Cliff's solo, 'Leave My Woman Alone'. The single is a cynical look at the modern age, where Britain is being turned into one large motorway.

FEBRUARY 14   *Disc and Music Echo* publish their poll results:

Mr Valentine
1 Cliff Richard
2 Scott Walker
3 Johnnie Walker

Best-Dressed Male Star
1 Cliff Richard
2 Barry Gibb
3 Tom Jones

Top British Male Singer
1 Tom Jones
2 Cliff Richard
3 Scott Walker (*American*)

Top World Male Singer
1 Elvis Presley
2 Tom Jones
3 Cliff Richard

Sincerely Cliff is voted sixth-best LP, and Cliff and Hank's 'Throw Down A Line' is voted tenth-best single.

FEBRUARY 20   Cliff is featured on Dave Cash's Radio 1 show.

MARCH ☐   Cliff attends a party at No.10 Downing Street given by the Prime Minister, Harold Wilson, in honour of West German Chancellor Willy Brandt. The gathering also includes Sandie Shaw and Una Stubbs.

■ Cliff, Una Stubbs and Willy Brandt

MARCH ☐	The final six songs for the Eurovision Song Contest are sung on Cliff's TV series and the winning song is revealed. Viewers voted Mary Hopkin's 'Knock Knock, Who's There?' into first place.
APRIL ☐	A paperback book, *Cliff Richard – Questions*, is published at the price of five shillings. In it Cliff sounds off on various topics:

Eurovision
The voting is right up the spout. Personally I think the only way to make any sense of this competition is to make it a bit more complicated. At the moment it's pretty obvious that many of the juries do not represent the tastes of their own countries anyway.

Girlfriends
I don't see how you can have a really close relationship with a girl unless you marry her. I doubt if it is possible – or very difficult – to have the sort of platonic relationship with a girl which two women may have or a man with a close male friend.

Racialism
No one race or skin colour is better than another in God's sight. Every individual has equal rights as a human being, and it's up to him to live with his neighbour be he black, yellow or white!

APRIL 6	Cliff appears at Batley Variety Club for a week of cabaret.
APRIL 11	It's announced that Cliff will sing and speak at a series of public meetings in London later in the year, to help launch a national campaign against the permissive society.
APRIL ☐	BBC Radio presents 'The Cliff Richard Story' with Robin Boyle.
APRIL ☐	Cliff grows a beard in preparation for his starring role in the forthcoming stage play *Five Finger Exercise*.
MAY 3	A bearded Cliff appears at the *NME* Poll Winners' Concert, backed by the Candies. His act includes 'The Girl Can't Help It', 'Great Balls Of Fire' and 'Throw Down A Line'. Cliff's trophy is presented to him by singer Malcolm Roberts.
MAY 11	*Five Finger Exercise* opens at the Bromley New Theatre – Cliff takes eight curtain calls on the first night.
MAY 19	Cliff records a contribution for BBC TV's 'Disney Show'.
MAY 30	Cliff releases his 50th single, a Mitch Murray-Peter Callarde-Geoff Stephens song, 'Goodbye Sam, Hello Samantha'. One critic says, 'Not a song of substance or durability, but one that's made for the charts.'
MAY ☐	A party to celebrate his 50th single is attended by a host of stars including Radio 1's John Peel. Cliff says that his favourite of the fifty singles is 'The Day I Met Marie'.
JUNE 13	Cliff and Clodagh Rogers appear in Roy Castle's BBC TV show.
JUNE 13	Cliff makes a guest appearance at the Bratislava Song Festival in Czechoslovakia. Other guests include Paul and Barry Ryan.
JULY ☐	DJ Terry Wogan says that 'Goodbye Sam, Hello Samantha' is not one of Cliff's strongest: 'By anyone else it wouldn't have a chance.'
JULY 4	The *NME* publish their half-yearly points table (30 points for a week at No.1 to 1 point for a week at No.30). Cliff is 54th with 91 points between the Beach Boys and Joe Dolan. The Jackson Five are top of the table with 342 points.

THE CLIFF RICHARD FILE **1970**

JULY ☐	Cliff flies to South Africa at the invitation of the Bishop of Natal to speak and sing in Durban at a series of youth meetings sponsored by Christian businessmen and aimed at the youth of the country.
JULY ☐	Journalist Andy Gray answers the question of how Cliff has outlasted all his rivals: '... Friendliness ... Cliff has always been so genuinely friendly with everyone. You never hear of him having a feud or a disagreement or being nasty to anyone. He never swears. His public relations are perfect ... he has never forgotten that it is the fan who has made him and retained him. He has been an inspiration to thousands who have chosen faith in Christ as their way of life. Instead of getting more tense as the years go by, Cliff has become more relaxed, more confident and more content with himself ... Cliff has started the seventies in great style, and just as he came through the sixties without a blemish, I'm sure he'll be with us in 1980, fresh as ever.'
AUGUST ☐	Cliff is holidaying and recording.
AUGUST 22	Cliff's 51st single, 'I Ain't Got Time Any More/Monday Comes Too Soon', is released. The song is scored and arranged by Mike Vickers of Manfred Mann fame.
AUGUST 24	Cliff says: 'I personally respect John Lennon for what he's trying to do for peace. He's doing what he thinks is right, in the same way that I make no secret that I'm using my career to promote Christianity. But Lennon has become a laughing-stock among so many people.'
SEPTEMBER ☐	Cliff is delayed for five hours at Copenhagen Airport, due to a bomb scare and the potential threat of a hijack.
SEPTEMBER ☐	Cliff spends some leisure time at the cinema. He sees *Rosemary's Baby*, *A Man Called Horse*, *The Wild Bunch* and *Bonnie and Clyde*.
SEPTEMBER 28	Cliff starts a four-week season at London's 'Talk of the Town'. His set includes, 'Move It', 'Jailhouse Rock', 'Great Balls Of Fire', 'Through The Eyes Of A Child' and 'I Who Have Nothing'. On stage, Cliff jokes about his religious convictions: 'I've heard it said that I've got stained-glass windows in my Mini, but that's ridiculous – they're in my Jensen!'
OCTOBER 4	Cliff appears in 'Sing a New Song' with the Settlers for BBC TV's department of religious programmes.
OCTOBER 9	Cliff receives the National Viewers' and Listeners' Association annual award for an 'Outstanding Contribution to Religious Broadcasting and Light Entertainment'. The award is presented by Malcolm Muggeridge and Mrs Mary Whitehouse tells Cliff: 'You really have made nonsense of this thing about the generation gap.'
OCTOBER 14	Cliff celebrates his 30th birthday.
OCTOBER ☐	Cliff considers buying a house in Weybridge, Surrey, on the same estate as Tom Jones, Engelbert Humperdinck and Gilbert O'Sullivan.
NOVEMBER 7	Cliff appears on Radio Luxembourg discussing his future with Ken Evans.
NOVEMBER 8	Cliff is featured on Dave Lee Travis' Radio 1 show with Cat Stevens and Peter Noone.
NOVEMBER 11-14	'Cliff in Concert' around Britain backed by Marvin, Welch and Farrar.
NOVEMBER 18-21	More concerts.

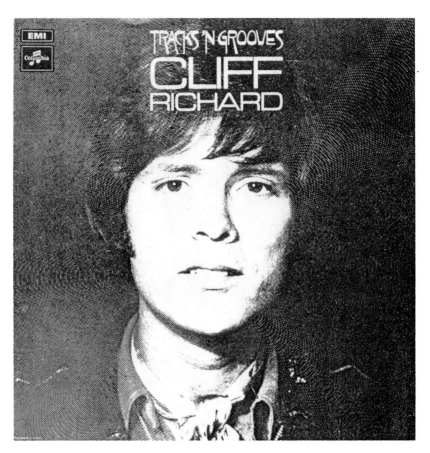

NOVEMBER 28	Having been described in an interview as 'mechanically charming', Cliff retorts: 'I'm not going to pretend it didn't hurt me because it did – deeply. But what really stung was the realisation that here was somebody knocking me for trying to be pleasant and friendly. If we really do live in a permissive society, then shouldn't it be the case that I should be allowed to be "mechanically charming" if I want to be? Shouldn't I be free too? The fact is, I'm only as human as the next person when it comes to criticism, and I don't mind admitting that I find it hard to take when I feel it's unjustified.'
DECEMBER 14-18	Cliff is featured on Terry Wogan's Radio 1 show with Billie Davis and the Casuals.
DECEMBER 17	BBC TV screen *The Young Ones*
DECEMBER 24	BBC TV screen a Special with Cliff, Hank Marvin and Una Stubbs.
DECEMBER ☐	It is reported that Cliff is to release a maxi-single.

1971

JANUARY 2 — *NME* publish their chart table for 1970 based on 30 points for a week at No.1 to 1 point for a week at No.30. Cliff comes 40th with 230 points, between the Beach Boys and Hot Legs. The chart leader is Elvis Presley with 799 points.

JANUARY 2 — Cliff's BBC TV series makes its debut – co-starring Una Stubbs and Hank Marvin.

JANUARY ☐ — Impresario Leslie Grade announces that he is keen to produce a big-budget musical starring Cliff.

JANUARY 9 — Cliff's 52nd single is released. 'Sunny Honey Girl' has two songs on the 'B' side – 'I Was Only Fooling Myself' and a duet with Olivia Newton-John 'Don't Move Away'. One reviewer says: 'It's likely to be one of Cliff's biggest hits for some time.' The 'A' side is a song jointly written by two songwriting teams – Roger Cook and Roger Greenaway teaming up with Johnny Goodison and Tony Hillier.

JANUARY 9 — The second in the BBC TV series 'It's Cliff Richard' features Marvin, Welch and Farrar.

JANUARY 16 — 'It's Cliff Richard' features the New Seekers. Cliff performs George Harrison's 'My Sweet Lord'.

JANUARY 18-22 — Cliff is featured on Jimmy Young's Radio 1 show with the Rockin' Berries, the Symbols and the Barron Knights.

JANUARY 23 — Elton John appears on 'It's Cliff Richard', singing 'Your Song'.

JANUARY ☐ — The *NME* poll results are published:

World Male Singer
1 Elvis Presley — 5,702
2 Cliff Richard — 3,697
3 Tom Jones — 2,420

World Musical Personality
1 Elvis Presley — 4,637
2 Cliff Richard — 2,708
3 Andy Williams — 1,789

Best TV/Radio Show
1 'Top of the Pops' — 11,237
2 'Disco 2' — 2,116
3 'It's Cliff Richard' — 1,816

British Vocal Personality
1 Cliff Richard — 3,547
2 Tom Jones — 2,385
3 Cilla Black — 1,696

British Male Singer

1 Cliff Richard	4,998
2 Tom Jones	3,777
3 Paul McCartney	1,536

Cliff's 'Goodbye Sam, Hello Samantha' is voted the 7th-best British single of 1970, and *Tracks 'n' Grooves* the 8th-best LP.

JANUARY 24 Cliff provides the commentary for 'Lollipop Tree', a section of 'The World About Us.' He talks about a home for 800 children at the foot of the Himalayas.

FEBRUARY 20 In Cliff's TV show, Clodagh Rogers performs the six final numbers in 'A Song for Europe'. Producer Michael Hurll makes public his problems with the usual voting system due to the current postal strike. The winning song is 'Jack in the Box'.

MARCH ☐ At the invitation of the Reverend Patrick Goodland, Cliff appears at the Stanmore Baptist Church in North London. The sermon is replaced by Cliff answering questions on his religious views from his close friend, Bill Latham, who is also Educational Officer of the Evangelical Alliance Relief Fund. The topics range from 'Did Una Stubbs wear a wig?' through to 'Drug taking and suicides in show business' and 'Cliff possibly being seen as a "Jekyll and Hyde" figure.' Cliff says during the interview that his Christian views are not a gimmick: 'With 99% of the population, a gimmick is something instantly commercial. This does not describe Christianity. I could have found a better gimmick.'

MARCH ☐ BBC1 and Cliff's management negotiate for another TV series.

MARCH ☐ Cliff buys a house in Essex for the Christian Arts Centre.

MARCH 6 Cliff duets with Petula Clark on his TV show.

MARCH 20 Derek Harvey from Headington, Oxford, attacks Cliff's TV show in a letter to the press: 'The comedy content is embarrassing – Cliff's versions of other people's hits always sound like inferior covers ... compare his programmes with those of Andy Williams, Petula Clark or Des O'Connor.'

MARCH 26 Cliff kicks off a European tour in Holland before appearing in Denmark, Germany, Austria, Switzerland and Belgium.

APRIL ☐ Cliff's 53rd single, 'Silvery Rain' (written by Hank Marvin), is described by reviewer Derek Johnson as 'one of the least commerical and uncharacteristic he has ever recorded'. Backed by 'Annabella Umbrella' and 'Time Flies', it is a social comment on the problems of pesticides and poisons. Cliff replies to the critics: 'There's no reason why a song shouldn't have something to say and still have an infectious beat – pop is an art form. You have to make complete use of it.'

APRIL 3 Derek Harvey's letter evokes replies from those in agreement and those who disagree. Lesley Short from Havant, Hampshire, replies: 'I thought the Cliff Richard shows knocked them for six. I find his family very entertaining, which is more than I can say for the Andy Williams production.' 'Senior Citizen' from Croydon, Surrey, writes: 'Cliff at thirty still seems to cling to his Harry Wharton of Greyfriars nice-chap image – the show is so juvenile it might as well switch slots with "Doctor Who".'

APRIL 11 Cliff is featured on the Dave Lee Travis show on Radio 1, with Dave Edmunds, Rockpile and Seals and Crofts.

THE CLIFF RICHARD FILE 1971

APRIL 17	Northern cabaret dates are announced for Cliff in June.
MAY 10-29	Cliff appears in the play *The Potting Shed* at the Bromley New Theatre.
MAY ☐	Plans are announced for Cliff's next film, *Xanadu*, which is to be shot entirely on location in Newcastle. The story is by Alan Plater, who wrote *The Virgin and the Gypsy*, with Peter Hammond of *Spring and Port Wine* fame directing. Producer Andrew Mitchell comments, 'This will not be a sugar-sweet out-and-out musical. Basically it's the tale of a romance between two young people in an industrial city.'
JUNE ☐	At the Dickie Valentine Memorial Concert, Cliff duets with Petula Clark.
JUNE 26	Cliff's 54th single 'Flying Machine' is released. One reviewer writes: '... days from now ... we shall all have joined the butchers' boys and milk roundsmen in whistling its happy tune.'
JUNE ☐	It is announced that shooting for Cliff's sixth film, *Xanadu*, will start in mid-September.
JULY 5	In the 1970/71 Ivor Novello Awards, Cliff receives an award for 'Outstanding Service to British Music'.
JULY 26-30	Cliff is featured on Radio 1's Tony Brandon show with Middle of the Road, Christie and the Searchers.
AUGUST 7	The BBC announces that the new Cliff series will start around Christmas. Hank Marvin will still be resident and the time will extend to 45 minutes.
AUGUST ☐	'Flying Machine' becomes Cliff's first-ever single not to make the Top 30.
AUGUST ☐	Cliff spends an evening watching the New Seekers at London's 'Talk of the Town'.

AUGUST 30	BBC1 screen 'Getaway with Cliff', a 50-minute programme featuring Olivia Newton-John and Marvin, Welch and Farrar.
AUGUST ☐	The shooting of *Xanadu* is postponed until the spring because of possible 'adverse weather conditions'.
SEPTEMBER ☐	Cliff's 'Flying Machine' tops the charts in Denmark.
OCTOBER ☐	Cliff's 'Flying Machine' tops the Malaysian charts.
OCTOBER 11-NOVEMBER 2	Cliff headlines a three-week show at the London Palladium supported by Marvin, Welch and Farrar and Olivia Newton-John.
OCTOBER 14	Cliff celebrates his 31st birthday.
OCTOBER 30	'Sing A Song Of Freedom/A Thousand Conversations' is Cliff's 55th single. One reviewer comments: 'Cliff plays it safe by treading the well-worn path to freedom.'
NOVEMBER 1-5	Cliff is featured on Dave Lee Travis's Radio 1 show with Peter Noone, Marmalade, the Drifters and Richard Barnes.
NOVEMBER 6	Jimmy Tarbuck and Cliff appear in Cilla Black's new BBC1 series 'Cilla'.
NOVEMBER ☐	Impresario Leslie Grade and theatre chief Louis Benjamin announce that Cliff's Palladium show has broken box-office records.
NOVEMBER ☐	'Sing A Song Of Freedom' is banned in South Africa because of political repressiveness.
NOV./DEC. ☐	Cliff undertakes several British dates supported by Marvin, Welch and Farrar and Olivia Newton-John.

DECEMBER ☐	Commenting on Christmas, Cliff says: 'I think it's foolish for people to moan about it being too commercial because it is treated in a non-religious way. You have to remember that the majority of the people don't believe in Christ, and Christmas is about Christianity. It certainly doesn't worry *me* that it's commercial – because I don't celebrate it in a commercial way. It is without a doubt the birth of the Messiah – and the only way to enjoy Christmas is to thoroughly believe in it. That's why so many people only enjoy it at one level.'
DECEMBER 24	BBC1 screen a 'Cliff Christmas Eve Special'.

1972

JANUARY ☐   Cliff begins a new 13-week BBC TV series 'It's Cliff Richard'. The Flirtations and Oliva Newton-John are resident but not Hank Marvin, and the critics seem to think that it lacks his humour. Una Stubbs is prevented from appearing in the first show because she is expecting a baby – Dandy Nichols appears in her place. The series is produced by Michael Hurll.

JAN./FEB. ☐   Among Cliff's guests on 'It's Cliff Richard' are Elton John, Labi Siffre and the New Seekers, who sing the six songs for Eurovision on the series.

JANUARY 22   Brian Wright from South Nutfield, Surrey, has a letter published in the music press: 'What has happened to Cliff? I've watched his show every week since it started, and I'm appalled at the utter rubbish I see and hear. Surely someone with Cliff's talent could do without the so-called comedy? Even the audience sounds false. If he goes on with such a shocking show, Cliff will lose a lot of fans, I'm sure.'

JANUARY 22   The *NME* poll results are published:

World Male Singer
1 Elvis Presley	4,748
2 Cliff Richard	1,645
3 Tom Jones/Rod Stewart	1,027

World Musical Personality
1 Elvis Presley	3,698
2 Cliff Richard	1,363
3 Rod Stewart	1,010

British Male Singer
1 Cliff Richard	3,883
2 Tom Jones	1,989
3 Rod Stewart	1,806

British Vocal Personality
1 Cliff Richard	2,864
2 Rod Stewart	2,177
3 Cilla Black	1,758

Best TV/Radio Show
1 Top of the Pops	5,577
2 Old Grey Whistle Test	1,816
3 It's Cliff Richard	905

JANUARY 5   Cliff's stablemate, Labi Siffre, reveals that unlike Cliff he is not a devout Christian: 'I went to a monastic institution, but I'm anti-religion. I find it degrading. I think it's time we all believed in ourselves rather than something of which we have no proof.'

FEBRUARY 26	Cliff's 56th single, 'Jesus/Mr Cloud', is released. Reviewer Danny Holloway writes: 'This is Cliff singing to his main man, asking him to come back to earth and save us from the scum and filth we live in. The song isn't exactly heavyweight, but that won't stop the mums and vicars from buying it.'
FEBRUARY ☐	Cliff presents a series for BBC Radio 1 and 2, 'Music for Sunday' on which he plays records by other Christian artists and some of his own.
MARCH ☐	Roy Wood, of the newly-formed Electric Light Orchestra and late of the Move, talks about writing songs for Cliff: '... the thing is, when you write material for the ELO, or the Move or whatever, you do occasionally get ideas that could never be used for those bands ... why not give songs to other artists, Cliff Richard and people like that?'
MARCH 11	Cliff gives a religious concert for Tear Fund at Manchester's new Century Hall.
MARCH 25	The Metropolitan Police promote a national young people's 'Help the Police' competition, and are helped by the support of Oliva Newton-John, Cliff Richard and DJs Tony Blackburn and Emperor Rosko.
APRIL 14-15	Cliff appears in a gospel concert at the Philharmonic Hall in Liverpool.
APRIL 14	The *Sun* newspaper presents Cliff with its award for 'Top Male Pop Personality' for the third year running.
APRIL-SEPT. ☐	Cliff undertakes a lot of work abroad, touring dozens of countries in Europe, the Middle East and the Far East.
MAY ☐	Cliff records at EMI's Abbey Road Studios – also there using the other studios are Argent, the Hollies, Roy Harper and Kevin Ayers.
MAY ☐	Radio 1 broadcasts the one hundred best-selling records of the last decade. Cliff's only placing is 'The Young Ones' at No.7.
MAY 27	An autumn tour of Britain for Cliff is announced.
MAY 27	The *New Musical Express* prints the following apology: 'We regret if we caused any distress to anyone by the suggestion made in this column that Cliff Richard was involved in the termination of the engagement between Olivia Newton-John and Bruce Welch.'
JUNE ☐	Elvis Presley's legendary vocal backing group, the Jordanaires, express a keenness to record with Cliff.
JULY ☐	Cliff's 57th single is released, 'Living In Harmony/Empty Chairs'. Reviewer Danny Holloway writes: 'Cliff is back with Norrie Paramor, who assisted his success in the beginning. The song is well-performed, although the subject matter is slightly trite. Cliff seems to force himself to keep up with the trends and I sometimes wonder why he bothers.'
SEPTEMBER 2	BBC2 TV screens *The Case*, a comedy thriller which includes eight songs. Produced by Michael Hurll, it stars Cliff, Olivia Newton-John and Tim Brooke-Taylor.
OCTOBER 18-DECEMBER 6	Backed by the Brian Bennett Orchestra, Cliff undertakes a 23-venue, 26-date tour of Britain.
NOVEMBER 6	The New Seekers, Vera Lynn, Henry Hall, Gilbert O'Sullivan, Lulu and Cliff appear in a BBC2 TV special '50 Years of Music' to mark the 50th anniversary of broadcasting in Britain.
NOVEMBER ☐	Reviewer Michael Parsons writes of Cliff's concert at Croydon: 'For an artist to stay at the top for as long as Cliff Richard has, he must adapt to the changing whims of his fans ... no one can doubt his showmanship and finesse –

THE CLIFF RICHARD FILE **1972**

even if his attempts at humour did fall on barren ground – nor the exuberant liveliness with which he injects his act. But there was something lacking . . . but the masses appeared to go home well-satisfied, so he's obviously lost nothing over the last fourteen years as far as they are concerned.'

DECEMBER **2**   Cliff's 58th single, 'A Brand New Song/The Old Accordion', is released and becomes Cliff's first 45 not to chart when it fails to reach the Top 50. Cliff tells the *Melody Maker*: 'I really can't understand why; I played it to my mother and she was sure it would be a hit.'

DECEMBER ☐   Cliff's personal manager, Pete Gormley, leaves hospital following an operation.

DECEMBER **6**   Cliff appears in a special concert with Dana, Gordon Giltrap, the Settlers, Larry Norman, the Brian Bennett Sound and Roy Castle to help raise money for the Arts Centre Group.

DECEMBER **11-23**   Cliff appears at the Batley Variety Club, Yorkshire.

DECEMBER ☐   Agent Arthur Howes announces that Cliff's tour was his biggest and most successful yet.

1973

JANUARY 2	BRT TIV in Belgium shows 'Cliff in Scotland'. Songs included are 'Hail Caledonia', 'Skye Boat Song', 'Courting In The Kitchen', 'Let's Have A Ceilidh', 'Bonnie Mary Of Argyll' and 'Scotland The Brave'.
JANUARY 6	Sire announce that they now issue Cliff's products in America.
JANUARY ☐	Cliff appears over six weeks on Cilla Black's BBC1 TV series, performing songs for the Eurovision Song Contest. The songs are 'Come Back, Billie Joe', 'Ashes To Ashes', 'Tomorrow's Rising', 'The Days Of Love', 'Power To All Our Friends' and 'Help It Along'.
JANUARY 13	Cliff is interviewed over the British Forces Broadcasting Service by Brian Cullingford.
JANUARY 19	Cliff appears on BBC2's 'They Sold a Million'.
JANUARY ☐	Cliff begins a three-week season at the 'Talk of the Town' in London.
JANUARY 27	The *NME* publish their 1972/73 readers' poll:

Male Singer
1 Rod Stewart
2 Gilbert O'Sullivan
3 David Bowie
4 Cliff Richard
5 Marc Bolan

Cliff comes 7th in the World Male Singer section behind Elvis Presley, Rod Stewart, Alice Cooper, Robert Plant, Neil Young and John Lennon.

FEBRUARY 25	Cliff appears in an eight-week series of contemporary Christian and general music concerts being held at St Paul's Cathedral.
FEBRUARY ☐	In an interview, Cliff says: 'Mary Whitehouse is ten years ahead of her time ... the cinema medium is being wasted. Morally something has got to be done about it. There's a need for censorship.'
MARCH 3	Reviewing Cliff's 'Talk of the Town' set, critic James Johnson writes: 'It's an easy enough task these days to make Cliff Richard seem slightly ridiculous. So easy in fact, it's hardly worthwhile. In between numbers he thankfully kept the chat to a minimum, even when he was telling us a little bit about Jesus ... which sounded rather incongruous over the clink of champagne glasses ...'
MARCH 9	Cliff's 59th single, 'Power To All Our Friends', is released. This winning song for Europe is coupled with 'Come Back, Billie Joe'. 'This I suppose,' said a reviewer, 'is what happens when cardboard radicalism meets sickening sentimentality at the Eurovision Song Contest ... Such is the criminal folly of the British singles market, however, that this hideous cringing piece of complacent mediocrity could very well sell.'
APRIL ☐	'Power To All Our Friends' becomes Cliff's first Top 10 single since 'Goodbye Sam, Hello Samantha' in 1970.

THE CLIFF RICHARD FILE 1973

APRIL 1 — In an interview with the *News of the World*, Cliff reveals: 'In the past two or three years I've not dated many girls at all, I don't know whether the inclination has gone or not . . . at the moment there's no one I want to date . . . I've not gone out saying to myself "I'll find a virgin." If I fall in love with a girl, it wouldn't matter how promiscuous she'd been; it wouldn't worry me. That's because the fantastic thing about Christianity is it doesn't matter what you were, but what you're going to be as a Christian.'

APRIL 2 — Cliff is the subject of 'My Top Twelve' on Brian Matthews' Radio 1 show.

APRIL 7 — Singing 'Power To All Our Friends', Cliff represents the United Kingdom in the Eurovision Song Contest, which is held at the Nouveau Theatre, Luxembourg; over 300 million people from 32 countries watch the competition.

APRIL □ — Having come third in the Eurovision Song Contest, Cliff says of the winning song, 'Tu te reconnaitras (Wonderful Dream)', by Luxembourg's Anne-Marie David: 'I just don't like the winning song . . . no, it's not sour grapes!'

APRIL 12-MAY 8 — Cliff appears in concerts across Australia as part of an evangelistic crusade under the banner of 'Help, Hope and Hallelujah'. His backing group is the Strangers, John Farrar's old group re-formed and including John and his wife Pat. Cliff's set includes 'Sing a Song of Freedom', 'How Great Thou Art', 'Day By Day', 'Silvery Rain', 'Everything Is Beautiful' and 'Jesus Loves You'.

MAY 4 — It's announced that Cliff is to make his first feature film since *Finders Keepers* in 1966. Shooting is due to start in Birmingham on June 4 for the musical tentatively titled *Hot Property*.

MAY □ — 'Power To All Our Friends' tops the chart in Holland.

JUNE □ — Cliff's 60th single is released: 'Help It Along/The Days Of Love/Tomorrow Rising/Ashes To Ashes.'

JUNE/JULY □ — Cliff on location in Birmingham, shooting his new film re-titled *Take Me High*. His co-stars include Debbie Watling, George Cole and Anthony Andrews.

AUGUST 8 — Cliff announces that he will appear on the bill of the 'Spiritual Re-emphasis' concert at Wembley with Johnny Cash and Billy Graham.

AUGUST □ — It is revealed that Cliff is to play Bottom in a version of *Midsummer Night's Dream*.

AUGUST 27-SEPTEMBER 1 — Johnny Cash, Parchment, Judy McKenzie and Cliff are among the musical contributors to the SPREE (Spiritual Re-emphasis) gathering at Earls Court, London, for a teach-in.

SEPTEMBER 1 — Cliff appears at Wembley with Johnny Cash and Billy Graham.

SEPTEMBER 8 — Reporter Nick Kent writes on attending the Cliff Richard/Johnny Cash Wembley festival: 'You see, the real success behind commercial Christianity is that it has to be moronic. Sure it can be a little pretentious, and it has to contain that neatly-packed bland message – basically, however, it simply needs to appeal to just that sort of mentality which comes from brainless submission to the Almighty. . . . looking like he'd just come out of rigorous training for the John Denver "Wimp of the Week" sweepstakes, Cliff bounced around, flashing his teeth and oozing good humour . . .'

NOVEMBER □ — Cliff's new film *Take Me High* is premièred in London. The music and lyrics are by Australian songwriter/producer Tony Cole, and the picture co-stars Debbie Watling, Moyra Fraser, George Cole, Hugh Griffith and

Cliff's tour of the Far East starts with a smile at the steps of a British Airways 747.

Anthony Andrews. Cliff plays the part of a young merchant banker, Tim Matthews, who ends up running a restaurant with his new-found girl-friend Sarah (Debbie Watling). The selling point of the establishment is their creation of the 'Brumburger', a hybrid of the abbreviation for Birmingham and a hamburger. The director is David Askey, producer is Kenneth Harper and the screenplay is by Charles Renfold.

NOVEMBER 26   Cliff's former bass player, ex-Shadow John Rostill, is found dead in his recording studio.

DECEMBER ☐   Cliff's 61st single is released – 'Take Me High/Celestial Houses'.

1974

CLIFF RICHARD
(You keep me) hangin' on
A new single - EMI 2150

JANUARY 1	At Southall, Cliff plays in his first football match for twenty years for the *Buzz* All Stars XI v Choralerna: *Buzz* being a British Christian youth monthly journal and Choralerna a Swedish Christian choir.
MARCH 2	The London Palladium announces that Cliff will headline a season at their theatre in the spring.
MARCH □	Cliff is awarded the Silver Clef trophy for outstanding services to the music industry at the second annual Music Therapy Committee lunch. The award is presented by the Duchess of Gloucester.
MARCH 23	On the Transatlantic label, the group Stray release a version of Cliff's 1958 hit 'Move It'. This was originally intended to be released the previous November, to coincide with the fifteenth anniversary of Cliff's chart debut.
APRIL 3	Backed by the Barry Guard Orchestra, Cliff begins a season at the London Palladium supported by Australian singer Pat Carroll, who formerly sang in a duo with Olivia Newton-John. Cliff's set includes 'Constantly', 'Take Me High', 'In The Country', 'Dancing Shoes', 'Do You Wanna Dance?' and a duet with Pat Carroll – 'You Got What It Takes'.
APRIL □	Rolf Harris deputises for three nights at the Palladium, as Cliff is ill with throat and chest problems.
MAY 4	Cliff's 62nd single, 'You Keep Me Hanging On/Love Is Here' is released. Reviewer Charlie Gillett comments: 'One of the best things about this is you'd never guess it was Cliff. Another is that the song is a winner all by itself. (Joe Simon had *the* version).
MAY 4	Cliff appears on BBC TV's 'Mike Yarwood Show' singing 'You Keep Me Hanging On'.
MAY 9	On the Nana Mouskouri Show on BBC TV, Cliff sings 'Constantly' and 'Give Me Back That Old Familiar Feeling', before dueting with Nana on 'I Believe In Music'.
MAY □	In Cheshunt, Cliff appears as Bottom in his old school's production of Shakespeare's *Midsummer Night's Dream*.
JUNE □	Cliff's *Help It Along* album is released, in aid of Tear Fund.
JUNE 17	Cliff chats on Radio 2's 'Pause For Thought'.
JULY 9	The International Cliff Richard Movement gathers members together at the United Reformed Church, Crouch End, London. Cliff gives a short concert and answers members' questions. Two films, *Love Never Gives Up* and *A Day In The Life Of Cliff Richard*, are shown.
AUGUST/SEPTEMBER □	BBC TV screens a new 'It's Cliff Richard' series.
AUGUST 3	Ex-New Seeker, Lyn Paul, guests on Cliff's BBC TV show.
AUGUST 28	Cliff appears in a special concert at the New Gallery, Regent Street, London for the Crusaders.

THE CLIFF RICHARD FILE 1974

■ The Morecambe and Wise show

SEPTEMBER 4   Cliff lends his support to the Romsey Abbey appeal, at which he meets and chats to Lady Mountbatten.

SEPTEMBER □   A list of venues for Cliff's forthcoming tour is published, on which he will be accompanied by a 20-piece orchestra.

OCTOBER 23-NOVEMBER 1   Cliff undertakes a series of gospel dates.

OCTOBER 27   Cliff and the Shadows reunite especially for a charity concert at the London Palladium in aid of the dependants of the late Colin Charman, who used to produce 'Top of the Pops'. Cliff sings 'Willie and The Hand Jive', 'Bachelor Boy', 'Don't Talk To Him', 'A Matter Of Moments' and 'Power To All Our Friends'. Also on the bill are Cilla Black, Dana, the Two Ronnies, Bruce Forsyth, Dick Emery, Harry Secombe, the Young Generation and the Ronnie Hazlehurst Orchestra.

OCTOBER □   The *Daily Express* reports that local Tory parties in Scotland using Cliff's 'Sing A Song Of Freedom' as their anthem have been told to pay performing rights.

NOVEMBER 7-DECEMBER 14   Cliff tours Britain, starting in Birmingham on November 7 and ending in Hull on December 14.

NOVEMBER 19   Cliff opens a Christian bookshop in Sutton.

NOVEMBER □   As a result of the concert with Cliff on October 27, the Shadows are invited to sing the United Kingdom's six Eurovision songs for 1975.

NOVEMBER □   In a *Daily Mirror* article, Cliff claims that God cured his slipped disc.

1975

JANUARY ☐	Cliff rehearses with Swedish Christian choir Choralerna.
JANUARY 18-22	Cliff appears with Choralerna in Manchester, Newcastle and Leicester.
JANUARY 25	'The Name of Jesus' concert at London's Albert Hall features Choralerna and Malcolm and Alwyn. Cliff sings.
JANUARY ☐	The *NME* publish their 1974 chart points survey, based on 30 points for 1 week at No. 1, to 1 point for 1 week at No. 30. In his lowest-ever showing in the table, Cliff comes 129th (sandwiched between Medicine Head and Donny Osmond) with 43 points. The table is headed by the Bay City Rollers, Alvin Stardust and Mud.
FEBRUARY 21	Cliff lunches with John Lang, the head of BBC Religious Programmes.
MARCH ☐	Cliff's 63rd single is released: 'It's Only Me You've Left Behind/You're The One'. It fails to register in the charts.
APRIL ☐	Cliff promotes his new single in Austria.
APRIL 9	Cliff is interviewed on the Bay City Rollers' Granada TV show 'Shang A Lang'.
APRIL 19	Sally James interviews Cliff on LWT's 'Saturday Scene'. During the programme, the original version of 'Travellin' Light' is played, whereupon Cliff mentions that there is a better version on his new album *The 31st of February Street*.
APRIL 19	Cliff attends the 'Way To Life' rally at Wembley's Empire Pool. With evangelist Dick Saunders and Bill Latham also on the platform, Cliff talks about his Christian conversion and his faith. He sings 'Love Never Gives Up', 'Why Me Lord' and 'Didn't He'.
APRIL ☐	'Sunday' – BBC Radio 4's religious current affairs magazine programme – broadcasts part of the previous week's 'Way To Life' rally.
APRIL 30	Cliff goes to the theatre to see *Joseph and the Amazing Technicolour Dreamcoat*.
MAY 1	Cliff receives a presentation from the World Record Club to mark the sale of 40,000 copies of the six-record boxed set *The Cliff Richard Story*.
JUNE 5	Cliff headlines a special charity concert at Manchester's Free Trade Hall, promoted by Piccadilly Radio, with all proceeds going to two Manchester policemen who died on duty – Sgt Williams and PC Rodgers. Sgt Williams had died after rioting which took place outside Granada's TV studios.
JULY ☐	Helen Moon of Cromer writes to the BBC's 'Jim'll Fix It' show to ask Jimmy Savile if she could meet her hero, Cliff, with the Shadows. Cliff sings 'Run Billy Run' and gives Helen a signed copy of *The 31st of February Street* album.
JULY 22	Cliff attends a Variety Club lunch at London's Savoy Hotel in honour of singer Vera Lynn.
AUGUST ☐	It's announced that Cliff is off to Moscow to record an album of Russian songs.

SEPTEMBER 6 — The first of a new BBC TV series 'It's Cliff and Friends' is screened. Guests include Su Shiffrin and David Copperfield and the producer is Phil Bishop. Cliff sings, 'All You Need Is Love', 'Good on the Sally Army', 'All I Wanna Do', 'I've Got Time' and 'Love Train'.

SEPTEMBER ☐ — Cliff's 64th single, 'Honky Tonk Angel/Wouldn't You Know It' is released, but does not make the charts.

SEPTEMBER 20 — On ITV's 'Supersonic', Cliff sings 'Honky Tonk Angel' and 'Let's Have A Party'.

OCTOBER 3 — A clip of Cliff is shown on Yorkshire TV's 'Pop Quest', hosted by Stevi Merike.

OCTOBER 14 — Noel Edmonds records Cliff's 35th birthday on his Radio 1 breakfast show and plays 'Please Don't Tease'.

OCTOBER ☐ — Alvin Stardust releases his version of Cliff's 'Move It' as a single.

OCTOBER ☐ — On ITV's 'Today' programme, Cliff is interviewed by Sandra Harris and declares that he had no idea that a 'honky-tonk angel' (the title of his current single) was a prostitute until somebody told him while he was in America. He reveals that he heard the song on an old country album a couple of years previously, liked it and recorded it. Cliff says that he had not wanted to upset anybody, and if DJs didn't want to play it he wouldn't particularly mind. He admits that he hadn't heard of American bars called 'honky-tonks' or the Rolling Stones single 'Honky-Tonk Women'.

OCTOBER ☐ — On the subject of Cliff's opinions on 'Honky Tonk Angel', critic Xavier Webster writes: 'It's hypocrisy to put prostitutes outside the cosy Christian circle, but cashing in on it is something else again.'

OCTOBER ☐ — Still on the subject of 'Honky Tonk Angel', Cliff says: 'I hope it's a flop. I never want to hear it again and I hope most of the public never hear it. I knew honky-tonks were something to do with bars, but I completely misconstrued the meaning. Okay, some people might say I'm naive – obviously it's very embarrassing for me. Now I know what I've been singing about, I've taken steps to do all I can to make it a flop. I hope no one buys it . . . If the record is a hit and I'm asked to sing it, I will refuse unless the words are changed.'

NOVEMBER ☐ — Cliff appears on Capital, London's commercial radio station with DJ Roger Scott in a nostalgia show reliving 1959. Cliff's second hit, 'High Class Baby', is played.

DECEMBER 3 — Cliff records a 'Christmas Day Special' produced by David Winter for BBC Radio.

DECEMBER 4 — Cliff begins recording for a series of 'Gospel Road' for BBC Radio 1 and Radio 2.

DECEMBER 27 — BBC1 TV screens 'Cliff and Friends'.

1976

JANUARY ☐   Cliff bans Aj Nebber from singing 'Dear Auntie Vera' on his TV show. The song is about a girl who asks an agony columnist how she can get a bigger bust.

JANUARY ☐   BBC's Radios 1 and 2 run a new series of 'Gospel Road', in which ex-Settler Cindy Kent reviews new records while Cliff contributes his own material and introduces songs by other people.

JANUARY 31   EMI release a box set of six cassettes, entitled *The Music and Life of Cliff Richard*. Tracks spanning his career and including the occasional Shadows number are linked by Cliff's thoughts and memories.

FEBRUARY ☐   EMI release 'Miss You Nights/Love Is Enough'. This is Cliff's 65th single and is produced by former Shadow Bruce Welch.

FEBRUARY 14   Cliff appears on ITV's 'Supersonic', singing 'Miss You Nights'.

FEBRUARY 28   Cliff enters the charts with 'Miss You Nights' – his first appearance on the singles charts since July 1974.

MARCH ☐   Cliff's intended visit to the Soviet Union is postponed.

MARCH ☐   Rocket Records release 'Miss You Nights' in the United States.

APRIL 15   Religious organisation Scope stages two charity concerts featuring Cliff and Larry Norman at Birmingham's Odeon Theatre. The concerts are in aid of the National Institute for the Healing of Addictions – an organisation subscribed to by the Who's Pete Townshend. Eric Clapton is among the celebrities to be cured by treatment offered by the Institute.

APRIL 23   Cliff's 66th single, 'Devil Woman/Love On', is released. One reviewer, Bob Edmonds, asks: 'Has Cliff been caught out again? He cut a previous single, "Honky Tonk Angel", without apparently knowing what it was about. This time someone may have forgotten to tell him what the words "devil" and "woman" mean. You see, Cliffie, a "devil" is a naughty person and a "woman" is more or less a person of the opposite sex. Now, is it right for an upstanding young man to sing about naughtiness and sex? Isn't this just setting a bad example to his followers?'

APRIL 26   Cliff records for Dutch television's 'Eddy Go Round' show, which is to be transmitted in June.

MAY 3   Radio Luxembourg previews Cliff's new album *I'm Nearly Famous*.

MAY 17   Cliff records 'Insight' for Radio 1 with producer Tim Blackmore.

MAY 20   Cliff is interviewed at Radio 210 in Reading – the latest ILR station to go on the air.

MAY ☐   A Hong Kong newspaper prints a bizarre piece of editorial under the heading 'Cliff Richard Circus Is Coming To Town': 'Clifford Richard Hong Kong's golden boy and Great Britain's answer to "Black Oak Arkansas" is expected for concert dates in Hong Kong sometime in June according to L'artiste's recording Labelle, EMI. Clifford the controversial heavy metal gun of rock; known for his bizarre stage regalia and eclectic cynicism is rumoured to

■ The author as a budding disc jockey and 'nearly famous' Cliff

be bringing with him 1,500 watt strobe lights, the Bolshoi Ballet and a herd of performing elephants.'

MAY 30   Radio's 'Insight' programme is transmitted, sub-titled 'Showmanship in Pop'. It features Alice Cooper, Rick Wakeman, Marc Bolan and Cliff.

JUNE 13   On 'Insight' Cliff and former Shadow Bruce Welch survey their 18-year association.

JUNE ☐   Among the celebrities seen sporting Cliff's 'I'm Nearly Famous' badges are guitarists Jimmy Page, Jeff Beck, Eric Clapton and Pete Townshend.

JUNE 19   Cliff appears on ITV's 'Supersonic', singing 'Honky Tonk Angel'.

JUNE 26   Cliff appears on ITV's 'Supersonic' singing 'Let's Have A Party'.

JULY ☐   'Devil Woman' picks up heavy 'FM' air-play on San Fransiscan radio stations.

THE CLIFF RICHARD FILE 1976

JULY 24 — BBC2 screens 'Cliff in Concert'.

JULY 31 — Cliff's 67th single, 'I Can't Ask for Anything More Than You, Babe/Junior Cowboy' is released. Reviewer Charles Shaar Murray writes: 'Cliff's record is a startling performance, sung almost entirely in a pubescent/feminine soul falsetto; it earns one's respect for the technique and execution, but ... let's just say that he's gonna seem very weird doing it on "Top of the Pops".'

JULY/AUGUST ☐ — Cliff is in America to promote the album *I'm Nearly Famous*.

AUGUST ☐ — In America, 'Devil Woman' enters the *Cashbox* and *Billboard* charts to give Cliff his third-ever hit Stateside and his first since 'It's All In The Game' in 1964.

SEPTEMBER 6 — Cliff is interviewed for BBC TV's 'Nationwide' and on Thames TV.

SEPTEMBER 9 — The *Guardian* newspaper publishes a letter from Brian Green of Epping in Essex: 'Sir, They got Cliff Richard – we got the Foxbat. At that rate of exchange, send them Jethro Tull and you could disband NATO.'

SEPTEMBER 15 — Cliff begins his visit to the Soviet Union, via Copenhagen and Stockholm.

SEPTEMBER 25 — Cliff attends a reception at the British Embassy in Moscow.

OCTOBER ☐ — 'Devil Woman' becomes Cliff's biggest-ever American hit – peaking at No. 6 in the *Billboard* chart and No. 5 in the *Cashbox* chart.

■ Elton John presents Cliff with a Gold Disc for 'I'm Nearly Famous'

OCTOBER 1 — Cliff kicks off a gospel tour in aid of Tear Fund, the British relief and development organisation.

OCTOBER 22-LATE NOVEMBER — Cliff gives a string of British pop concerts.

OCTOBER 31 — BBC TV screens *The Young Ones*.

NOVEMBER 5 — Talking to Sandy Harrod of the *Croydon Advertiser* before a Tear Fund concert, Cliff explains that the fund was set up eight or nine years ago to provide money for Third World projects. Of his August tour of Russia, Cliff says: 'I suppose they chose me because I'm fairly middle-of-the-road,' and of his revived recording career: 'I've broken out of the polythene bag ...'

NOVEMBER ☐	At Cliff's Tear Fund concerts, songs include 'Devil Woman', 'Miss You Nights', 'Willie and the Hand Jive'.
NOVEMBER ☐	It's announced that Cliff intends to 'have another go' at the Eurovision Song Contest.
NOVEMBER ☐	Cliff reveals that he is to visit India – his birthplace.
NOVEMBER 14	The *Sunday People* prints an article by Peter Bishop, questioning the prolific use of four-letter words in the pop paper *New Musical Express* under the heading: 'Should we Fling this Filth at our Pop Kids?' The article complains that in one recent *NME* article, the four-letter word for sexual relations appeared no fewer than seven times. Alongside the banner headline the *Sunday People* prints a picture of Cliff who 'refuses to have the *NME* in the house'.
NOVEMBER 22	Cliff performs at London's Royal Albert Hall with the Brian Bennett Band.
NOVEMBER ☐	Cliff's 68th single, 'Hey Mr Dream Maker/No One Waits' is released.
DECEMBER ☐	In India, Cliff meets Mother Teresa of Calcutta and her missionaries of charity. He visits the homes for the destitute and dying.

DECEMBER 7/8	Cliff gives two performances at the Kalamandir Auditorium, New Delhi.
DECEMBER ☐	Cliff visits Tear Fund projects in Bangladesh.
DECEMBER 30	On Belgian TV's 'Adamo Special', Cliff sings 'Power To All Our Friends', 'Honky Tonk Angel' and duets with Adamo on 'Livin' Doll'.
DECEMBER 31	BBC1's 'A Jubilee of Music' is screened, featuring Vera Lynn, Lulu, Acker Bilk and Cliff.

1977

JANUARY 1 — The *NME* jokingly award Cliff 'The First Annual Mary Whitehouse Seal of Good Housekeeping Award' for refusing to have the *NME* in the house.

JANUARY ☐ — In the *NME* 1976 singles chart table (30 points for 1 week at No. 1, 1 point for 1 week at No. 30) Cliff is placed 28th with 229 points, between Diana Ross and Hot Chocolate. Abba come top with 995 points, followed by Rod Stewart and Demis Roussos. In the album yearly chart, *I'm Nearly Famous* comes 45th.

JANUARY 8 — Cliff appears on BBC TV's 'Multi-Coloured Swap Shop' with Noel Edmonds.

FEBRUARY 10 — For World Records 25th Anniversary, Cliff is their guest of honour.

FEBRUARY 26 — ITV's 'Supersonic' features Cliff, Guys 'n' Dolls, Racing Cars, Golden Earring and Dennis Weaver.

MARCH 6 — The Cliff Richard Movement magazine *Dynamite* reports that Cliff's Tear Fund concerts in 1976 raised over £37,000, the money providing six vehicles for Argentina, the Yemen, Arab Republic, Nigeria, Haiti and Burundi, as well as a generator for a hospital in India, a rural development centre in Kenya and a nutritional training centre in Zaire.

MARCH ☐   EMI release Cliff's 69th single, 'My Kinda Life/Nothing Left For Me To Say' and reviewer Steve Clarke writes: 'It's twelve years if it's a day since Cliff exchanged his quiff and leather jacket for all things wholesome, and to hear him sing a song eulogising the life of the guitar picker is about as convincing as Margaret Thatcher telling us how she'll put things right before you can say "Sir Keith Joseph". The rock 'n' roll backing is not exactly stuffed with raunch.'

■ From the pages of *New Musical Express* 25 June 1977

MARCH ☐   Cliff attends a dinner party at Elton John's house. Former 'Ready Steady Go' compère Cathy McGowan is also present.

MARCH 21-APRIL 10   Cliff spends 3 weeks in South Africa.

APRIL ☐   Journalist Monty Smith writes of Cliff: 'Besides being a neat riposte to America's apparent indifference, the *I'm Nearly Famous* album had an entirely deserved regenerative effect on Cliff's career. He was hardly at a make or break point but, give the lad credit, he could easily have gone the way of most mainstream performers at that stage – to the great cabaret club in the West End.'

APRIL ☐   Cliff appears on 'Top Of The Pops' singing 'My Kinda Life'.

MAY 2-25   Cliff tours Australasia.

MAY 7   ITV's 'All You Need Is Love' looks at the early days of rock'n'roll. Cliff is featured, along with Elvis Presley, Bill Haley, Jerry Lee Lewis, Carl Perkins, Chuck Berry, Chubby Checker, Gene Vincent, Tommy Steele, Terry Dene, Little Richard and Lonnie Donegan.

MAY 29   London Weekend Television screens Cliff's 1966-made film *Finders Keepers*.

JUNE 6   As part of the Queen's Silver Jubilee celebrations, Cliff speaks at a youth rally in Windsor Great Park.

JUNE ☐   On the subject of the new punk rock explosion, Cliff comments: 'I don't like what punk rockers do – especially to themselves ... Some like Tom Robinson and Elvis Costello are great, but most of them are lousy and I find it all a bit repulsive that people should want to look so ugly. The punks think they own the pop scene, but they forget they're just leasing it from us ... What we've got going now is the first generation of forty-year-olds who dig rock 'n' roll. When I was eighteen, people of forty hated rock. Now, when we're sixty ... it may sound ridiculous, but I'm going to love rock, the music will still be our music.'

THE CLIFF RICHARD FILE 1977

JUNE 13-27	Cliff undertakes a promotional visit to the USA.
JUNE 27	EMI release Cliff's 70th single, 'When Two Worlds Drift Apart/That's Why I Love You.'
JUNE 29	Cliff records 'When Two Worlds Drift Apart' for 'Top of the Pops'.
JULY 2	Cliff guests on ITV's 'Saturday Scene'.
JULY 20	Cliff attends a reception at Buckingham Palace.
AUGUST 2-16	Cliff holidays in Portugal.
AUGUST ☐	The Sunday Mirror asks celebrities who they'd like to be stranded with on a desert island. Frankie Howerd chooses Mary Whitehouse, newscaster Reginald Bosanquet chooses Muppet Miss Piggy, and Cliff selects actress Farrah Fawcett-Majors ... 'so that she can give me tennis lessons.'
AUGUST 17	LBC 'Newsbeat' and the BBC World Service both interview Cliff.
SEPTEMBER ☐	Hodder & Stoughton publish Cliff's own book Which One's Cliff? written in conjunction with Bill Latham, in which he relates his Christian beliefs.
SEPTEMBER 9-24	Cliff tours Europe.
SEPTEMBER ☐	In the Sunday Times colour supplement, journalist Gordon Burn writes of Cliff: 'Just because he's 37, well-preserved and not ashamed to admit to being celibate for the past twelve years, doesn't necessarily mean a thing.'
SEPTEMBER 28	On his Radio 1 show, Dave Lee Travis talks to Cliff for an hour and plays tracks.
OCTOBER 1	Along with Robert Morley, Cliff appears on Michael Parkinson's BBC1 chat show.
OCTOBER 7	Cliff starts his 1977 gospel tour at Redworth Leisure Centre.
OCTOBER 7-22	Touring England on the gospel tour.
OCTOBER ☐	At EMI's sales conference dinner, singer Roger Chapman makes loud and rude comments about Cliff's self-imposed twelve years' celibacy.
OCTOBER 14	Cliff's 37th birthday is spent playing at the Manchester Free Trade Hall.
OCTOBER 18	To celebrate the Queen's Silver Jubilee and the centenary of the invention of the gramophone, the British Phonographic Institution in its Britannia Awards names Cliff 'Best British Male Artist'. Queen's 'Bohemian Rhapsody' is 'Best British Pop Single' and Julie Covington and Graham Parker tie for 'Most Outstanding New British Recording Artist'.
OCTOBER 24	Cliff gives a gospel show in Rotterdam.
OCTOBER 28	The Songwriters' Guild of Great Britain presents Cliff with the Gold Badge Award.
NOVEMBER 9	Cliff kicks off a pop tour at the Southampton Gaumont.
NOVEMBER 9-DECEMBER 12	Cliff on tour in England and Scotland.
NOVEMBER ☐	Cliff is interviewed by Sally James on ATV's Saturday morning programme 'TisWas' and becomes involved in the messy slapstick routine treatment that's synonymous with the show.
NOVEMBER ☐	EMI issue Small Corners, an album of religious songs by Cliff.

NOVEMBER ☐	Miss Margica Caraghin writes a rather over-the-top letter to the music press from Galati, Roumania: 'What could be more beautiful and more wonderful than to celebrate Cliff Richard today when he celebrates his birthday. How wonderful it is Cliff Richard's birthday! Let's be next to him, my friends, from all over the world! Let's be next to him as we have always been, so he should feel the warmth of our endless and burning love for him. The English nation celebrates him, and at the same time the entire world, the entire musical world, celebrates him since Cliff belongs to the entire musical world, loving him and appreciating him ...'

■ Cliff reads 13-year-old *New Musical Express* on the pages of November 1977 *NME*

NOVEMBER ☐	History does not record whether this was written with effusive gushing sincerity or was the work of a wag! Cliff is photographed with Tony James and Bob Andrews from Generation X.
NOVEMBER 9-DECEMBER 12	Cliff starts a secular tour of Britain.
NOVEMBER ☐	Journalist Bob Woffinden writes of Cliff: 'He's still neat, deferential and responsible; he still hasn't moved on to higher things ... in fact, Richard might be capable of much more yet, but he's so determinedly inoffensive that we're never likely to find out what.'
NOVEMBER 12	Cliff appears on the Saturday morning TV show 'TisWas'.
NOVEMBER 21	Cliff is interviewed by the press from 11 am to 6 pm.
NOVEMBER 26	Cliff and the Shadows announce that they will play together in February for the first time in ten years.
DECEMBER ☐	Cliff attends the Record Industry Ball at London's Dorchester Hotel.
DECEMBER 17	Cliff appears on BBC TV's live 'Swap Shop Christmas Show'. They screen the video of *My Kinda Life* and Cliff takes one of his belts as a 'Swap'.

1978

JANUARY 31	Along with Roy Castle and his wife Fiona, Cliff takes part in a Booksellers' Convention at Wembley. Among the songs he sings are 'Every Face Tells A Story', 'When I Survey the Wondrous Cross' and 'Why Should The Devil Have All The Good Music'.
JANUARY ☐	Cliff releases his 71st single, 'Yes He Lives/Good On The Sally Army'.
FEBRUARY 4	Singer Ian Dury says of Cliff's new single: 'The work of a great entertainer in his prime. Stevie Wonder and John Coltrane have both done music about Jesus as well. Every time Cliff comes on, time stands still to this very day . . . some say he lives in Hendon.'
FEBRUARY 15	Cliff sings two songs from his *Small Corners* album on BBC TV's 'Pebble Mill At One'.
FEBRUARY 16	The Arts Centre Group stage a special concert at Croydon featuring Cliff, Roy Castle, Dana and Neil Reid.
FEBRUARY 27-MARCH 11	Cliff and the Shadows reunite to play a two-week 20th Anniversary Show at the London Palladium.
MARCH 2	Mike Read interviews Cliff at the London Palladium for Radio Luxembourg.
MARCH 6	EMI Records host a special dinner for Cliff at 'Rags' Restaurant in London.
MARCH 7	Cliff dines with Elton John.
APRIL ☐	EMI France release 'Why Should The Devil Have All The Good Music' and 'Hey Watcha Say'.
JUNE 27	Cliff attends the opening of the Arts Centre's new headquarters in Short Street, London, near the Old Vic.
JUNE 20	Cliff attends a Music Therapy Committee lunch.
JULY ☐	Cliff's 72nd single is released: 'Please Remember Me/Please Don't Tease'. The 'A' side is a song written by American singer/composer Dave Loggins and comes from Cliff's forthcoming album *Green Light*; the 'B' side is an update of Cliff's 1960 hit.
SUMMER ☐	Cliff records the album *Green Light* at EMI's Abbey Road Studios and visits South Africa, Australia and Hong Kong.
SEPTEMBER 1	Cliff meets pensioners in Weybridge, Surrey to present them with budgerigars.
SEPTEMBER 2	Cliff joins evangelist Dick Saunders on stage and sings 'Up in Canada', 'Lord I Love You' and 'When I Survey the Wondrous Cross'.
SEPTEMBER ☐	In an interview with the magazine *Dynamite*, Cliff admits that although the Rolling Stones make great records, their lyrics are ridiculous.
SEPTEMBER 21	On German TV's 'Star Parade', Cliff sings 'Please Remember Me' and 'Lucky Lips'.

THE CLIFF RICHARD FILE **1978**

■ 'Top of the Pops' running order 1978

■ Kelly generously shares her rubber ring with Cliff

149

THE CLIFF RICHARD FILE 1978

OCTOBER 1   BBC Radio 1 starts running '20 Golden Years' – a series which relates Cliff's success story in five parts. It is narrated by Tim Rice.

OCTOBER 9/10   Under the banner of 'Help, Hope & Hallelujah', Cliff gives two concerts to celebrate the tenth anniversary of Tear Fund. His songs include 'Such Is The Mystery', 'Song For Sarah', 'Yes He Lives', 'Up in Canada', 'You Can't Get To Heaven By Living Like Hell', 'Yesterday Today Forever' and 'Why Should The Devil Have All The Good Music'.

OCTOBER 10   Hilversum Radio in Holland broadcasts the Albert Hall concert.

OCTOBER ☐   Tear Fund's tenth anniversary and the ninth anniversary of Cliff's involvement. Since his initial donation of two gospel concerts in 1969, Cliff has undertaken an annual concert tour, membership of its Board, narration of three promotional trips and visits to the Fund's projects in Sudan, Nepal and Bangladesh.

OCTOBER ☐   Of the Tear Fund concerts, Cliff says: 'You know, it never fails to encourage me when I think that at this very moment, somewhere in the world a Christian is using an X-ray unit or a Land-Rover or even a building paid for by one of these concerts.'

OCTOBER 30   On an Australian TV show, 'Australian Music to the World', Cliff sings 'Devil Woman'. A clip filmed at Cliff's home in Weybridge, in which he chats about John Farrar and Olivia Newton-John, is also shown.

NOVEMBER 6   Cliff attends a party in London's Belgrave Square for the launch of the first *Guinness Book of British Hit Singles* along with Elton John, Bob Geldof, Vera Lynn, Hank Marvin, the Drifters, Billy Idol, Paul Jones, Mike D'Abo and Russ Conway, amongst others. A photograph of all present is taken for the cover of the *Second Guinness Book of British Hit Singles*.

NOVEMBER ☐   Cliff's 73rd single is released: 'Can't Take the Hurt Any More/Needing A Friend'.

1979

JANUARY 1	KBS TV in Korea screens *The Young Ones*.
JANUARY □	The UK Scripture Union launches a series of cassettes which feature Cliff reading from the scriptures.
FEBRUARY 1	At a special lunch at Claridges Hotel in London, EMI present Cliff with a gold clock and a gold replica of the key to their headquarters in Manchester Square, to celebrate their twenty-one-year partnership.
FEBRUARY 13	At the Music Week Awards, Cliff and the Shadows receive an award for twenty-one years as major British recording artists.
FEBRUARY 27	Cliff lunches at New Scotland Yard.
MARCH □	'Green Light/Imagine Love' becomes Cliff's 74th British single. Written by Alan Tarney, it is produced by Bruce Welch.
APRIL 20	At St Alban's Cathedral, Cliff takes part in a special youth festival.
MAY 1	Cliff is present at the Local Radio Awards at the Grosvenor House Hotel, London. This is an event organised by *Radio & Record News*.
MAY 31/JUNE 1	Cliff records for Dutch TV.
JUNE 10	Cliff talks of his Christian faith at a Liverpool Theatre chat show.
JUNE 12	Cliff takes part in more Bible readings for the Scripture Union cassettes. On the same day, to celebrate the fiftieth anniversary of the Dutch Youth Hostel Organisation, he appears on Dutch TV's 'Auro Gala Special' singing 'Miss You Nights' and 'When Two Worlds Drift Apart'.
JUNE 28	Cliff attends the European Baptist Congress at the Brighton Centre, Sussex. He talks about the work of Tear Fund and his visit to the Soviet Union, as well as singing nine songs.
JULY 5	At a Variety Club of Great Britain lunch, Cliff is guest of honour in celebration of his twenty-one years in show business. The function is attended by the Duke of Kent, the Shadows and Joan Collins amongst others.

■ 5 July 1979: Cliff celebrates twenty-one years in showbusiness with (left to right) Anita Harris, Elaine Paige, Joan Collins and Patti Boulaye

THE CLIFF RICHARD FILE 1979

JULY ☐   Cliff's 75th single is released: 'We Don't Talk Any More/Count Me Out'. The 'A' side is written by Alan Tarney and produced by Bruce Welch. The Terry Britten-Bruce Welch 'B' side is taken from the *Green Light* album.

AUGUST **25**   Eleven years and 124 days since he last topped the chart with 'Congratulations', Cliff gets to No. 1 with 'We Don't Talk Any More', deposing The Boomtown Rats with 'I Don't Like Mondays'.

■ 25 August 1979: Cliff celebrates his seventy-fifth single 'We Don't Talk Anymore' topping the chart

AUGUST **25**   An historic moment as Cliff becomes the second singer who discarded the surname Webb to top the chart in the same year – Cliff's real name being Harry Webb. The other is Gary Numan (Gary Webb).

AUGUST ☐   Cliff launches his own gospel label Patch Records in association with EMI. The first release is a Cliff produced album by Garth Hewitt, which is launched at the Greenbelt Festival in Hertfordshire.

AUGUST **26**   Cliff appears at the Greenbelt Christian Music Festival, where he sings for 90 minutes backed by George Ford, Graham Jarvis, Mart Jenner, Snowy White, Mike Moran, Tony Rivers, Stu Calver and John Perry. He is also interviewed by poet and writer Steve Turner about his faith.

■ Summer Holiday '79 style

AUGUST	27	BBC Radio 1 broadcast a special programme on Greenbelt.
SEPTEMBER	5	Cliff is a guest on Capital Radio's Roger Scott show in London.
SEPTEMBER	18	Cliff attends a Filey Christian Holiday Crusade meeting, where he participates in discussions and signs books.
SEPTEMBER	□	Cliff's original producer Norrie Paramor dies.
SEPTEMBER	19	On Manchester's Piccadilly Radio, Cliff is the guest of DJ Roger Day.
SEPTEMBER	22	Cliff takes part in 'Hosannah '79', an anti-racist festival held in Birmingham.
SEPTEMBER	22	After one month at No. 1, 'We Don't Talk Any More' is knocked off the top of the chart by Gary Numan's 'Cars'.
OCTOBER	4	Kate Bush and Cliff appear with the London Symphony Orchestra at the Royal Albert Hall in aid of the LSO's 75th Birthday Appeal.
NOVEMBER	□	Cliff's 76th single is released: 'Hot Shot/Walking In The Light'. Produced

THE CLIFF RICHARD FILE **1979**

by Cliff and Terry Britten, the 'A' side is taken from the *Rock 'n' Roll Juvenile* album, being one of seven tracks where Terry Britten collaborated with Scots singer/songwriter B.A. Robertson.

NOVEMBER 17   'We Don't Talk Any More' becomes Cliff's fourth single to enter the American Top 40, the others being 'Livin' Doll' (1959), 'It's All In The Game' (1964), and 'Devil Woman' (1976).

DECEMBER 2   In Camberley, Surrey, Cliff takes part in a concert in aid of the International Year of the Child.

DECEMBER 16   Following a torchlight procession from London's Trafalgar Square, along the Mall to Buckingham Palace, Cliff leads a crowd of tens of thousands as he sings carols, accompanying himself on guitar on a specially constructed stage facing Buckingham Palace. The Queen and Prince Charles join in the carols from the balcony and later Cliff is received in Buckingham Palace after the celebrations to mark the end of the Year of the Child.

DECEMBER 18   Cliff sings at a special concert in aid of the International Year of the Child.

DECEMBER 23   Cliff turns DJ for two hours on BBC Radio 1's 'Star Special' when he plays his favourite records.

DECEMBER 26   On BBC Radio 2's 'Two Sides Of Cliff', Cliff plays records by himself and the Shadows.

DECEMBER ☐   'We Don't Talk Any More' breaks into the American Top 10, finally peaking at No. 7.

DECEMBER ☐   *Record Collector* magazine prints the going rate for some of Cliff's old records:

'32 minutes and 15 seconds LP'	– £12
'Serious Charge EP'	– £10
'Express Bongo EP'	– £10

1980

JANUARY 7   Cliff is interviewed by Mike Douglas on his USA TV show about his OBE and his American career.

JANUARY 8   On USA TV's 'Dinah Shore Show', Cliff chats about his childhood, his OBE and American girls.

FEBRUARY ☐   Cliff's 77th single is released: 'Carrie/Moving In'.

FEBRUARY 6   Cliff appears at a special tribute concert to Norrie Paramor, his long-time friend and producer who died the previous year. Backed by the Ron Goodwin Orchestra and Tony Rivers, John Perry and Stu Calver, Cliff sings six numbers which are closely associated with Norrie: 'Bachelor Boy', 'Constantly', 'The Day I Met Marie', 'Congratulations', 'The Young Ones' and 'Summer Holiday'.

■ At the Norrie Paramor tribute cabaret with the Duchess of Kent

FEBRUARY 7   Cliff attends a 'Christians in Sport' dinner in London.

FEBRUARY 10   Cliff takes part in an evangelist meeting in Cambridge with Dr Billy Graham, and in the evening speaks at Great St Mary's, the University Church.

FEBRUARY 20   In an article in the *Daily Star*, Cliff says: 'Sex outside marriage is wrong ... I believe that people who are promiscuous do find it much more difficult to have a stable relationship, and that is what marriage is. Marriage is a special thing, and quite simply I haven't found the right girl yet. I've only been in love twice and it was a long time ago.'

FEBRUARY 27   In the National Rock and Pop Awards organised by Radio 1, 'Nationwide' and the *Daily Mirror*, Cliff receives the Nationwide Golden Award as 'Best Family Entertainer'.

MARCH ☐	ITV's 'Pop Gospel' series begins, during which Cliff appears in two programmes.
MARCH ☐	'Carrie' enters the British Top 10, peaking at No. 4 to become Cliff's 43rd Top 10 hit single in Britain.
SPRING ☐	Cliff is voted 'Top Pop Star' by the viewers of Noel Edmonds' Saturday morning TV show 'Swap Shop'.
SPRING ☐	Cliff wins the *TV Times* award for 'The Most Exciting Male Singer On Television'.
MARCH ☐	Cliff goes on a business trip to America.
MARCH 27	Cliff appears in front of 5,500 people at London's Albert Hall at the 'Sing Good News' event, honouring the top writers in a contest organised by the Bible Society. Cliff sings 'Why Should The Devil Have All The Good Music' and 'When I Survey The Wondrous Cross'.
APRIL 5	'Carrie' enters the USA chart to become Cliff's fifth big American hit.
APRIL 15	Cliff records for the 'Pop Gospel' show in Manchester.
APRIL 16	During Capital Radio's 'Help a London Child' campaign, listener Kim Kayne beats off other bidders with a £1,400 pledge to the charity in exchange for lunch with Cliff. The lunch – in Cliff's office in Upper Harley Street – consists of melon, fillet steak with Spanish sauce, green beans with ham, new potatoes, aubergines, salad, strawberry shortcake, champagne, wine and coffee.
MAY ☐	'Carrie' reaches the American Top 40.
JULY 18	July gospel tour begins.
JULY 23	On Mike Read's Radio 1 'Breakfast Show', Cliff expresses his gratitude to all his fans before going to Buckingham Palace to collect his OBE from the Queen. As Cliff and his mother Dorothy arrive at Buckingham Palace in his Rolls-Royce, the crowd sings 'Congratulations'. In the white and gold Buckingham Palace ballroom, before being presented to the Queen, Cliff – dressed in sober black suit with red tie, red rose and bright red trainer shoes – explains the reason for his eccentric garb: 'I haven't got any morning dress, so I thought I would wear something colourful! I've been to the Palace before and I knew there was a lot of red about the place. I have always been a very firm Royalist and have followed the Royal family since I was a kid.' Two hours later at 12.30 Cliff leaves Buckingham Palace for a champagne lunch.
SUMMER ☐	Cliff appears in Germany with his group, now known as the Sky Band, and includes in his set 'The Rock That Doesn't Roll', 'The Twelfth Of Never', 'The Minute You're Gone', 'Sci-Fi', 'Devil Woman' and 'Green Light'.
AUGUST ☐	'Dreamin'/Dynamite' becomes Cliff's 78th single. The 'B' side is a new version of the 21-year-old 'B' side to 'Travellin' Light', which became a hit in its own right.
SEPTEMBER 1,8,15	Cliff contributes to BBC World Services 'Reflections', in which he selects and reads biblical texts.
SEPTEMBER ☐	'Dreamin'' climbs into the British Top 10, peaking at No. 8 to become Cliff's 44th single to make the British Top 10.
SEPTEMBER ☐	A lunchtime press launch is held in London's West End to promote *Happy Christmas From Cliff*, a slim volume published by Hodder & Stoughton. It

■ Cliff with Olivia Newton-John

THE CLIFF RICHARD FILE 1980

■ Cliff at home

contains many seasonal colour photographs of Cliff at home and abroad, as well as puzzles, quizzes and accounts of Christmas around the world.

SEPTEMBER **23** Cliff is a guest on Radio 2's 'John Dunn Show'.

OCTOBER ☐ Cliff takes part in a television show to raise money for charity.

OCTOBER **14** Cliff commences a five-night stand at London's Apollo Theatre, where the crowd sing 'Happy Birthday' to him on the opening night. Numbers in the set include 'Move It', 'Carrie', 'Miss You Nights', 'Give A Little Bit More' 'Everyman', 'The Young Ones', 'Livin' Doll' and 'A Little In Love'.

SEPTEMBER **27** Noel Edmonds chats to Cliff on BBC TV's Saturday morning show 'Swap Shop'.

OCTOBER ☐ EMI release Cliff's 79th single, 'Suddenly', with Olivia Newton-John. The 'B' side is performed by Olivia alone: 'You Made Me Love You'.

DECEMBER **13** On BBC TV's Michael Parkinson show, Cliff sings Elvis's 'Heartbreak Hotel' and in the finale 'All The Way' with the other guests.

CHRISTMAS ☐ Top London store Selfridges invite Cliff and several other major celebrities to design their own shop window. Cliff's window is on the traditional religious theme – 'Christmas Through The Eyes Of A Child'.

1981

JANUARY	☐	'A Little In Love' is in the American charts, peaking at No.17.
JANUARY	☐	Cliff undertakes a promotional visit to the United States for his forthcoming March tour.
JANUARY	4	Cliff appears on the John Kelly show on Los Angeles TV.
JANUARY	5	Cliff appears on the John Davison show on Los Angeles TV.
JANUARY	6	Cliff appears on US TV in the 'Dionne Warwick Solid Gold Show' in Los Angeles.
JANUARY	7	Cliff appears on the Merv Griffin show on Los Angeles TV.
JANUARY	10	Cliff in Ontario, Canada.
JANUARY	11	Cliff travels to New York.
JANUARY	12	Cliff in New York. At home his 80th single, 'A Little In Love/Keep On Looking', is released.
JANUARY	☐	Cliff returns to London on Concorde from New York's Kennedy Airport.
JANUARY	16	Cliff has a meeting with Billy Graham at the Royal Albert Hall, London. On the same day he attends the twenty-fifth birthday celebrations of the major British evangelical magazine *Crusade*, where he talks about his recent American trip, his forthcoming concerts and the death of John Lennon.
JANUARY	18-21	Cliff rehearses for his gospel tour.
JANUARY	22	Cliff's manager, Peter Gormley, meets with Dave Clark who is laying the foundations for his musical *Time*.
JANUARY 22-FEBRUARY	7	Cliff undertakes several gospel tour dates.
JANUARY	27	Cliff films a video for 'A Little In Love' at Farningham in Kent with producer David Mallett.
JANUARY	☐	New York journalist David Fructs describes Cliff as 'looking like a hip seminary student in an unassuming cardigan sweater, aviator glasses and brown suede sneakers'.
FEBRUARY	3	BBC producer Norman Stone films Cliff at home.
FEBRUARY	☐	Cliff is interviewed after his gospel concert at Sheffield by German magazine *Bravo*.
FEBRUARY	9	Cliff records for 'Top of the Pops' and the Kenny Everett Show at Riverside Studios, London. Musicians are Alan Tarney, Trevor Spencer, Mark Jenner and Mark Griffiths.
FEBRUARY	10	Cliff sings with a choir of 400 girls to raise money for St Brendan's School, Clevedon, Bristol. The school's headmaster, John Davey, had been Cliff's teacher who helped him to pass his 'O' level in religious studies in 1965.
FEBRUARY	14	Cliff attends a Crusaders meeting at Central Hall, Westminster, London.

THE CLIFF RICHARD FILE **1981**

■ Front cover of *International Cliff Richard Movement Magazine*, 1981

FEBRUARY **15**	Cliff attends a 'Christians in Sport' dinner in Watford.
FEBRUARY **16-22**	Cliff rehearses at Shepperton Studios.
FEBRUARY **17**	Cliff records for Kenny Everett's TV show.
FEBRUARY **24**	At London's Café Royal, Cliff receives the *Daily Mirror* Readers' Award as 'Outstanding Musical Personality of the Year', which is presented to him by Una Stubbs.
FEBRUARY **26**	Cliff goes to see the première of the film about Agatha Christie.
FEBRUARY **27**	Cliff flies from Heathrow Airport, bound for Canada and the United States on a month-long tour.
MARCH □	While rehearsing in Hollywood, a tour truck loaded with equipment and instruments worth £40,000 is stolen.
MARCH **3**	Cliff and his group Thunder open at the Paramount Theatre, Seattle – the first

	date of the tour. Among songs included are: 'Move It', 'Green Light', 'Dreaming', 'Miss You Nights', 'A Little In Love', 'The Rock That Doesn't Roll', 'Do You Wanna Dance', 'Devil Woman', and 'We Don't Talk Any More'.
MARCH ☐	Cliff's month-long tour of the USA and Canada is extended to seven weeks.
MARCH ☐	Cliff's first UK video is released: *The Young Ones*, retailing at £28.30.
MARCH 20	BBC TV screens 'Cliff in London' – excerpts from Cliff's autumn concerts at the Apollo.
MARCH 31	Cliff's mother Dorothy and Bill Latham fly to New York to join Cliff.
APRIL 20	Cliff flies back to England, arriving at Heathrow's Terminal 3.
APRIL 27-30	Cliff rehearses at Shepperton Studios for his show at the Hammersmith Odeon.
MAY 1	Cliff stars in a 'Rock Special' at the Hammersmith Odeon, which is filmed by BBC producer Norman Stone to go out on television at a later date. Live songs from the concert are later inter-cut with reminiscences by Cliff's friends and show business colleagues such as Adam Faith, Marty Wilde and the Shadows.
MAY ☐	Phil Everly comments that Cliff was one of the very few artists who ranked just below Elvis Presley in the rock 'n' roll pantheon.
MAY ☐	'Give A Little Bit More' is released as a single in America and reaches No.39 in the charts.
MAY 3	The BBC films Cliff, backed by the Fantoms, at London's Hard Rock Café.
SPRING ☐	Cliff is voted 'Top Pop Star' in the *Sunday Telegraph* Readers' Poll.
MAY 21-23	Cliff filming on location for EMI.
JUNE ☐	Cliff's *Love Songs* album is released and becomes his fifth chart-topping LP.
JUNE 13	Cliff attends the opening of a new hairdressing salon in Surrey.
JUNE 30	Cliff guests on Michael Aspel's Capital Radio show.
JULY 8	Cliff appears on Radio London.
JULY 10	Cliff is interviewed on the Weybridge Hospital Radio Station, Radio Wey.
JULY 16	Cliff mixes 'Daddy's Home', 'Shakin' All Over' and 'Stood Up' at Shepperton Studios.
JULY 23	The *Wired for Sound* video is shot in Milton Keynes.
JULY 24	Cliff has a barbecue at home.
JULY 27	Cliff flies to Portugal for a two-week holiday.
AUGUST 11	Cliff flies from Portugal to South Africa to continue his holiday.
AUGUST 15-22	Cliff in Mauritius.
AUGUST 15	After five weeks at No.1, Cliff's *Love Songs* LP is knocked off the top of the charts by *The Official BBC Album of the Royal Wedding*.
AUGUST 17	Cliff's 81st single, 'Wired For Sound/Hold On' is released and becomes his 6th single to peak at No.4 in the charts.

THE CLIFF RICHARD FILE **1981**

AUGUST **23-27**	Cliff rehearses at Shepperton Studios.
AUGUST **28**	Cliff flies to Amsterdam for one concert.
AUGUST **30**	Cliff appears at the Greenbelt Christian Festival in Hertfordshire.
SEPTEMBER **1&2**	Cliff undertakes two gospel shows at London's Wembley Conference Centre.
SEPTEMBER **1**	Get It Together screen the *Wired For Sound* video.
SEPTEMBER **10**	Cliff sings 'Wired For Sound' on 'Top of the Pops.'
SEPTEMBER **12-20**	Cliff spends a week in Wales.
SEPTEMBER **14**	'Wired For Sound/Hold On' is released in America, but doesn't get higher than No.77.
SEPTEMBER **26**-OCTOBER **10**	Cliff spends two weeks in New York and Los Angeles.
OCTOBER **13**	Cliff dines with Rick Parfitt, guitarist with rock group Status Quo.
OCTOBER **14**	Cliff's 41st birthday.
OCTOBER **15**	Cliff records for 'Musik Laden' on German TV.
OCTOBER **20**	The video for 'Daddy's Home' is shot at Ewarts Studio in Wandsworth. Cliff's brief is to look unshaven and wear tight jeans, a white T-shirt and black leather jacket.
OCTOBER **24**	At Addlestone Police Station in Surrey, Cliff presents awards to local children.
NOVEMBER **2**-DECEMBER **19**	Cliff on a UK tour.
NOVEMBER **4**	'Service for the Blind' interview Cliff.
NOVEMBER **23**	Cliff appears on the bill of the Royal Variety Performance at Drury Lane, London.
NOVEMBER **23**	BBC TV start to screen a four-part series which looks at Cliff's twenty-three years in show business; this includes gospel and orthodox concerts, religion, life on the road, his charity work and interviews with business and personal friends including Olivia Newton-John, Adam Faith, Marty Wilde and disc jockeys Kenny Everett, Dave Lee Travis and Mike Read. Cliff's friend and religious adviser, Bill Latham, discusses the gospel tours and reveals that they made £50,000-£60,000 a year for Tear Fund. Religious broadcaster David Winter talks about Cliff's conversion to Christianity.
NOVEMBER ☐	Cliff and one of Britain's top lady tennis players, Sue Barker, become friends and start spending a lot of time in each other's company.
NOVEMBER ☐	Cliff's 82nd single, 'Daddy's Home', is a song which has long been one of his favourites – the original by Shep and the Limelites featuring on Cliff's Bel-Ami jukebox at his home. The 'B' side is the old Johnny Kidd song 'Shakin' all over'. 'Daddy's Home' becomes Cliff's 9th single to come to rest at the No.2 spot in the charts.
NOVEMBER **28**	Sally James interviews Cliff on the Saturday morning TV programme 'TisWas'.
NOVEMBER **30**	Cliff undertakes a book-signing session at London's Heathrow Airport (Terminal 1).

■ Cliff and the Shadows study their chart success in *The Guinness Book of Hit Singles*

Cliff and Shakin' Stevens

■ 13 October 1981: Cliff and Rick Parfitt rock

NOVEMBER **30**   BBC2 screen the second part of 'Cliff'.
DECEMBER **7**   BBC2 transmit the third in the series 'Cliff'.
DECEMBER **14**   BBC2 transmit the fourth and last in the series 'Cliff'.
DECEMBER **22**   Cliff records for BBC TV's 'Pop Quiz.'
DECEMBER **23**   Cliff flies to Miami to spend Christmas in Florida.

1982

JANUARY ☐	Cliff arrives back in England from Miami.
JANUARY 4-15	Cliff records at Strawberry Studios.
JANUARY 21	Cliff is interviewed on the telephone by eight Australian newspapers and nine Australian radio stations over a period of fourteen hours.
FEBRUARY 1-6	Cliff appears at Blazers night club in Windsor, Berkshire.
FEBRUARY 10	Cliff departs for a world tour with ever-present tour manager, David Bryce.
FEBRUARY 12-19	Cliff appears in Bangkok, Singapore and Hong Kong.
FEBRUARY 22-MARCH 13	Cliff appears in Perth, Adelaide, Melbourne, Brisbane, Sydney, Christchurch and Auckland.
MARCH 17-19	Cliff appears in Los Angeles and New York.
MARCH 22	Cliff arrives back in England.
MARCH 31	Weetabix hold a press conference in the Derby & Queensbury Room at London's Café Royal with Cliff, who is spearheading a campaign with them to raise money for underprivileged children.
APRIL 4	Cliff visits Cranleigh School in Surrey.
APRIL 10	Cliff assists in Capital Radio's 'Help a London Child'.
APRIL 18	Cliff attends the 'Christians in Sport' dinner in Watford.
APRIL 21	Cliff is interviewed by *Family* magazine, the *Surrey Herald* and the *Guildford Church Magazine* prior to attending the *TV Times* awards at Thames TV's Teddington Studios.
APRIL 29- MAY 2	Cliff visits Northern Ireland.
MAY 9-15	Cliff and Bill Latham visit Kenya on behalf of Tear Fund.
MAY 27	Photographer Brian Aris takes new shots of Cliff at his Holborn Studios in London.
JUNE 2	Cliff is scheduled to record his new single 'The Only Way Out', but the studio is struck by lightning and the session is put back a week.
JUNE 7	Cliff records 'The Only Way Out' at Townhouse Studios.
JUNE 9	At Wokingham in Berkshire, Cliff opens a new Dr Barnardo's home.
JUNE 13	Radio 2's Nick Page interviews Cliff at home.
JUNE 15	Cliff watches Sue Barker play in a tennis tournament at Eastbourne.
JUNE 19	Cliff sees Andrew Lloyd Webber's musical *Cats*.

Cliff and Sue Barker

THE CLIFF RICHARD FILE 1982

■ Britain's two most successful pop artists

JULY 5	EMI release Cliff's 83rd single, 'The Only Way Out/Under The Influence' which reaches No.10 in the charts.
JULY 5-31	Cliff tours the USA and Canada.
AUGUST 5-27	Cliff holidays in Bermuda with Bill Latham and both their mothers.
SEPTEMBER 6	Cliff's 84th single, 'Where Do We Go From Here/Discovering', is released but only reaches No.60 – Cliff's lowest-ever chart placing.
SEPTEMBER 8	'Where Do We Go From Here' video is shot in London.
SEPTEMBER 14-15	Cliff is interviewed by Capital Radio, British Forces Network, Radio 1's Talkabout, Radio 1's Andy Peebles and Guildford Hospital Radio.
SEPTEMBER 27	EMI film Cliff for a Christmas record token commercial.
OCTOBER 9-NOVEMBER 2	Cliff tours Europe and Scandinavia.
NOVEMBER 7	Cliff attends the 'Christmas in Sport' dinner in Liverpool.
NOVEMBER 15	EMI release Cliff's 85th single, 'Little Town/Love and a Helping Hand/You and Me and Jesus'.
NOVEMBER 23	Cliff performs at the Royal Albert Hall, London with the Royal Philharmonic Orchestra.
NOVEMBER 24-27	Cliff produces Sheila Walsh at Rick Parfitt's studios in Surrey.
NOVEMBER 27	Noel Edmonds chats to Cliff on his live TV show.
DECEMBER 1	Phil Everly and Cliff have photographs taken together.
DECEMBER □	'Little Town' climbs to No.11 in the charts.
DECEMBER 23	Cliff sings 'Little Town' on 'Top of the Pops.'
DECEMBER 23	Cliff attends the Arts Centre Group carol service.

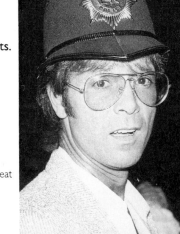

■ On the beat

19**83**

JANUARY **13**   The film *Cliff in Kenya* is premièred at the BAFTA cinema in London's Piccadilly.

JANUARY **15-16**   Cliff takes part in a tennis tournament in Holland.

THE CLIFF RICHARD FILE 1983

JANUARY 20-26	Cliff appears at Blazers night club in Windsor, Berkshire.
JANUARY 28	As part of the Weetabix appeal, Cliff presents a cheque to the children of the Great Ormond Street Hospital in London.
JANUARY 31-MARCH 14	Cliff tours Hong Kong, Bangkok, Singapore, Manila, Melbourne, Canberra, Brisbane, Sydney, Adelaide and Perth.

FEBRUARY ☐	Cliff's 86th single 'She Means Nothing To Me', on which Cliff duets with Phil Everly, is released. The 'B' side, 'A Man and a Woman', features Phil Everly only. The single is produced by Stuart Colman.
MARCH ☐	'She Means Nothing To Me' peaks at No.9.
MARCH 21,22&23	Cliff records with record producer/songwriter Mike Batt. The session includes a song called 'Please Don't Fall in Love'.
MARCH 24	At St Martin-in-the-Fields church in London, Cliff attends a memorial service for comedian Arthur Askey.

THE CLIFF RICHARD FILE **1983**

APRIL **9-29**   Cliff on a European and Scandinavian gospel tour taking in Lisbon, Barcelona, Stuttgart, Hamburg, Essen, Malmo, Gothenburg, Rotterdam, Antwerp and Brussels.

APRIL ☐   EMI release Cliff's 87th single, 'True Love Ways/Galadriel'. 'True Love Ways' had previously been a hit for Buddy Holly in 1960 and for Peter and Gordon in 1965.

MAY **21-29**   Cliff and Terry Britten record 'Never Say Die (Give a Little Bit More)'.

MAY ☐   Cliff's 88th single, 'Drifting' (with Sheila Walsh) is released. The 'B' side, 'Lovely When the Lights Go Out', is by Sheila Walsh only.

JUNE **6**   Lord Snowdon photographs Cliff at a 4-hour session in London.

JUNE **7**   Cliff records for BBC TV's 'Pop Quiz.'

JUNE **11**   Cliff records for 'Time of Your Life' at BBC TV centre with Noel Edmonds and Una Stubbs.

JUNE **23**   Cliff attends the retirement party for a Baptist minister in Walton-on-Thames, Surrey.

JUNE **27**   Radio 1 broadcaster/journalist Paul Gambaccini and Cliff take part in a rock seminar at the Arts Centre Group in London.

JULY **1**   BBC TV screen 'Time of Your Life'.

JULY **2-3**   Cliff watches the tennis finals at Wimbledon.

JULY **18**   Cliff goes to Holland for an international conference with Billy Graham.

JULY **19**   Cliff records the video for 'Never Say Die/Give a Little Bit More'.

AUGUST **3-24**   Cliff holidays in Portugal.

AUGUST **22**   Cliff's 89th single, 'Never Say Die/Give a Little Bit More' is released. The 'B' side is Cliff's version of the Little Richard/Everly Brothers classic 'Lucille'.

AUGUST **27**   Cliff appears at the Greenbelt Christian Festival.

SEPTEMBER **8**   Cliff sends a congratulatory telegram to the Shadows at a 'Silver Luncheon' to celebrate their 25 years in the business and the publication of their autobiography with Mike Read.

```
                                                     06 September 1983

         TELEMESSAGE LXP        GREETINGS-B
         THE SHADOWS
         MUSIC THERAPY LUNCHEON
         CARLTON TOWER HOTEL CADOGAN PLACE
         LONDON
         SW1

                 DEAR HANK BRUCE BRAIN

                 YOU KNOW THAT I ALWAYS BEEN PROUD TO BE ASSOCIATED WITH YOU
                 SORRY I CANT BE WITH YOU TODAY TO SAY SO PERSONALLY.
                 25 YEARS AND NOT OUT YET. WE DID IT TOGETHER, WE DID IT
                 SEPARATELY. SEE YOU IN THE CHARTS
```

THE CLIFF RICHARD FILE **1983**

SEPTEMBER 14-23	Cliff in Los Angeles and Salt Lake City.
OCTOBER 5-DECEMBER 10	Cliff undertakes dozens of concerts around Britain, ending with a long run at London's Apollo Theatre.
OCTOBER 10	Cliff co-hosts the 'Radio 1 Breakfast Show' live from Mike Read's house in Weybridge, Surrey.
OCTOBER 14	Cliff's 43rd birthday.
OCTOBER 25	Cliff attends a charity lunch at London's Dorchester Hotel in the presence of Princess Anne, in aid of the Bone Marrow Unit at Westminster Hospital.
OCTOBER 27	Cliff records for TV's 'Pebble Mill at One'.
NOVEMBER 1	Cliff attends the 'Tin Pan Alley Ball' at London's Royal Lancaster Hotel.
NOVEMBER 5	Olivia Newton-John and her sister are guests of Cliff's at his Apollo concert.
NOVEMBER 7	EMI release Cliff's 90th single, 'Please Don't Fall in Love/Too Close To Heaven', which climbs to No.7 in the charts.
NOVEMBER 7	Princess Alexandra and Angus Ogilvy watch Cliff at the Apollo.
NOVEMBER 11	After his show at the Apollo, Cliff dines with Princess Anne and Tim Rice.
NOVEMBER 13	Cliff watches the Benson & Hedges tennis final at Wembley.
NOVEMBER 17	TV AM film Cliff at David Lloyd's Tennis Centre.
DECEMBER 8	Cliff attends a Variety Club lunch at London's Hilton Hotel.
DECEMBER 19	Cliff's own pro-celebrity tennis tournament is staged at the Conference Centre, Brighton. Participants are Cliff, Hank Marvin, actor Trevor Eve, Mike Read, Sue Barker, Sue Mappin, Jo Durie and Anne Hobbs. The round-robin tournament is won by Trevor Eve and Anne Hobbs.
DECEMBER 20	Cliff attends the Arts Centre Group carol service at All Souls' Church in Langham Place, London.

1984

JANUARY 7-8	Cliff watches tennis from a private box at London's Royal Albert Hall.
JANUARY 15-18	Cliff holidays in Portugal.
JANUARY 24-FEBRUARY 10	Cliff is in the Far East and America for two weeks.
FEBRUARY 21-23	Cliff holidays in Portugal.
FEBRUARY 29	Cliff appears live on BBC Radio 4's 'Woman's Hour'.
MARCH 13-17	Cliff goes to Scandinavia for a promotional visit.
MARCH 19	EMI release Cliff's 91st single, 'Baby You're Dynamite/Ocean Deep', which peaks at No.27 in the charts. It is subsequently 'flipped', with the 'B' side 'Ocean Deep' becoming the 'A' side which then re-enters the charts and peaks at No.72.
MARCH 26	Cliff records his vocals for 'Two to the Power', a duet with Janet Jackson.
MARCH 30	Cliff records for Terry Wogan's BBC TV show.
APRIL 1-15	Cliff and Bill Latham go to Haiti, where they visit Port-au-Prince and La Gonave. During the visit, Cliff is moved to write a song about La Gonave.
APRIL 26	Cliff sees Andrew Lloyd Webber's musical *Starlight Express*.
MAY 9	Cliff attends a service at Westminster Abbey for 'Christian Heritage Year'.
MAY 10	Cliff is filmed in Switzerland for the Golden Rose of Montreux festival.
JUNE 2	Cliff takes part in a charity concert for the Elmbridge Hospice appeal in Surrey.
JUNE 11	Cliff records for BBC TV's 'Rock Gospel Show.'
JUNE 13	Cliff attends 'Mission to London', a Christian evening at Queen's Park Rangers football ground in London.
JUNE 16-21	Cliff spends five days in Portugal.
JULY 1-6	Cliff and the Shadows appear at the Empire Pool, Wembley.
JULY 7-12	Cliff and the Shadows appear at the NEC Centre, Birmingham.
JULY 23-28	Cliff records the rock 'n' roll *Silver* album.
AUGUST 2-23	Cliff holidays in Portugal.
AUGUST 28	Cliff and Dave Clark meet to discuss the musical *Time*.
SEPTEMBER 7	TVS film Cliff at the David Lloyd Tennis Centre.
SEPTEMBER 1-29	Cliff undertakes a British gospel tour.
SEPTEMBER ☐	EMI release Cliff's 92nd single, 'Two To The Power' with Janet Jackson. The 'B' side, 'Rock 'n' Roll', features Janet Jackson only.

THE CLIFF RICHARD FILE   **1984**

OCTOBER **8-13**	Cliff in concert at Blazers night club, Windsor, Berkshire.
OCTOBER **14**	Cliff leaves for Australia on his 44th birthday.
OCTOBER **15**-NOVEMBER **29**	Cliff in Australia and New Zealand.
OCTOBER **22**	Cliff's 93rd single, 'Shooting From The Heart/Small World' is released, but only reaches No.51 in the charts.
DECEMBER **8**	Cliff attends the Silver Wedding party of Shadows drummer Brian Bennett and his wife Margaret, at their home in Hertfordshire.
DECEMBER **9**	Cliff records at the BBC TV Centre for a 'Rock Gospel Show' Christmas special.
DECEMBER **10**	Cliff records for Mike Yarwood's Christmas show.
DECEMBER **15**	The second pro-celebrity tennis tournament organised by Cliff takes place at the Brighton Conference Centre. The eight players are Cliff, Hank Marvin, Mike Yarwood, Terry Wogan, Annabel Croft, Sarah Gomer, Julie Salmon and Sue Mappin.

■ Martina Wogan and Virginia Yarwood warm up at Brighton

DECEMBER **17-19**	Cliff records at EMI's Abbey Road Studios with Dave Clark.
DECEMBER ☐	Cliff attends the Arts Centre Group carol service at All Souls' Church, Langham Place, in London.
DECEMBER **26**-JANUARY **14**	Cliff and Bill Latham fly to South Africa for 3 weeks.

1985

JANUARY 14	Cliff returns from South Africa.
JANUARY 21	Cliff's 94th single is released: 'Heart User/I Will Follow You'. It peaks at No.46.
JANUARY 25	Cliff appears live on pop TV programme 'The Tube', singing 'Lovers and Friends', 'Lucille' and 'Heart User'.
FEBRUARY 1	Cliff is interviewed for Radio 1's 'History of Pop,' *Newsbeat*, Gloria Hunniford on Radio 2, Capital Radio's Roger Scott and Radio Luxembourg.
FEBRUARY 2	Cliff appears on Michael Aspel's TV show 'Aspel and Friends'.
FEBRUARY 9	Cliff appears on 'Saturday Superstore.'
FEBRUARY 11	Cliff attends a reception at 10 Downing Street, the London home of Prime Minister Margaret Thatcher.
FEBRUARY 17-18	Cliff records at the BBC TV Centre for an Easter special.

THE CLIFF RICHARD FILE 1985

FEBRUARY 19-28	Cliff holidays in Portugal.
MARCH 17-25	Cliff holidays in Portugal.
MARCH 30	Cliff, along with many other celebrities, attends broadcaster/journalist Paul Gambaccini's birthday party in North London.
APRIL 1	Alan Tarney and Cliff start recording new material.
APRIL 16	At the David Lloyd Tennis Centre, Cliff participates in a Pro-Am tournament.
APRIL 30	Cliff films in Bath for 'Jim'll Fix It'.
MAY 1	Along with Alvin Stardust, Andrew Lloyd Webber, Mike McCartney, Bobby Davro and Dave Lee Travis, Cliff attends the launch of the Waddingtons board game 'Mike Read's Pop Quiz' at Stringfellows night club in London.
MAY 5	Cliff takes part in LWT's '40 Years of Peace' at London's Palace Theatre.
MAY 15	Elton John and Cliff record together at Maidenhead, Berkshire.
MAY 16	Cliff is given a demonstration of the latest laser lights available.
MAY 19-28	Cliff holidays in Portugal.
MAY 29	BBC Wales use David Lloyd's Tennis Centre to shoot a health film *Don't Break Your Heart* in which Cliff takes part.
MAY 30	Along with Lonnie Donegan, Vera Lynn, Hank Marvin, David Cassidy and Bob Geldof, Cliff attends a 'Guinness Book of Hit Singles' presentation by Norris McWhirter at a lunch at the Savoy Hotel for authors Tim and Jo Rice, Paul Gambaccini and Mike Read.
MAY 30	Cliff puts the finishing touches to 'She's So Beautiful' at EMI's Abbey Road Studios.
JUNE 8	Cliff sends a wedding congratulations telegram to Nick Beggs of the pop group Kajagoogoo and his wife Boo.
JUNE 9	Cliff plays in Bernard Cribbins' pro-celebrity tennis tournament at Foxhills, Surrey.
JUNE 10/11	Cliff records 'It's In Every One Of Us' for the musical *Time*.
JUNE 17-21	Ken Russell produces Cliff's *She's So Beautiful* video in the Lake District.
JUNE 25	Cliff dines at the House of Commons.
JUNE 30	Cliff attends a 'Christians in Sport' service.
JULY 1	Cliff opens the new Addlestone District Health Centre in Surrey.
JULY 9-27	Cliff undertakes a gospel tour of Britain and the Channel Islands, which is cut short due to a throat infection.
JULY 16	While playing in Guernsey, Cliff and Bill Latham spend a day on the island of Herm renewing their friendship with Major and Mrs Wood and their family, as they had camped on the island with the Crusaders in the late sixties.
JULY 29-AUGUST 3	Cliff spends a few days in the USA.

■ Cliff and Bill Latham grace the front cover of 'Cliff Uniteds' summer magazine

AUGUST **5-22**	Cliff holidays in Portugal.
AUGUST **23-25**	Cliff spends two days in Norway filming for a TV gala.
AUGUST **25**	Cliff starts recording 'Born to Rock 'n' Roll' from the musical *Time*.
AUGUST **31**	Cliff attends a Polish Youth Conference in Warsaw.
SEPTEMBER **2**	EMI release Cliff's 95th single, 'She's So Beautiful/She's So Beautiful', the 'B' side being a different mix. The single reaches No.17 in the charts.
SEPTEMBER **6-13**	Cliff does TV, press and radio promotion in Germany, Belgium, Holland and Denmark.
SEPTEMBER **16**	In Birmingham, Cliff attends the launch of the publication *You and Me and Jesus*, volume 2.

THE CLIFF RICHARD FILE   1985

■ Potential Wimbledon Stars of '96 at Bisham Abbey. Spot the two no-hopers

SEPTEMBER **23-25**	Cliff spends three days at Bisham Abbey Sports Centre in connection with the 'Cliff Richard Tennis Hunt'.
SEPTEMBER **28**	Cliff appears on BBC TV's 'Saturday Superstore'.
OCTOBER **8-29**	Cliff tours Scandinavia.
NOVEMBER **5**-DECEMBER **14**	Cliff undertakes many concerts in England and Scotland.
NOVEMBER **7**	Cliff meets singer Van Morrison at London's Hammersmith Odeon.
NOVEMBER **25**	EMI release Cliff's 96th single, 'It's In Every One Of Us/Alone'. This is the first time that a Cliff single has had a wholly instrumental 'B' side. It's Cliff's second single to be released from the musical *Time* and it peaks at No.45.
DECEMBER **1**	Cliff appears on BBC TV's 'Pebble Mill at One'.
DECEMBER **19**	Cliff opens a new X-ray unit at Weybridge Hospital in Surrey.
DECEMBER **21**	Cliff appears on BBC TV's 'Saturday Superstore.'
DECEMBER **21**	Cliff's third annual pro-celebrity tennis tournament at the Brighton Conference Centre. Players are Cliff, Hank Marvin, Shakin' Stevens, Mike Read, Annabel Croft, Anne Hobbs, Virginia Wade and Sara Gomer.

1986

JANUARY 11-19   Cliff and Bill Latham fly to America for a tennis tournament.

JANUARY 29   Cliff records a new version of his 1959 No.1 'Livin' Doll' for Comic Relief with the cast of the TV comedy series 'The Young Ones'. The single is produced by Stuart Colman, who was also responsible for Cliff's single with Phil Everly.

■ 'Darling, we're the Young Ones'

THE CLIFF RICHARD FILE 1986

JANUARY 30	Cliff and the Young Ones make a video for the new version of 'Livin' Doll'.
FEBRUARY ☐	Cliff takes dancing lessons.
FEBRUARY 10	Rehearsals begin for the musical *Time*.
FEBRUARY 14	*TV Times* presents Cliff with the 'Best Male Singer' award at Thames Television.
FEBRUARY 22	Cliff appears on Michael Aspel's TV show 'Aspel and Friends'.
MARCH ☐	EMI release Cliff's 97th single, 'Livin' Doll'.
MARCH 27	The previews of the musical *Time* begin.
APRIL 7	The Duchess of Kent sees *Time*.
APRIL 9	The musical *Time* is premièred and followed by a celebrity-ridden launch party at the Hippodrome in London.
APRIL ☐	'Livin' Doll' becomes Cliff's eleventh No.1 hit single nearly 27 years after it first topped the charts.
MAY ☐	EMI release Cliff's 98th single and the third from his musical *Time*: 'Born to Rock and Roll/Law of the Universe.'

CLIFF RICHARD
DISCOGRAPHY

SINGLES   *RELEASED*

Title	Month	Year
Move It / Schoolboy Crush	August	1958
High Class Baby / My Feet Hit The Ground	November	1958
Living Lovin' Doll / Steady With You	January	1959
Mean Streak / Never Mind	April	1959
Living Doll / Apron Strings	July	1959
Travelling Light / Dynamite	October	1959
A Voice In The Wilderness / Don't Be Mad At Me	January	1960
Fall In Love With You / Willie And The Hand Jive	March	1960
Please Don't Tease / Where Is My Heart	June	1960
Nine Times Out Of Ten / Thinking Of Our Love	September	1960
I Love You / 'D' In Love	December	1960
Theme For A Dream / Mumblin' Mosie	February	1961
A Girl Like You / Now's The Time To Fall In Love	June	1961
Gee Whiz It's You / I Cannot Find a True Love	August	1961
When The Girl In Your Arms Is The Girl In Your Heart / Got A Funny Feeling	October	1961
The Young Ones / We Say Yeah	January	1962
I'm Lookin' Out The Window / Do You Want To Dance	May	1962
It'll Be Me / Since I Lost You	August	1962
The Next Time / Bachelor Boy	November	1962
Summer Holiday / Dancing Shoes	February	1963
Lucky Lips / I Wonder	May	1963
It's All In The Game / Your Eyes Tell On You	August	1963
Don't Talk to Him / Say You're Mine	November	1963
I'm The Lonely One / Watch What You Do With My Baby	January	1964
Constantly / True Lovin'	April	1964
On The Beach / A Matter Of Moments	June	1964
The Twelfth Of Never / I'm Afraid To Go Home	October	1964
I Could Easily Fall In Love With You / I'm In Love With You	November	1964
The Minute You're Gone / Just Another Guy	March	1965
On My Word / Just A Little Bit Too Late	June	1965
Time In Between / Look Before You Move	August	1965
Wind Me Up (Let Me Go) / The Night	October	1965
Blue Turns To Grey / Somebody Loses	February	1966
Visions / What Would I Do (For The Love of A Girl)	July	1966
Time Drags By / La La La Song	October	1966
In The Country / Finders Keepers	December	1966
It's All Over / Why Wasn't I Born Rich	March	1967
I'll Come Runnin' / I Get The Feelin'	June	1967
The Day I Met Marie / Our Story Book	September	1967
All My Love / Sweet Little Jesus Boy	November	1967
Congratulations / High 'n' Dry	March	1968
I'll Love You Forever Today / Girl You'll Be A Woman Soon	June	1968
Marianne / Mr Nice	September	1968

THE CLIFF RICHARD FILE **SINGLES**

Title	Month	Year
Don't Forget To Catch Me / What's More (I Don't Need Her)	November	1968
Good Times / Occasional Rain	February	1969
Big Ship / She's Leaving You	May	1969
Throw Down A Line / Reflections	September	1969
With The Eyes Of A Child / So Long	November	1969
The Joy Of Living / Boogatoo, Leave My Woman Alone	February	1970
Goodbye Sam Hello Samantha / You Never Can Tell	May	1970
I Ain't Got Time Any More / Monday Comes Too Soon	August	1970
Sunny Honey Girl / Don't Move Away (Cliff & Olivia) / I Was Only Fooling Myself	January	1971
Silvery Rain / Annabella Umbrella / Time Flies	March	1971
Flying Machine / Pigeon	June	1971
Sing A Song Of Freedom / A Thousand Conversations	October	1971
Jesus / Mr Cloud	February	1972
Living In Harmony / Empty Chairs	August	1972
Brand New Song / The Old Accordion	November	1972
Power To All Our Friends / Come Back Billie Joe	March	1973
Help It Along / Tomorrow Rising / The Days Of Love / Ashes to Ashes	April	1973
Take Me High / Celestial Houses	November	1973
(You Keep Me) Hanging On / Love Is Here	April	1974
It's Only Me You've Left Behind / You're The One	March	1975
Honky Tonk Angel / Would You Know It (Got Myself A Girl)	September	1975
Miss You Nights / Love Enough	November	1975
Devil Woman / Love On (Shine On)	April	1976
I Can't Ask For Any More Than You / Junior Cowboy	July	1976
Hey Mr Dream Maker / No One Waits	November	1976
My Kinda Life / Nothing Left For Me To Say	February	1977
When Two Worlds Drift Apart / That's Why I Love You	June	1977
Yes He Lives / Good On The Sally Army	January	1978
Please Remember Me / Please Don't Tease	July	1978
Can't Take The Hurt Any More / Needing A Friend	November	1978
Green Light / Imagine Love	February	1979
We Don't Talk Any More / Count Me Out	July	1979
Hot Shot / Walking In The Light	October	1979
Carrie / Moving In	January	1980
Dreamin' / Dynamite	August	1980
Suddenly (with Olivia Newton-John) / You Made Me Love You (ONJ only)	October	1980
A Little In Love / Keep On Looking	January	1981
Wired For Sound / Hold On	August	1981
Daddy's Home / Shakin' All Over	November	1981
The Only Way Out / Under The Influence	July	1982
Where Do We Go From Here / Discovering	September	1982
Little Town / Love And A Helping Hand / You And Me And Jesus	November	1982
She Means Nothing To Me (with Phil Everly) / A Man And A Woman (PE only)	February	1983
True Love Ways / Galadriel	April	1983
Drifting (with Sheila Walsh) / Lonely When The Lights Go Out (SW only)	May	1983
Never Say Die (Give A Little Bit More) / Lucille	August	1983
Please Don't Fall In Love / Too Close To Heaven	November	1983
Baby You're Dynamite / Ocean Deep	March	1984
Two To The Power (with Janet Jackson) / Rock 'n' Roll (JJ only)	September	1984
Shooting From The Heart / Small World	October	1984
Heart User / I Will Follow You	January	1985

She's So Beautiful / She's So Beautiful	September	1985
It's In Every One Of Us / Alone (instrumental)	November	1985
Living Doll (with 'The Young Ones) /	March	1986
Born to Rock 'n' Roll / Law Of The Universe	May	1986

EPs *RELEASED*

SERIOUS CHARGE — May 1959
Living Doll / No Turning Back / Mad About You / (The Shadows: Chinchilla)

CLIFF NO.1 — June 1959
Apron Strings / My Babe Down The Line / I Gotta Feeling / Baby I Don't Care

CLIFF NO.2 — July 1959
Donna / Move It / Ready Teddy / Too Much / Don't Bug Me Baby

EXPRESSO BONGO — January 1960
Love / A Voice In The Wilderness / The Shrine On The Second Floor / (The Shadows: Bongo Blues)

CLIFF SINGS NO.1 — February 1960
Here Comes Summer / I Gotta Know / Blue Suede Shoes / The Snake And The Bookworm

CLIFF SINGS NO.2 — March 1960
Twenty Flight Rock / Pointed Toe Shoes / Mean Woman Blues / I'm Walkin'

CLIFF SINGS NO.3 — June 1960
I'll String Along With You / Embraceable You / As Time Goes By / The Touch Of Your Lips

CLIFF SINGS NO.4 — September 1960
I Don't Know Why (I Just Do) / Little Things Mean A Lot / Somewhere Along The Way / That's My Desire

CLIFF'S SILVER DISCS — December 1960
Please Don't Tease / Fall In Love With You / Nine Times Out Of Ten / Travellin' Light

ME AND MY SHADOWS NO.1 — February 1961
I'm Gonna Get You / You And I / I Cannot Find a True Love / Evergreen Tree / She's Gone

ME AND MY SHADOWS NO.2 — March 1961
Left Out Again / You're Just The One To Do It / Lamp Of Love / Choppin' And Changin' / We Have It Made

ME AND MY SHADOWS NO.3 — April 1961
Tell Me / Gee Whiz It's You / I'm Willing To Learn / I Love You So / I Don't Know

THE CLIFF RICHARD FILE — EPs

LISTEN TO CLIFF NO.1 — October 1961
What'd I Say / True Love Will Come To You / Blue Moon / Lover

DREAM — November 1961
Dream / All I Do Is Dream Of You / I'll See You In My Dreams / Then Grow Too Old To Dream

LISTEN TO CLIFF NO.2 — December 1961
Unchained Melody / First Lesson In Love / Idle Gossip / Almost Like Being In Love / Beat Out Dat Rhythm On A Drum

CLIFF'S HIT PARADE — February 1962
I Love You / Theme For A Dream / A Girl Like You / When The Girl In Your Arms Is The Girl In Your Heart

CLIFF RICHARD NO.1 — April 1962
Party Days / Catch Me / How Wonderful To Know / Tough Enough

HITS FROM 'THE YOUNG ONES' — May 1962
The Young Ones / Got A Funny Feeling / Lessons In Love / We Say Yeah

CLIFF RICHARD NO.2 — June 1962
Fifty Tears For Every Kiss / The Night Is So Lonely / Poor Boy / Y'Arriva

CLIFF'S HITS — November 1962
It'll Be Me / Since I Lost You / Do You Want To Dance / I'm Looking Out The Window

TIME FOR CLIFF AND THE SHADOWS — March 1963
So I've Been Told / I'm Walkin' The Blues / When My Dreamboat Comes Home / Blueberry Hill / You Don't Know

HOLIDAY CARNIVAL — May 1963
Carnival / Moonlight Bay / Some Of These Days / For You And Me

HITS FROM 'SUMMER HOLIDAY' — June 1963
Summer Holiday / The Next Time / Dancing Shoes / Bachelor Boy

MORE HITS FROM 'SUMMER HOLIDAY' — September 1963
Seven Days To A Holiday / Stranger In Town / Really Waltzing / All At Once

CLIFF'S LUCKY LIPS — October 1963
It's All In The Game / Your Eyes Tell On You / Lucky Lips / I Wonder

LOVE SONGS — November 1963
I'm In The Mood For Love / Secret Love / Love Letters / I Only Have Eyes For You

WHEN IN FRANCE — February 1964
La Mer / Boum / J'attendrai / C'est Si Bon

CLIFF SINGS DON'T TALK TO HIM   March   1964
Don't Talk To Him / Say You're Mine / Spanish Harlem / Who Are We To Say / Falling In Love With Love

CLIFF'S PALLADIUM SUCCESSES   May   1964
I'm The Lonely One / Watch What You Do With My Baby / Perhaps Perhaps Perhaps / Frenesi

WONDERFUL LIFE NO.1   August   1964
Wonderful Life / Do You Remember / What've I Gotta Do / Walkin'

A FOREVER KIND OF LOVE   September   1964
A Forever Kind Of Love / It's Wonderful To Be Young / Constantly / True True Lovin'

WONDERFUL LIFE NO.2   October   1964
Matter Of Moments / Girl In Every Port / A Little Imagination / In The Stars

HITS FROM WONDERFUL LIFE   December   1964
On The Beach / We Love A Movie / Home / All Kinds Of People

WHY DON'T THEY UNDERSTAND   February   1965
Why Don't They Understand / Where The Four Winds Blow / The Twelfth Of Never / I'm Afraid To Go Home

CLIFF'S HITS FROM ALADDIN & HIS WONDERFUL LAMP   March   1965
Havin' Fun / Evening Comes / Friends / I Could Easily Fall (In Love With You)

LOOK IN MY EYES MARIA   May   1965
Look In My Eyes Maria / Where Is Your Heart / Maria / If I Give My Heart To You

ANGEL   September   1965
Angel / I Only Came To Say Goodbye / On My Word / The Minute You're Gone

TAKE FOUR   October   1965
Boom Boom / My Heart Is An Open Book / Lies and Kisses / Sweet And Gentle

WIND ME UP   February   1966
Wind Me Up / The Night / The Time In Between / Look Before You Love

HITS FROM 'WHEN IN ROME'   April   1966
Come Prima (For The First Time) / Nel Blue Di Pinto Di Blu (Volare) / Dicitoncella Vuve (Just Say I Love Her) / Arrivederci Roma

LOVE IS FOREVER   April   1966
My Colouring Book / Fly Me To The Moon / Someday / Everyone Needs Someone To Love

LA LA LA LA LA — December 1966
La La La La La / Solitary Man / Things We Said Today / Never Knew What Love Could Do

CINDERELLA — May 1967
Come Sunday / Peace and Quiet / She Needs Him More Than Me / Hey Doctor Man

CAROL SINGERS — November 1967
God Rest You Merry Gentlemen / In The Bleak Midwinter / Unto Us A Boy Is Born / While Shepherds Watched / O Little Town Of Bethlehem

ALBUMS — *RELEASED*

CLIFF — April 1959
Apron Strings / My Babe / Down The Line / I Got A Feeling / Jet Black (The Drifters) / Baby I Don't Care / Donna / Move It / Ready Teddy / Too Much / Don't Bug Me Baby / Driftin' (The Drifters) / That'll Be The Day / Be Bop A Lula (The Drifters) / Danny / Whole Lotta Shakin' Goin' On

CLIFF SINGS — November 1959
Blue Suede Shoes / The Snake And The Bookworm / I Gotta Know / Here Comes Summer / I'll String Along With You / Embraceable You / As Time Goes By / The Touch Of Your Lips / Twenty Flight Rock / Pointed Toe Shoes / Mean Woman Blues / I'm Walking / I Don't Know Why / Little Things Mean A Lot / Somewhere Along The Way / That's My Desire

ME AND MY SHADOWS — October 1960
I'm Gonna Get You / You And I / I Cannot Find A True Love / Evergreen Tree / She's Gone / Left Out Again / You're Just The One To Do It / Lamp Of Love / Choppin' 'n' Changin' / We Have It Made / Tell Me / Gee Whiz It's You / I Love You So / I'm Willing To Learn / I Don't Know / Working After School

LISTEN TO CLIFF — May 1961
What'd I Say / Blue Moon / True Love Will Come To You / Lover / Unchained Melody / Idle Gossip / First Lesson In Love / Almost Like Being In Love / Beat Out Dat Rhythm On A Drum / Memories Linger On / Temptation / I Live For You / Sentimental Journey / I Want You To Know / We Kiss In A Shadow / It's You

21 TODAY — October 1961
Happy Birthday To You / Forty Days / Catch Me / How Wonderful To Know / Tough Enough / Fifty Tears For Every Kiss / The Night Is So Lonely / Poor Boy / Y'Arriva / Outsider / Tea For Two / To Prove My Love For You / Without You / A Mighty Lonely Man / My Blue Heaven / Shame On You

THE YOUNG ONES — December 1961
Friday Night / Got A Funny Feeling / Peace Pipe / Nothing's Impossible / The Young Ones / All For One / Lessons In Love / No One For Me But Micky / What Do You Know We've Got A Show And Vaudeville Routine / When The

Girl In Your Arms Is The Girl In Your Heart / Just Dance / Mood Mambo / The Savage / We Say Yeah

32 MINUTES AND 17 SECONDS WITH CLIFF RICHARD   October   1962
It'll Be Me / So I've Been Told / How Long Is Forever / I'm Walkin' The Blues / Turn Around / Blueberry Hill / Let's Make A Memory / When My Dreamboat Comes Home / I'm On My Way / Spanish Harlem / You Don't Know / Falling In Love With Love / Who Are We To Say / I Wake Up Cryin'

SUMMER HOLIDAY   January   1963
Seven Days To A Holiday / Summer Holiday / Let Us Take You For A Ride / Les Girls / Round And Round / Foot Tapper / Stranger In Town / Orlando's Mime / Bachelor Boy / A Swingin' Affair / Really Waltzing / All At Once / Dancing Shoes / Jugoslav Wedding / The Next Time / Big News

CLIFF'S HIT ALBUM   July   1963
Move It / Living Doll / Travellin' Light / A Voice In The Wilderness / Fall In Love With You / Please Don't Tease / Nine Times Out Of Ten / I Love You / Theme For A Dream / A Girl Like You / When The Girl In Your Arms / The Young Ones / I'm Looking Out The Window / Do You Wanna Dance

WHEN IN SPAIN   September   1963
Perfidia / Amor Amor Amor / Frenesi / You Belong To My Heart / Vaya Con Dios / Sweet And Gentle / Maria No Mas / Kiss / Perhaps Perhaps Perhaps / Magic Is The Moonlight / Carnival / Sway

WONDERFUL LIFE   July   1964
Wonderful Life / A Girl In Every Port / Walkin' / A Little Imagination / Home / On The Beach / In The Stars / We Love A Movie / Do You Remember / What've I Gotta Do / Theme For Young Lovers / All Kinds Of People / A Matter Of Moments / Youth And Experience

ALADDIN AND HIS WONDERFUL LAMP   December   1964
Emperor Theme / Chinese Street Scene / Me Oh My / I Could Easily Fall (In Love With You) / Little Princess / This Was My Special Day / I'm In Love With You / There's Gotta Be A Way / Ballet: (Rubies, Emeralds, Sapphires, Diamonds) / Dance Of The Warriors / Friends / Dragon Dance / Genie With The Light Brown Lamp / Make Ev'ry Day A Carnival Day / Widow Twankey's Song / I'm Feeling Oh So Lovely / I've Said Too Many Things / Evening Comes / Havin' Fun

CLIFF RICHARD   April   1965
Angel / Sway / I Only Came To Say Goodbye / Take Special Care / Magic Is The Moonlight / House Without Windows / Razzle Dazzle / I Don't Wanna Love You / It's Not For Me To Say / You Belong To My Heart / Again / Perfidia / Kiss / Reelin' And Rockin'

MORE HITS BY CLIFF   July   1965
It'll Be Me / The Next Time / Bachelor Boy / Summer Holiday / Dancing Shoes / Lucky Lips / It's All In The Game / Don't Talk To Him / I'm The Lonely One / Constantly / On The Beach / A Matter Of Moments / The Twelfth Of Never / I Could Easily Fall (In Love With You)

THE CLIFF RICHARD FILE **ALBUMS**

WHEN IN ROME
Come Prima / Volare / Autumn Concerto / The Questions / Maria's Her Name / Don't Talk To Him / Just Say I Love Her / Arriverderci Roma / A Little Grain Of Sand / House Without Windows / Che Cosa Del Farai Mia Amour / Me You're Mine

August 1965

LOVE IS FOREVER
Everyone Needs Someone To Love / Long Ago And Far Away / All Of A Sudden My Heart Sings / Have I Told You Lately That I Love You / Fly Me To The Moon / A Summer Place / I Found A Rose / My Foolish Heart / Through The Eye Of A Needle / My Colouring Book / I Walk Alone / Someday (You'll Want Me To Love You) / Paradise Lost / Look Homeward Angel

November 1965

KINDA LATIN
Blame It On The Bossa Nova / Blowing In The Wind / Quiet Nights Of Quiet Stars / Eso Beso / The Girl From Ipanema / One Note Samba / Fly Me To The Moon / Our Day Will Come / Quando Quando Quando / Come Closer To Me / Meditation / Concrete And Clay

May 1966

FINDERS KEEPERS
Finders Keepers / Time Drags By / Washerwoman / La La La Song / My Way / Oh Senorita / Spanish Music / Fiesta / This Day / Paella / Finders Keepers / My Way / Paella / Fiesta / Run To The Door / Where Did The Summer Go / Into Each Life Some Rain Must Fall

December 1966

CINDERELLA
Welcome To Stoneybroke / Why Wasn't I Born Rich / Peace And Quiet / The Flyder And The Spy / Poverty / The Hunt / In The Country / Come Sunday / Dare I Love Him Like I Do / If Our Dreams Come True / Autumn / The King's Place / Peace And Quiet / She Needs Him More Than Me / Hey Doctor Man

January 1967

DON'T STOP ME NOW
Shout / One Fine Day / I'll Be Back / Heartbeat / I Saw Her Standing There / Hang On To A Dream / You Gotta Tell Me / Homeward Bound / Good Golly Miss Molly / Don't Make Promises / Move It / Don't / Dizzy Miss Lizzy / Baby It's You / My Babe / Save The Last Dance For Me

April 1967

GOOD NEWS
Good News / It Is No Secret / We Shall Be Changed / 23rd Psalm / Go Where I Send Thee / What A Friend We Have In Jesus / All Glory Laud And Honour / Just A Closer Walk With Thee / The King Of Love My Shepherd Is / Mary What You Gonna Name That Pretty Little Baby / When I Survey The Wondrous Cross / Take My Hand Precious Lord / Get On Board Little Children / May The Good Lord Bless And Keep You

October 1967

CLIFF IN JAPAN
Shout / I'll Come Running / The Minute You're Gone / On The Beach / Hang On To A Dream / Spanish Harlem / Finders Keepers / Visions / Evergreen Tree / What'd I'd Say / Dynamite / Medley: Let's Make A Memory, The Young Ones, Lucky Lips, Summer Holiday, We Say Yeah

May 1968

TWO A PENNY August 1968

Two A Penny / I'll Love You Forever Today / Questions / Long Is The Night / Lonely Girl / And Me (I'm On The Outside Now) / Daybreak / Twist and Shout / Celeste / Not from the film: Wake Up Wake Up / Cloudy / Red Rubber Ball / Close To Kathy / Rattler

ESTABLISHED 1958 September 1968

Don't Forget To Catch Me / Voyage To The Bottom Of The Bath / Not The Way That It Should Be / Poem / The Dreams I Dream / The Average Life Of A Daily Man / Somewhere By The Sea / Banana Man / Girl On The Bus / The Magical Mrs Clamps / Ooh La La / Here I Go Again Loving You / What's Behind The Eyes Of Mary / Maggie's Samba

THE BEST OF CLIFF June 1969

The Minute You're Gone / On My Word / The Time In Between / Wind Me Up (Let Me Go) / Blue Turns To Grey / Visions / Time Drags By / In The Country / It's All Over / I'll Come Running / The Day I Met Marie / All My Love / Congratulations / Girl You'll Be A Woman Soon.

SINCERELY October 1969

In The Past / Always / Will You Love Me Tomorrow / You'll Want Me / I'm Not Getting Married / Time / For Emily Whenever I May Find Her / Baby I Could Be So Good At Loving You / Sam / London's Not Too Far / Take Action / Take Good Care Of Her / When I Find You / Punch And Judy

IT'LL BE ME November 1969

It'll Be Me / So I've Been Told / How Long Is Forever / I'm Walkin' The Blues / Turn Around / Blueberry Hill / Let's Make A Memory / When My Dreamboat Comes Home / I'm On My Way / Spanish Harlem / You Don't Know / Falling In Love With Love / Who Are We To Say / I Wake Up Cryin'

CLIFF LIVE AT THE TALK OF THE TOWN July 1970

Introduction / Congratulations / Shout / All My Love / Ain't Nothing But A House Party / Something Good / If Ever I Should Leave You / Girl You'll Be A Woman Soon / Hank's Medley / London's Not Too Far / The Dreams That I Dream / The Day I Met Marie, La La La La La / A Taste Of Honey / The Lady Came From Baltimore / When I'm 64 / What's More I Don't Need Her / Bows And Fanfare / Congratulations / Visions / Finale: Congratulations

ABOUT THAT MAN October 1970

The Birth Of John The Baptist / Sweet Little Jesus Boy / The Visit Of The Wise Men And The Escape Into Egypt / John The Baptist Points Out Jesus / Jesus Recruits His Helpers And Heals The Sick / Where Is That Man / Jesus Addresses The Crowd On The Hillside / Can It Be True / Jesus Is Betrayed And Arrested / The Trial Of Jesus / His Execution And Death / The First Easter – The Empty Tomb / Reflections

HIS LAND November 1970

Ezekiel's Vision / Dry Bones / His Land / Jerusalem Jerusalem / The New 23rd / His Land / Hava Nagila / Over In Bethleham / Keep Me Where Love Is / He's Everything To Me / Narration And Hallelujah Chorus

TRACKS 'N' GROOVES
November 1970

Early In The Morning / As I Walk Into The Morning Of Your Life / Love Truth And Emily Stone / My Head Goes Around / Put My Mind At Ease / Abraham Martin And John / The Girl Can't Help It / Bang Bang (My Baby Shot Me Down) / I'll Make It All Up To You / I'd Just Be Fool Enough / Don't Let Tonight Ever End / What A Silly Thing To Do / Your Heart's Not In Your Love / Don't Ask Me To Be Friends / Are You Only Fooling Me

THE BEST OF CLIFF VOLUME TWO
November 1972

Goodbye Sam Hello Samantha / Marianne / Throw Down A Line / Jesus / Sunny Honey Girl / I Ain't Got Time Any More / Flying Machine / Sing A Song Of Freedom / With The Eyes Of A Child / Good Times / I'll Love You Forever Today / The Joy Of Living / Silvery Rain / Big Ship

TAKE ME HIGH
December 1973

It's Only Monday / Midnight Blue / Hover (Instrumental) / Why (duet with Anthony Andrews) / Life / Driving / The Game / Brumburger Duet (duet with Deborah Watling) / Take Me High / The Anti-Brotherhood Of Man / Winning / Driving (Instrumental) / Join The Band / The Word Is Love / Brumburger (Finale)

HELP IT ALONG
June 1974

Day By Day / Celestial Houses / Jesus / Silvery Rain / Jesus Loves You / Fire And Rain / Yesterday Today Forever / Mr Business Man / Help It Along / Amazing Grace / Higher Ground / Sing A Song Of Freedom

THE 31ST OF FEBRUARY STREET
November 1974

31st Of February Street Opening / Give Me Back That Old Familiar Feeling / The Leaving / Travellin' Light / There You Go Again / Nothing To Remind Me / Our Love Could Be So Real / No Matter What / Fireside Song / Going Away / Long Long Time / You Will Never Know / The Singer / 31st of February Street Closing

I'M NEARLY FAMOUS
May 1976

I Can't Ask For Any More Than You / It's No Use Pretending / I'm Nearly Famous / Lovers / Junior Cowboy / Miss You Nights / I Wish You'd Change Your Mind / Devil Woman / Such Is The Mystery / You've Got To Give Me All Your Lovin' / Alright It's Alright

EVERY FACE TELLS A STORY
March 1977

My Kinda Life / Must Be Love / When Two Worlds Drift Apart / You Got Me Wondering / Every Face Tells A Story (It Never Tells A Lie) / Try A Smile / Hey Mr Dream Maker / Give Me Love Your Way / Up In The World / Don't Turn The Light Out / It'll Be Me Babe / Spider Man

40 GOLDEN GREATS
September 1977

Move It / Livin' Doll / Travellin' Light / Fall In Love With You / Please Don't Tease / Nine Times Out Of Ten / Theme For A Dream / Gee Whiz It's You / When The Girl In Your Arms Is The Girl In Your Heart / A Girl Like You / The Young Ones / Do You Wanna Dance / I'm Looking Out The Window / It'll Be Me / Bachelor Boy / The Nex Time / Summer Holiday / Lucky Lips / It's All In The Game / Don't Talk To Him / Constantly / On The Beach / I Could Easily Fall (In Love With You) / The Minute You're Gone / Wind Me Up (Let Me Go)

/ Visions / Blue Turns To Grey / In The Country / The Day I Met Marie / All My Love / Congratulations / Throw Down A Line / Goodbye Sam Hello Samantha / Sing A Song Of Freedom / Power To All Our Friends / (You Keep Me) Hanging On / Miss You Nights / Devil Woman / I Can't Ask For Any More Than You / My Kinda Life

SMALL CORNERS February 1978

Why Should The Devil Have All The Good Music / I Love / Why Me / I've Got News For You / Hey Watcha Say / I Wish We'd All Been Ready / Joseph / Good On The Sally Army / Goin' Home / Up In Canada / Yes He Lives / When I Survey The Wondrous Cross

GREEN LIGHT September 1978

Green Light / Under Lock And Key / She's A Gipsy / Count Me Out / Please Remember Me / Never Even Thought / Free My Soul / Start All Over Again / While She's Young / Can't Take The Hurt Any More / Ease Along

THANK YOU VERY MUCH (Cliff & The Shadows) February 1979

The Young Ones / Do You Wanna Dance / The Day I Met Marie/ Shadoogie / Atlantis / Nivram / Apache / Please Don't Tease / Miss You Nights / Move It / Willie And The Hand Jive / All Shook Up / Devil Woman / Why Should The Devil Have All The Good Music / End Of The Show

ROCK 'N' ROLL JUVENILE September 1979

Monday Thru Friday / Doing Fine / Cities May Fall / You Know That I Love You / My Luck Won't Change / Carrie / Hot Shot / Language Of Love / We Don't Talk Any More / Sci Fi

I'M NO HERO September 1980

Take Another Look / Anything I Can Do / A Little In Love / Here (So Doggone Blue) / Give A Little Bit More / In The Night / I'm No Hero / Dreamin' / A Heart Will Break / Everyman

LOVE SONGS July 1981

Miss You Nights / Constantly / Up In The World / Carrie / A Voice In The Wilderness / The Twelfth Of Never / I Could Easily Fall (In Love With You) / The Day I Met Marie / Can't Take The Hurt Any More / A Little In Love / The Minute You're Gone / Visions / When Two Worlds Drift Apart / The Next Time / It's All In The Game / Don't Talk To Him / When The Girl In Your Arms Is The Girl In Your Heart / Theme For A Dream / Fall In Love With You / We Don't Talk Any More

WIRED FOR SOUND September 1981

Wired For Sound / Once In A While / Better Than I Know Myself / Oh No Don't Let Go / 'Cos I Love That Rock 'n' Roll / Broken Doll / Lost In a Lonely World / Summer Rain / Young Love / Say You Don't Mind / Daddy's Home

NOW YOU SEE ME . . . NOW YOU DON'T August 1982

The Only Way Out / First Date / Thief In The Night / Where Do We Go From Here / Son Of Thunder / Little Town / It Has To Be You It Has To Be Me / The Water Is Wide / Now You See Me Now You Don't / Be In My Heart / Discovering

DRESSED FOR THE OCCASION May 1983
Green Light / We Don't Talk Any More / True Love Ways / Softly As I Leave You / Carrie / Miss You Nights / Galadriel / Maybe Someday / Thief In The Night / Up In The World / Treasure Of Love / Devil Woman

SILVER October 1983
Silver's Home Tonight / Hold On / Never Say Die (Give A Little Bit More) / Front Page / Ocean Deep / Locked Inside Your Prison / Please Don't Fall In Love / Baby You're Dynamite / The Golden Days Are Over / Love Stealer

ROCK 'N' ROLL SILVER
Makin' History / Move It / Donna / Teddy Bear / It'll Be Me / Lucille / Little Bitty Pretty One / There'll Never Be Anyone Else But You / Be Bop A Lula / Tutti Frutti

CLIFF & THE SHADOWS September 1984
On The Beach / Do You Wanna Dance / Lucky Lips / Don't Talk To Him / A Voice In The Wilderness / A Girl Like You / Fall In Love With You / Gee Whiz It's You / Mean Streak / In The Country / Move It / Nine Times Out Of Ten / Dancing Shoes / Theme For A Dream / Willie And The Hand Jive / I'm The Lonely One / When The Girl In Your Arms / Time Drags By / I Could Easily Fall / We Say Yeah

THE ROCK CONNECTION November 1984
Heart User / Willie And The Hand Jive / Lovers And Friends / Never Be Anyone Else But You / La Gonave / Over You / Shooting From The Heart / Learning How To Rock 'n' Roll / Lucille / Be Bop A Lula / Donna / Dynamite / She Means Nothing To Me / Makin' History

TIME
Born to Rock 'n' Roll / Time Talkin' / Time / Music of the Spheres / Law of the Universe / The Time Lord Theme / The Charge / One Human Family / What on Earth / *I Know* I Know / Your Brother in Soul / Case for the Prosecution / Starmaker / Time Will Teach Us All / I Object / In My Defence / Within My World / Because / Move the Judge / She's So Beautiful / Beauty, Truth, Love, Freedom, Peace / If You Only Knew / We're The U.F.O. / The Theme from 'Time' / Harmony / The Return / Time (Reprise) / It's in Every One of Us

COMPILATIONS
WALKING IN THE LIGHT
Better Than I Know Myself / Such Is The Mystery / Every Face Tells A Story / Love And A Helping Hand / You Got Me Wondering / Walking In The Light / Why Should The Devil Have All The Good Music / Under The Influence / Lost In A Lonely World / You Me And Jesus / Summer Rain / Thief In The Night

FROM THE HEART
Livin' Doll / Please Don't Tease / Bachelor Boy / I Love You / The Next Time / The Young Ones / Summer Holiday / The Day I Met Marie / Visions / Congratulations / The Minute You're Gone / Move It / Green Light / I'm Nearly Famous / Miss You Nights / Up In The World / She's A Gypsy / Baby You're Dynamite / Heart User / The Water Is Wide / Devil Woman / We Don't Talk Any More / Donna / La Gonave / Nothing Left For Me To Say / Up In Canada / Ocean Deep

IT'S A SMALL WORLD
Tiny Planet / Small World / Devil Woman / Moving in / It Has To Be You, It Has To Be You / La Gonave / I Will Follow You / The Only Way Out / Rock 'n' Roll Juvenile / Where Do We Go From Here